RED STATE

The Confused Citizen's
Guide to Surviving
in the Other America

Justin Cord Hayes

Adams Media
Avon, Massachusetts

Published by Adams Media, an F+W Publications Company
57 Littlefield Street
Avon, MA 02322
www.adamsmedia.com

ISBN: 1-59337-642-1

J I H G F E D C B A

Printed in Canada.

Library of Congress Cataloging-in-Publications Data
Hayes, Justin Cord.
Blue state ; Red state / Justin Cord Hayes.
p.   cm.
Added t.p. title: Red state
Flip book. No collective t.p.; titles transcribed from individual title pages.
Includes bibliographical references and index.
ISBN 1-59337-642-1 (alk. paper)
1. United States—Politics and government—2001—Humor. 2. United States—Social life
and customs—1971—Humor. 3. Conservatism—United States—Humor. 4. Liberalism—
United States—Humor. 5. American wit and humor. I. Title. II. Title: Red state.
E902.H395 2006
973.93102'07—dc22
2006007454

Interior art ©iStockphoto.com/Emanuele Gnani

This book is available at quantity discounts for bulk purchases.
For information, please call 1-800-872-5627.

Contents

PART 1

Help!
I'm Trapped
in a Red
State!

Introduction

Malice in Jesusland

THEY MAY NOT ALWAYS act like it, but rest assured, the folks who live in Red States really are Americans. You haven't been banished to the ninth circle of Hades. You're just surviving in a Red State, that's all.

True, Red States bear a sometimes striking resemblance to the topsy-turvy world of Lewis Carroll's Wonderland, rather than to your beloved Blue States. Red Staters, for example, are patriotic to the nth degree. They wrap themselves in the flag and will beat you as senseless as they, should you have the temerity to question the president's judgment in waging war, not on a country, but on an abstract noun: "terrorism."

On the other hand, Red Staters are surprisingly quick to adopt a scorched-earth policy when it comes to the very freedoms upon which the United States was founded. They would happily play villagers in a Frankenstein film and apply torches to free speech and the separation of church and state.

Don't despair. What follows is a guide to the way those Red Staters think—if they can, in fact, be said to think at all. You'll learn about their not-very-likely-to-change-in-this-lifetime views on hot-button issues like abortion, capital punishment, and gun control. After a quick lesson in Red State knee-jerk thought, you'll discover where to find pockets of beloved Blue State favorites within your new Red State.

Next, you'll be introduced to the nutty politicians who represent your new state. You'll find out about the part your new state played in our nation's political history and/or the part it played in the more scandalous moments of "public service."

You can survive and even thrive in your Red state. But, just to be safe, visit your local barista and stock up now on cartons of fair-trade coffee beans.

A Guide to Red State Thought

ABORTION

For the time being at least, a woman's right to choose is protected by the Supreme Court. That's just a reminder for you, since in your new Red State home—you'll swear the entire population has, Big Brother-like, removed *Roe v. Wade* from its collective memory banks. Yes, abortion is legal in Red States, though with various restrictions. The average abortion rate for the United States is 21.3 per 1,000 women of child-bearing age.

Alabama Alabama's rate is 14.3. The state's restrictions are: A) Parental consent for minors, B) A woman must receive state-directed counseling and wait twenty-four hours before getting an abortion, and C) Public funding is available for abortion only in cases of life endangerment, rape, or incest.

Alaska Alaska's rate is 11.7. The state's only restriction requires a woman to have state-directed counseling before getting an abortion.

Arizona Arizona's rate is 16.5. The state's only restriction is parental consent for minors.

Arkansas Arkansas's rate is 9.8. The state's restrictions are: A) Parental notification for minors, B) A woman must receive state-directed counseling and wait until the next day before getting an abortion, and C) Public funding for abortions is available only in cases of life endangerment, rape, or incest.

Colorado Colorado's rate is 15.9. The state's restrictions are: A) Parental notification for minors, B) Public funding is available only in cases of life endangerment, rape, or incest, and C) Abortion is not covered in public employees' insurance policies.

Florida Florida's rate is 31.9. The state's only restriction is that public funding is available only in cases of life endangerment, rape, or incest.

Georgia Georgia's rate is 16.9. The state's restrictions are: A) Parental notification for minors and B) Public funding is available only in cases of life endangerment, rape, or incest.

Idaho Idaho's rate is 7.0. The state's restrictions are: A) Parental consent for minors, B) A woman must receive state-directed counseling and wait twenty-four hours before getting an abortion, C) Public funding is available only in cases of life endangerment, rape, or incest, and D) Abortion is covered in private insurance policies only in cases of life endangerment, unless an optional rider is purchased.

Indiana Indiana's rate is 9.4. The state's restrictions are: A) Parental consent for minors, B) A woman must receive state-directed counseling and wait eighteen hours before getting an abortion, and C) Public funding for abortions is available only in cases of life endangerment, health, rape, or incest.

Iowa Iowa has a rate of 9.8. The state's restrictions are: A) Parental notification for minors and B) Public funding for abortions is available only in cases of life endangerment, rape, incest, or fetal abnormality.

Kansas Kansas has a rate of 21.4. The state's restrictions are: A) Parental notification for minors, B) A woman must receive state-directed counseling and wait twenty-four hours before getting an abortion, and C) Public funding is available only in cases of life endangerment, rape, or incest.

Kentucky Kentucky's rate is 5.3. The state's restrictions are: A) Parental consent for minors, B) A woman must receive state-directed counseling and wait twenty-four hours before getting an abortion, C) Public funding is available only in cases of life endangerment, rape, or incest, D) Abortion is not covered in insurance policies for public employees, and E) Abortion is covered in private insurance policies only in cases of life endangerment, unless an optional rider is purchased.

Louisiana Louisiana's rate is 13.0. The state's restrictions are: A) Parental consent for minors, B) A woman must receive state-directed counseling and wait twenty-four hours before getting an abortion, and C) Public funding is available only in cases of life endangerment, rape, or incest.

Mississippi Mississippi's rate is 6.0. The state's restrictions are: A) Parental consent for minors, B) A woman must receive state-directed counseling and wait twenty-four hours before getting an abortion, C) Public funding is available for abortion only in cases of life endangerment, rape, incest, or fetal abnormality, and D) Abortion is covered in insurance policies for public employees only in cases of life endangerment, rape, incest, or fetal abnormality.

Missouri Missouri's rate is 6.6. The state's restrictions are: A) Parental consent for minors, B) Public funding is available only in cases of life endangerment, rape, or incest, and C) Abortion is covered in private insurance policies only in cases of life endangerment, unless an optional rider is purchased.

Montana Montana's rate is 13.5. Montana is one of two Red States without any of the common forms of abortion restrictions. The other reasonable Red State is New Mexico.

Nebraska Nebraska has a rate of 11.6. The state's restrictions are: A) Parental notification for minors, B) A woman must receive state-directed counseling and wait twenty-four hours before getting an abortion, C) Public funding is available only in cases of life endangerment, rape, or incest, and D) Abortion is covered in insurance policies for public employees only in cases of life endangerment.

Nevada Nevada's rate is 32.2. The state's restrictions are: A) A woman must receive state-directed counseling before getting an abortion, and B) Public funding for abortions is available only in cases of life endangerment, rape, or incest.

New Mexico New Mexico's rate is 14.7. New Mexico is one of two Red States without any of the common forms of abortion restrictions. The other is Montana.

North Carolina North Carolina's rate is 21.0. The state's restrictions are: A) Parents must give consent for minors, and B) Public funding is available only in the case of life endangerment, rape, or incest.

North Dakota North Dakota's rate is 9.9. The state's restrictions are: A) Parental consent for minors, B) A woman must receive state-directed counseling and wait twenty-four hours before getting an abortion, C) Public funding for abortions is available only in cases of life endangerment, rape, or incest, D) Abortion is covered in insurance policies for public employees only in cases of life endangerment, and E) Abortion is covered in private insurance policies only in cases of life endangerment, unless an optional rider is purchased.

Ohio Ohio has a rate of 16.5. The state's restrictions are: A) Parental notification for minors, B) A woman must receive state-directed counseling and wait twenty-four hours before getting an abortion, C) Public funding is available only in cases of life endangerment, rape, or incest, and D) Abortion is covered in insurance policies for public employees only in cases of life endangerment, rape, or incest.

Oklahoma Oklahoma's rate is 10.1. The state's only restriction is: A) Public funding for abortion is available only in cases of life endangerment, rape, or incest.

South Carolina South Carolina's rate is 9.3. The state's restrictions are: A) Parental consent for minors, B) A woman must receive state-directed counseling and wait an hour before getting an abortion, and C) Public funding is available only in cases of life endangerment, rape, or incest.

South Dakota South Dakota's rate is 5.5. The state's restrictions are: A) Parental notification for minors, B) A woman must receive state-directed counseling and wait twenty-four hours before getting an abortion, and C) Public funding is available only in cases of life endangerment.

Tennessee Tennessee's rate is 15.2. The state's restrictions are: A) Parental consent for minors and B) Public funding for abortions is available only in cases of life endangerment, rape, or incest.

Texas Texas has a rate of 18.8. The state's restrictions are: A) Parental notification for minors, B) A woman must receive state-directed counseling and wait twenty-four hours before getting an abortion, and C) Public funding is available only in cases of life endangerment, rape, or incest.

Utah Utah's rate is 6.6. The state's restrictions are: A) Parental notification for minors, B) A woman must receive state-directed counseling and wait twenty-four hours before getting an abortion, and C) Public funding for abortions is available only in cases of life endangerment, rape, or incest.

Virginia Virginia's rate is 18.1. The state's restrictions are: A) The parent of a minor must give his or her consent before the minor can get an abortion, B) A woman must receive state-directed counseling, then wait twenty-four hours before getting an abortion, C) Public funding for abortions are only given in cases of life endangerment, rape, incest, or fetal abnormality, and D) Insurance for public employees covers abortion only in the case of life endangerment, rape, incest, or fetal abnormality.

West Virginia West Virginia's rate is 6.8. The state's restrictions are: A) Parental notification for minors and B) A woman must receive state-directed counseling and wait twenty-four hours before getting an abortion.

Wyoming Wyoming's rate is 1.0. The state's restrictions are: A) Parental consent for minors and B) Public funding is available only in cases of life endangerment, rape, or incest.

DEATH PENALTY

Boy, do they love the death penalty in your Red State. If you live in Texas, you'll swear it's the state pastime, more beloved than the Spurs or the Rangers.

Keep in mind that cooler heads prevailed for a short time in 1972. The Supreme Court essentially struck down the death penalty as unconstitutional. Your neighbors didn't have to resort to vigilante justice for very long, though. The death penalty returned across America in 1976, and in some Red States, it returned with a vengeance.

Below is a guide to the forms of state-sanctioned murder your new state finds acceptable. You'll notice that lethal injection is the execution method of choice in most states. And you'll see that only four Red States don't have the death penalty.

Just for laughs, death penalty information for your state is followed by each state's violent crime rates. Only Ohio actually has seen a drop in violent crime since the death penalty was reinstated. In some states, violent crime rates doubled between 1976 and 2000. But ask anyone in your new state, and they'll tell you: The death penalty is a great deterrent to violent crime.

Alabama Since 1976, Alabama has executed thirty-two death row inmates. The state's death row population is around 200, and the minimum age in Alabama for death penalty eligibility is sixteen. Inmates can choose between electrocution and lethal injection. There were 14,201 violent crimes committed in Alabama in 1975, the year before the death penalty was reinstated. There were 14,248 in 1976 and 21,620 in 2000.

Alaska Alaska does not have the death penalty.

Arizona Since 1976, Arizona has executed twenty-two death row inmates. The state's death row population is just over 130, and the minimum age in Arizona for death penalty eligibility is sixteen. Arizona favors lethal injection, but inmates sentenced before November of 1992 can opt for the gas chamber. Arizona experienced a drop in violent crime between 1975 and 1976. In 1975, it was 12,184. It dropped to 10,335 in 1976. Rates soon began to rise again, however. There were 27,281 violent crimes committed in Arizona in 2000.

Arkansas Since 1976, Arkansas has executed twenty-six death row inmates. The state's death row population is a low thirty-eight, and the minimum age in Arkansas for death penalty eligibility is sixteen. The state uses lethal injection, but inmates sentenced before July 4, 1983, can opt for electrocution. Arkansas experienced a drop in violent crime between 1975 and 1976. In 1975, the rate was 7,369. It was 6,410 in 1976. The state's violent crime rate hit a high of 14,072 in 1991. In 2000, Arkansas's violent crime rate was 11,904.

Colorado Colorado should just admit it's really a Blue State at heart. It has the death penalty, but the state has only executed one person since 1976. Colorado's death row population is three, and the minimum age for death penalty eligibility is eighteen. The state uses lethal injection. Colorado experienced a drop in violent crime between 1975 and 1976. And the state's doing something right. Between 1992 and 2000, the violent crime rate in Colorado dropped from 20,086 to 14,367.

Florida Florida has been busy since 1976: The state has executed sixty death row inmates. The state's death row population is 382, and the minimum age in Florida for death penalty eligibility is seventeen. The state offers inmates a choice of lethal injection or electrocution. Criminals also have been busy in Florida. The state did experience a drop in violent crime between 1975 and 1976. But the rate of violent crime more than doubled between 1976 and 2000. It rose from 54,597 to 129,777.

Georgia Since 1976, Georgia has executed thirty-eight death row inmates. The state's death row population is 113, and the minimum age in Florida for death penalty eligibility is seventeen. The state uses lethal injection. Georgia experienced a drop in violent crime between 1975 and 1976, but the rate nearly doubled between 1976 and 2000. It rose from 21,030 to 41,319.

Idaho Idaho is another of those Blue States in Red State clothing. It has executed one death row inmate since 1976. The state's death row population is twenty, and the minimum age in Idaho for death penalty eligibility is sixteen. The state favors lethal injection, but a firing squad is available. Idaho's violent crime rate rose between 1975 and 1976, and it's been rising pretty steadily since between 1976 and 2000. It rose from 1,884 to 3,267.

Indiana Since 1976, Indiana has executed fourteen death row inmates. The state's death row population is thirty-five, and the minimum age in Indiana for death penalty eligibility is eighteen. The state uses lethal injection. Indiana's violent crime rate dropped between 1975 and 1976. Its rate rose between 1976 and 2000, with several significant drops between some years. The violent crime rate in 1976 was 16,721. It rose to 21,230 in 2000.

Iowa Iowa does not have the death penalty.

Kansas Kansas has the death penalty, but it has not executed anyone since 1976. The state's death row population is seven, and the minimum age in Kansas for death penalty eligibility is eighteen. The state uses lethal injection. Kansas's violent crime rate rose slightly between 1975 and 1976, and it rose steadily between 1976 and 2000. It jumped from 283 to 390.

Kentucky Since 1976, Kentucky has executed two people. The state's death row population is thirty-six, and the minimum age in Kentucky for death penalty eligibility is sixteen. The state uses lethal injection, but death row inmates sentenced before June 1, 1998, can opt for the electric chair. Kentucky's violent crime rate rose slightly between 1975 and 1976, and it rose slightly between 1976 and 2000. It jumped from 8,987 to 11,903.

Louisiana Louisiana has executed twenty-seven people since 1976. The state's death row population is ninety-four, and the minimum age in Louisiana for death penalty eligibility is sixteen. The state uses lethal injection. Louisiana's violent crime rate rose slightly between 1975 and 1976. Between 1976 and 2000, the state hit an all-time violent crime high of 45,600 in 1993. In 2000, Louisiana's rate was 30,440.

Mississippi Mississippi has executed six people since 1976. The state's death row population is seventy, and the minimum age in Mississippi for death penalty eligibility is sixteen. Lethal injection is the state's execution method. Mississippi's violent crime rate dropped from 7,411 in 1975 to 6,954 in 1976. The rate in 2000 was 10,267.

Missouri Missouri has executed sixty-four people since 1976. The state has fifty-seven inmates on death row, and the minimum age in Missouri for death penalty eligibility is eighteen. Inmates can choose to die by lethal injection or in the gas chamber. Missouri's violent crime rate dropped from 23,521 in 1975 to 21,470 in 1976. The rate in 2000 was 27,419.

Montana Montana has executed two people since 1976. The state only has four inmates on death row, and the minimum age in Montana for death penalty eligibility is eighteen. The state uses lethal injection. Montana's violent crime rate dropped from 1,418 in 1975 to 1,358 in 1976. The rate in 2000 was 2,171.

Nebraska Nebraska has executed three people since 1976. The state has eight death row inmates, and the minimum age in Nebraska for death penalty eligibility is eighteen. The state executes inmates with the electric chair. Nebraska's violent crime rate dropped from 3,986 in 1975 to 3,269 in 1976. The rate in 2000 was 5,606.

Nevada Nevada has executed eleven people since 1976. The state has eighty-six death row inmates, and the minimum age in Nevada for death penalty eligibility is sixteen. The state uses lethal injection. Nevada's violent crime rate rose from 4,018 in 1975 to 4,215 in 1976. The rate in 2000 was 10,474.

New Mexico New Mexico has executed only one person since 1976. The state has two death row inmates, and the minimum age in New Mexico for death penalty eligibility is eighteen. The state executes criminals by lethal injection. New Mexico's violent crime rate rose from 6,134 in 1975 to 6,475 in 1976. The rate in 2000 was 13,786.

North Carolina North Carolina has executed thirty-six people since 1976. The state has 197 death row inmates, and the minimum age in North Carolina for death penalty eligibility is seventeen. The state uses lethal injection. North Carolina's violent crime rate dropped from 23,791 in 1975 to 22,061 in 1976. The rate in 2000 was 40,051.

North Dakota North Dakota does not have the death penalty.

Ohio Ohio has executed sixteen people since 1976. The state has 202 inmates on death row, and the minimum age in Ohio for death penalty eligibility is eighteen. The state uses lethal injection. Ohio's violent crime rate dropped from 43,901 in 1975 to 41,553 in 1976. The rate in 2000 was 37,935, making it the only Red State to experience a decline in violent crime between 1976 and 2000.

Oklahoma Oklahoma obviously has been taking lessons from its border state of Texas. It has executed seventy-seven people since 1976. The state has ninety-eight inmates on death row, and the minimum age in Oklahoma for death penalty eligibility is sixteen. Oklahoma allows for a smorgasbord of execution options: lethal injection, electrocution, and firing squad. Oklahoma's violent crime rate dropped from 8,225 in 1975 to 7,926 in 1976. The rate in 2000 was 17,177.

South Carolina South Carolina has executed thirty-three people since 1976. The state has seventy-four inmates on death row, and the minimum age in South Carolina for death penalty eligibility is sixteen. The state offers a choice of lethal injection or electrocution. South Carolina's violent crime rate rose from 14,412 in 1975 to 17,065 in 1976. The rate in 2000 was 32,293.

South Dakota South Dakota has the death penalty but has not executed anyone since 1976. The state has four inmates on death row, and the minimum age in South Dakota for death penalty eligibility is eighteen. The state uses lethal injection. South Dakota's violent crime rate dropped from 1,402 in 1975 to 1,277 in 1976. The rate went nuts after that. In 2000, it was 17,511.

Tennessee Tennessee has executed only one person since 1976. The state has 106 inmates on death row, and the minimum age in Tennessee for death penalty eligibility is eighteen. The state uses lethal injection, but death row inmates sentenced before January 1, 1999, can opt for the electric chair. Tennessee's violent crime rate dropped slightly from 16,627 in 1975 to 16,574 in 1976. The rate in 2000 was 40,233.

Texas Texas is, by far, the Red State leader in executing people. The Lone Star state has put to death 345 people since 1976. The state has 447 inmates on death row, and the minimum age in Texas for death penalty eligibility is seventeen. The state uses lethal injection.

Texas's violent crime rate dropped from 47,803 in 1975 to 44,422 in 1976. But, what's this? It can't be! The rate has more than doubled since then? The rate in 2000 was 113,653.

Utah Utah has executed six people since 1976. The state has ten inmates on death row, and the minimum age in Utah for death penalty eligibility is sixteen. The state uses lethal injection, but Utah used the firing squad until banning it in 2004. Inmates sentenced prior to the ban can opt for that method. Utah's violent crime rate dropped from 2,795 in 1975 to 2,709 in 1976. The rate in 2000 was 5,711.

Virginia Virginia has executed ninety-four people since 1976. The state has twenty-three inmates on death row, and the minimum age in Virginia for death penalty eligibility is sixteen. The state offers inmates a choice of lethal injection or the electric chair. Virginia's violent crime rate dropped from 18,917 in 1975 to 15,485 in 1976. The rate in 2000 was 19,943.

West Virginia West Virginia does not have the death penalty.

Wyoming Wyoming has the death penalty, but the state has executed only one person since 1976. The state has two death row inmates, and the minimum age in Wyoming for death penalty eligibility is eighteen. The state offers lethal injection or the gas chamber. Wyoming's violent crime rate rose from 764 in 1975 to 851 in 1976. The rate in 2000 was 1,316.

ENVIRONMENTAL ISSUES

You're not going to believe this, but it's true. Red States are among America's leaders in environmental protection. They may love their guns in your new state. They may joyfully fry hardened criminals. They may disagree with your negative assessment of Dub-Yuh's abilities and intelligence quotient. But they are practicing

"Compassionate Conservativism" on flora and fauna. Quick! Someone call *Ripley's Believe It or Not*!

Arizona Arizona brought together all its environmental agencies in 1985, creating the cabinet-level Arizona Department of Environmental Quality. In 1985, the new department had about 135 employees. It has grown into an agency of more than 700 people, and the department routinely levies large fines on companies that harm Arizona's air, water, and land.

In January 2005 alone, the department penalized the Arizona Water Company $45,000 for hazardous waste violations; penalized Kinder Morgan $500,000 for a 2003 water spill; received an $80,000 settlement from Envirosolve for hazardous waste violations; and received a $392,400 settlement from Bayless Company for groundwater contamination.

Colorado Colorado's Department of Public Health and Environment is considered a leader in innovations among state regulatory agencies. In 2004, Colorado's state legislature passed and Governor Bill Owens later signed a bill into law that allowed the state's department of public health to create a pilot project that brought together members of the department's air quality, hazardous and solid waste, radiation, sustainability, and water quality teams.

This group was joined by members of the community, environmental and community organizations, and the local and federal government. All work together to create plans for regulating environmental controls and measures and for fostering community involvement in improving the environment across Colorado.

Texas Yes. Texas. Dub-Yuh's old stomping grounds. In the 1990s, Texas streamlined its environmental agencies by consolidating their programs. The Texas Commission on Environmental Quality was in place by 2002. It has approximately 3,000 employees and a budget of $463.9 million in 2005. The 2002 name change, from the Texas Natural Resource Conservation Commission, was designed to focus on the commission's main purpose: protecting the environment.

GUN CONTROL

No, "gun control" isn't an oxymoron in a Red State. Yes, your neighbors consider the Second Amendment one of the books of the Bible, one of the Gospels, in fact. And it's true that Red States have the majority of "right to carry" states. But even most Red States have *some* restrictions, and they're often amusing ones.

Alabama In Alabama, you need a permit to carry a handgun. That's about it. The state doesn't require a permit for the purchasing or registration of rifles, shotguns, and handguns. Owners don't have to be licensed. And you don't need a permit to carry rifles or shotguns. But good news! According to state law, gun sellers break the law if they let a "habitual drunkard" purchase a gun.

Alaska Be very polite to your colleagues and neighbors. The state has none of the typical restrictions on firearms, and you don't need a permit to carry a concealed handgun.

Arizona In Arizona, you need a permit to carry a handgun. And on election day, you can rest easily. The state expressly prohibits anyone from carrying a firearm into a polling place on the day of an election.

Arkansas You need a permit to carry a handgun in Arkansas. And don't get any ideas about road rage. The state expressly prohibits shooting from or across a public highway or right of way.

Colorado In Colorado, you only need a permit to carry a concealed handgun. But litigious folks, beware. The state prohibits bringing a lawsuit against a firearm manufacturer, importer, or dealer, if a gun brings tragedy to your life.

Florida You need a permit to carry a handgun in the Sunshine State. And keep your temper in check, bub. According to state law, "It is unlawful to have or carry a firearm in the presence of one or more persons and exhibit the firearm in a rude, careless, angry, or threatening manner, except in cases of self defense."

Georgia In Georgia, you need a permit to carry a handgun. And just in case you ever get the notion to send your child to school with a firearm, don't do it. In Georgia, guns are prohibited on school buses and within 1,000 feet of any school property.

Idaho In Idaho, you need a permit to carry a handgun. And apparently, you *can* shoot a firearm on or across a public right of way in Idaho—something you can't do in Arkansas. Idaho's law only prohibits shooting from or across a public *highway*.

Indiana Hoosiers only need a permit to carry a handgun. And if a coworker's short on cash, make sure he keeps his firearms out of his empty pockets. Indiana prohibits making a loan "secured by a mortgage, deposit, or pledge of a handgun."

Iowa In Iowa, you need a permit to purchase and a permit to carry a firearm. And remember, in Iowa, hunting and flying don't mix. The state prohibits "hunting, wounding, or pursuing any game from or with an aircraft in flight."

Kansas Kansas is another "courtesy state." It has none of the typical restrictions on firearms, except that civilians are not able to carry concealed handguns. Openly brandishing one? That's pretty much okay.

Kentucky In Kentucky, you need a permit to carry a handgun. And you might want to consider buying a boat. It's illegal in Kentucky to shoot a game animal from a car. But you can shoot one from a boat.

Louisiana In Louisiana, you need a permit to carry a handgun. And if you go drinking on Bourbon Street, leave your weapon at home. Firearms are expressly prohibited from being used "on the premises of an alcoholic beverage outlet"—that is, anywhere Hurricanes and Mint Juleps are sold.

Mississippi In Mississippi, you need a permit to carry a handgun. And if you find out a coworker's hobby is making and selling her own guns, turn her in to authorities. Only recognized manufacturers' products can be sold in Mississippi.

Missouri You need a permit to purchase and a permit to carry a handgun in Missouri. And if you get bitten by the gun bug and purchase one yourself, show it to your new friends with a smile on your face. By state law, it's illegal to exhibit a gun in an angry or threatening manner.

Montana In Montana, you only need a permit to carry a concealed handgun. Otherwise, anything goes . . . unless you're on a snowmobile. It's illegal in Montana to "discharge a firearm from or upon a snowmobile."

Nebraska In Nebraska, you need a permit to purchase a handgun.

Nevada In Nevada, you need a permit to carry a handgun. The state doesn't prohibit the open carrying of a firearm, but its laws warn you to "exercise caution when carrying a firearm in public." Duh, thank you, duh, very much.

New Mexico In New Mexico, you need a permit to carry a handgun. And in a nod to "warnings" like, "Caution! Coffee is hot!" or "Swallowing poison is not recommended," New Mexico prohibits "endangering the safety of another by handling or using a firearm in a negligent manner."

North Carolina In North Carolina, you need a permit to purchase and a permit to carry a handgun. And, just to remind you that you're in the South now, brother, Sundays are the Lord's Day. Hunting with a rifle, shotgun, or handgun on Sunday is against the law.

North Dakota In North Dakota, you only need a permit to carry a concealed handgun.

Ohio In Ohio, you need a permit to carry a handgun. And no driving and shooting . . . unless you do it accidentally. It's unlawful in Ohio to "knowingly" shoot a gun while in or on a motor vehicle.

Oklahoma In Oklahoma, you need a permit to carry a handgun. And remember this handy rule of thumb: It's okay to discharge a firearm from a motorboat, but *not* from "a boat under sail."

South Carolina In South Carolina, you need a permit to carry a handgun.

South Dakota South Dakota enforces a forty-eight-hour waiting period before you can purchase a gun, though you don't need a permit to purchase it. And you only need a permit to carry a concealed handgun. If you get a traffic ticket and decide to contest it in court, leave your gun at home. Guns are expressly prohibited from being brought into courthouses.

Tennessee In Tennessee, you need a permit to carry a handgun. And in yet another "Duh Law," Tennessee prohibits "carrying a weapon into a meeting where the owner has posted prominent signs at all entrances banning weapon possession."

Texas In Texas, you need a permit to carry a handgun. And make sure you're ingenuous when displaying a gun in Dub-Yuh country. Don't be calculating in your firearm-brandishing. In Texas, "it is unlawful to display a firearm in a public place in a manner calculated to alarm."

Utah In Utah, you only need a permit to carry a concealed handgun.

Virginia In Virginia, you only need a permit to carry a concealed handgun.

West Virginia You need a permit to carry a handgun in West Virginia. And if you buy a gun and then regret doing so, don't try to palm it off at your next garage sale. In West Virginia, it is expressly prohibited to "publicly display firearms for sale . . . in such a manner as a passerby on a street, road, or alley may see them."

Wyoming In Wyoming, you need a permit to carry a handgun.

HOMOSEXUALITY

The Supreme Court struck down the country's sodomy laws in 2003. Prior to that ruling, fourteen states had sodomy laws, and—surprise, surprise—nearly all of them were Red States. And three of those fourteen states had laws that specifically targeted homosexuals. That's right. In those states, law-abiding citizens could be targeted just because they practiced an alternative lifestyle. It sounds like the Puritan era, doesn't it?

In the other eleven states, it was just understood that the laws were meant to "protect" heterosexuals from the private activities of some 10 percent of each state's population. Thanks to the Supreme Court's ruling, gay people are no longer targeted in your new Red State. What follows is a list of the states that had sodomy laws on their books well into the twenty-first century. The language in some of these laws is unintentionally hilarious.

Alabama In Alabama, it was a misdemeanor to "engage in deviate sexual intercourse with another person."

Florida In Florida, "a person who commit(ed) any unnatural and lascivious act with another person commit(ed) a misdemeanor of the second degree." Moms could breathe easily. The law specifically okayed breastfeeding. But note the law had to make clear that breastfeeding is a natural and nonlascivious act.

Idaho In Idaho, you could get five years for committing "the infamous crime against nature . . . with mankind or with any animal." It did not specify *which* infamous crime is *the* infamous crime, however.

Kansas Kansas's laws specifically targeted homosexuals.

Louisiana In Louisiana, you could get five years of hard labor for "the unnatural carnal copulation of a human being with another of the same or opposite sex or with an animal."

Mississippi Mississippi was hard core: "Every person who shall be convicted of the detestable and abominable crime against nature committed with mankind or with a beast shall be punished by imprisonment in the penitentiary for a term of not more than ten years."

Missouri Missouri's laws specifically targeted homosexuals.

North Carolina Sodomy was a felony in North Carolina.

Oklahoma Oklahoma's laws specifically targeted homosexuals.

South Carolina South Carolina's statute used the "b" word: "Whoever shall commit the abominable crime of buggery, whether with mankind or with beast, shall, on conviction, be guilty of a felony and shall be imprisoned in the Penitentiary for five years."

Texas Texas's laws specifically targeted homosexuals.

Utah In Utah, a reform bill to decriminalize sodomy between spouses failed in 1997.

Virginia You'll want to take a cold shower after you read Virginia's old law: "If any person carnally knows in any manner any brute animal, or carnally knows any male or female person by the anus or by or with the mouth, or voluntarily submits to such carnal knowledge, he or she shall be guilty of a Class 6 felony."

How to (Almost) Feel at Home in a Red State

A Blue Stater Survival Guide

INDEPENDENT BOOK STORES

When they're not busy banning or burning them, Red Staters actually do read books. Of course, they prefer stirring fare like "end-time" novels to "trash" like *The Catcher in the Rye* and the work of Toni Morrison. But don't worry.

If you want to find modern literature and the writings of Al Franken, they're as close as your nearest independent book shop. Independent stores can be found all across America, even in Red States. Most are members of the American Booksellers Association, which has regional offices deep in Red State territory. Many even have the guts to serve both Blue *and* Red States. Contact one of them to find the independent bookstore nearest you.

★ Chesapeake Regional Area Booksellers: ✆202-554-5070
★ Great Lakes Booksellers Association: ✍*www.books-glba.org*
★ Midwest Booksellers Association: ✍*www.abookaday.com*

- ★ Mountains & Plains Booksellers Association: ✉ *www.mountainsplains.org*
- ★ New Orleans Gulf South Booksellers Association: ✉ *www.nogsba.com*
- ★ Oklahoma Independent Booksellers Association: ☎ 918-743-5912
- ★ Pacific Northwest Booksellers Association: ✉ *www.pnba.org*
- ★ Southeast Booksellers Association: ✉ *www.sibaweb.org*

ART HOUSE AND CLASSIC CINEMAS

Red States aren't to blame for the mind-numbing morass that motion pictures have become. Major studios want to grab those dollars all over the world. Big explosions and steamy sex scenes translate better than the brilliance of Samuel Beckett or even the intelligent steaminess of Jacqueline Susann. Just throw in a whole bunch of four-letter words shouted by pretty people, and voila! C'est cinema.

Foreign, independent, and classic films are the escape from these doldrums. Blue States are more likely to have art house cinemas. But they're not unheard of in Red States. The following list, culled mostly from the wonderful Cinematreasure.com Web site, can direct you to movie houses that won't lower your IQ. Several of these classic cinemas have been turned into performing arts theaters, but they still feature classic, independent, and/or foreign films on a regular basis.

Alabama
- ★ **Birmingham** Alabama Theatre, 1817 Third Avenue North:
  ✉ *www.alabamatheatre.com*
- ★ **Montgomery** Capri Theatre, 1045 East Fairview Avenue: ✉ *www.capritheatre.org*
- ★ **Tuscaloosa** Bama Theatre, 600 Greensboro Avenue: ✉ *www.bamatheatre.com*

Alaska
- ★ **Anchorage** Bear Tooth Theatre Pub, 1230 W. 27th Avenue:
  ✉ *www.beartooththeatre.net*

Arizona

- ★ **Tempe** Valley Art, 509 Mill Avenue: ☎ 480-446-7272
- ★ **Yuma** Yuma Theater, 254 Main Street: ☎ 928-373-5243

Arkansas

- ★ **Blytheville** Ritz Civic Center, 306 Main Street: ☎ 870-762-1744
- ★ **Harrison** Lyric Theatre, 113 East Rush Avenue: ☎ 870-391-3504
- ★ **Hot Springs** Malco Theatre, 817 Central Avenue: ☎ 501-623-6200
- ★ **Pine Bluff** Saenger Theatre, 207 West Second Street: ☎ 870-434-8880

Colorado

- ★ **Boulder** Boulder Theater, 2032 14th Street: ✐ *www.bouldertheater.com*
- ★ **Colorado Springs** Twin Peak Theatre, 115 East Pikes Peak Avenue: ✐ *www.kimballstwinpeak.com*
- ★ **Denver** Mayan Theatre, 110 Broadway: ✐ *www.landmarktheatres.com/ Market/Denver/MayanTheatre.htm*
- ★ **Denver** Oriental Theatre, 4335 West 44th Avenue: ✐ *www.orientaltheatre.net*
- ★ **Telluride** Nugget Theatre, 207 West Colorado Avenue: ✐ *www.telluride2. com/cgi-shl/page.pl?1192*
- ★ **Westcliffe** Jones Theater, 16 Lea Lane: ✐ *www.jonestheater.com*

Florida

- ★ **Fort Lauderdale** Cinema Paradiso, 503 SE 6th Street: ✐ *www. cinemaparadiso.org*
- ★ **Fort Lauderdale** Gateway Theatre, 1820 East Sunrise Boulevard: ✐ *www. sunrisecinemas.com*
- ★ **Jacksonville** Florida Theatre, 128 East Forsyth Street: ✐ *www.floridatheatre. com*
- ★ **Plantation** Mercede Cinema 4, 1870 North University Drive: ✐ *www. sunrisecinemas.com*
- ★ **St. Petersburg** Beach Theatre, 315 Corey Avenue: ✐ *www.beachtheatre.com*
- ★ **Sarasota** Burns Court Theater, 506 Burns Lane: ✐ *www.filmsociety.org*
- ★ **Tampa** Tampa Theatre, 711 Franklin Street: ✐ *www.tampatheatre.org*

RED STATE

Georgia

- ★ **Americus** Rylander Theater, 310 West Lamar Street: ✑ *www.rylander.org*
- ★ **Atlanta** Garden Hills Theatre, 2835 Peachtree Road NE: ✑ *www. lefonttheaters.com*
- ★ **Dalton** Wink Theater, 115 West Crawford Street: ✑ *www.winktheatre.org*
- ★ **Macon** Douglass Theater, 355 Martin Luther King Jr. Boulevard: ✑ *www. douglasstheatre.org*
- ★ **Savannah** Trustees Theater, 216 East Broughton Street: ✑ *www.scad.edu/filmfest*

Idaho

- ★ **Boise** Egyptian Theater, 700 West Main Street: ✆ 208-345-0454
- ★ **Moscow** Kenworthy Performing Arts Centre, 508 Main Street: ✑ *www. kenworthy.org*
- ★ **Sandpoint** Panida Theater, 300 North 1st Avenue: ✑ *www.panida.org*

Indiana

- ★ **Danville** Royal Theater, 59 South Washington Street: ✑ *www. royaltheaterdanville.com*
- ★ **Franklin** Artcraft Theatre, 57 North Main Street: ✑ *www.franklinheritage.org*
- ★ **Highland** Town Theatre, 8616 Kennedy Avenue: ✑ *www.towntheatre.net*
- ★ **Whiting** Hoosier Theatre, 1335 119th Street: ✆ 219-659-0567

Iowa

- ★ **Des Moines** Varsity Theatre, 1207 25th Street: ✆ 515-277-0404
- ★ **Sioux City** Sioux City Orpheum, 520 Pierce Street: ✑ *www.orpheumlive.com*

Kansas

- ★ **Dodge City** Dodge Theatre, 108 Gunsmoke Street: ✆ 620-225-4421
- ★ **Lawrence** Liberty Hall Theatre, 644 Massachusetts Street: ✑ *www. libertyhall.net*
- ★ **Overland Park** Rio Theatre, 7204 West 80th Street: ✑ *www.fineartsgroup.com*
- ★ **Salina** Stiefel Theatre for the Performing Arts, 159 South Santa Fe Avenue: ✑ *www.stiefeltheatre.org*
- ★ **Shawnee** Fine Arts, 1119 Johnson Drive: ✑ *www.fineartsgroup.com*

★ **Wichita** Orpheum Theater, 200 North Broadway, Suite 102: ✎*www.wichitaorpheum.com*

Kentucky
★ **Glasgow** Plaza Theatre, 115 East Main Street: ✎*www.glasgowplazatheatre.com*
★ **Lexington** Kentucky Theatre, 214 East Main Street: ☏859-231-6997

Louisiana
★ **Franklin** Teche Theatre for the Performing Arts, 501 Main Street: ✎*www.techetheatre.org*
★ **New Orleans** Canal Place Cinema, 333 Canal Street: ☏504-525-1254
★ **New Orleans** Sanger Theatre, 143 North Rampart Street: ✎*www.saengertheatre.com*
★ **New Orleans** State Palace Theatre, 1108 Canal Street: ✎*www.statepalace.com*

Mississippi
★ **Meridian** Temple Theatre, 2320 Eighth Street: ☏601-693-5353

Missouri
★ **Bolivar** Walnut Street Theatre, 114 West Walnut Street: ✎*www.geocities.com/wsta_bolivarmo/*
★ **Kansas City** Tivoli Square, 4050 Pennsylvania: ☏913-383-7756
★ **St. Louis** Landmark Hi Pointe Theatre, 1005 McCausland Avenue: ✎*www.landmarktheatres.com*
★ **St. Louis** Landmark Tivoli Theatre, 6350 Delmar Boulevard: ✎*www.landmarktheatres.com*

Montana
★ **Bozeman** 10 West Main Street: ✎*www.carmike.com*
★ **Missoula** The Wilma Theatre, 131 South Higgins Avenue: ✎*www.thewilma.com*
★ **Troy** Lincoln Theatre, 312 Kootenai Avenue: ☏406-295-9345

Nebraska
★ **Lincoln** Rococo Theater, 134 North 13th Street: ✎*www.rococotheatre.com*

★ **Omaha** Cinema Center, 2828 South 82nd Avenue: ☏402-397-9684
★ **Omaha** Dundee Theater, 4952 Dodge Street: ☏402-551-3595

Nevada
★ **Las Vegas** Century 16 Suncoast, 9090 Alta Drive: ✎www.coastmovies.com
★ **Las Vegas** Regal Village Square 18, 9400 West Sahara Avenue: ☏702-838-0490

New Mexico
★ **Albuquerque** Century 14 Downtown Albuquerque, 100 Central Avenue: ☏505-243-7469
★ **Albuquerque** Guild Cinema, 3405 Central Avenue NE: ✎www.guildcinema.com
★ **Mesilla** Fountain Theatre, 2469 Calle de Guadalupe: ✎www.fountaintheatre.org

North Carolina
★ **Asheville** Fine Arts Theatre, 36 Biltmore Avenue: ✎www.fineartstheatre.com
★ **Cary** Galaxy Cinema, 770 Cary Towne Boulevard: ✎www.mygalaxycinema.com
★ **Chapel Hill** Carolina Theatre, 108 East Franklin Street: ☏919-933-8464
★ **Charlotte** Manor Theatre, 607 Providence Road: ☏704-334-2727
★ **Greensboro** Carolina Theatre, 310 South Greene Street: ✎www.carolinatheatre.com
★ **Raleigh** Rialto Theatre, 1620 Glenwood Avenue: ✎www.therialto.com
★ **Southern Pines** Sunrise Theater, 250 Northwest Broad Street: ✎www.sunrisetheater.com
★ **Tryon** Tryon Theatre, 45 South Trade Street: ✎www.tryontheatre.com
★ **Winston-Salem** Roger L. Stevens Center, 407 West Fourth Street: ☏336-631-1212

North Dakota
★ **Fargo** The Historic Fargo Theatre, 314 Broadway: ✎www.fargotheatre.org
★ **Grand Forks** Empire Arts Center, 415 DeMers Avenue: ✎www.empireartscenter.org

Ohio
★ **Akron** Akron Civic Theatre, 182 South Main Street: ✎www.destinationdowntownakron.com

★ **Canton** Canton Palace Theatre, 605 Market Avenue North: ✎*www.cantonpalacetheatre.org*

★ **Cincinnati** Mariemont Theater, 6906 Wooster Pike: ✎*www.mariemonttheatre.com*

★ **Cleveland** Shaker Square Cinemas, 13116 Shaker Square: ✎*www.clevelandcinemas.com*

★ **Cleveland Heights** Cedar Lee Theatre, 2163 Lee Road: ✎*www.clevelandcinemas.com*

★ **Columbus** Drexel Theatre, 2256 East Main Street: ✎*www.drexel.net*

★ **Columbus** Drexel Grandview, 1247 Grandview Avenue: ✎*www.drexel.net*

★ **Yellow Springs** Little Art Theatre, 247 Xenia Avenue: ✎*www.littleart.com*

Oklahoma

★ **Oklahoma City** Oklahoma City Museum of Art, 415 Couch Drive: ✎*www.okcmoa.com*

★ **Tulsa** AMC Southroads 20, 4923 East 41st Street: ✆918-622-9544

South Carolina

★ **Charleston** Terrace Theatre, 1956-D Maybank Highway: ✎*www.terracetheater.com*

★ **Columbia** Nickelodeon Theater, 937 Main Street: ✎*www.nickelodeon.org*

South Dakota

★ **Rapid City** The Elks Theatre, 512 6th Street: ✎*www.elkstheatre.com*

Tennessee

★ **Knoxville** Regal Downtown West Cinema 8, 1640 Downtown West Boulevard: ✆865-693-0505

★ **Knoxville** Tennessee Theatre, 604 South Gay Street: ✎*www.tennesseetheatre.com*

★ **Maryville** The Palace Theater, 113 West Broadway: ✎*www.palacetheater.com*

★ **Memphis** Malco Highland Quartet, 3473 Poplar Avenue: ✎*www.malco.com*

★ **Memphis** Malco Ridgeway 4, 5853 Ridgeway Center Parkway: ✎*www.malco.com*

★ **Nashville** The Belcourt Theatre, 2102 Belcourt Avenue: ✎*www.belcourt.org*

★ **Nashville** Regal Green Hills 16, 3815 Green Hills Village Drive: ✆615-269-5910

Texas

★ **Abilene** Paramount Theatre, 352 Cypress Street: ✉ *www.paramount-abilene.org*

★ **Austin** Alamo Drafthouse Cinema, 409 Colorado Street: ✉ *www.originalalamo.com*

★ **Austin** Dobie Theatre, 2025 Guadalupe Street: ✆ 512-472-3456

★ **Austin** Paramount Theatre, 713 Congress Avenue: ✉ *www.austintheatre.org*

★ **Dallas** Inwood Theatre, 5458 West Lovers Lane: ✆ 214-764-9106; ✉ *www.landmarktheatres.com*

★ **Dallas** Lakewood Theater, 1825 Abrams Parkway: ✉ *www.lakewoodtheater.com*

★ **Eastland** Majestic Theatre, 108 North Lamar Street: ✆ 254-629-2102

★ **Houston** Brown Auditorium Theater, 1001 Bissonnet Street: ✉ *www.mfah.org*

★ **Houston** River Oaks Theater, 2009 West Gray Street: ✆ 713-866-8881

★ **San Antonio** Santikos Bijou at the Crossroads, 4522 Fredericksburg Road: ✉ *www.santikos.com*

Utah

★ **Bicknell** Wayne Theatre, 11 East Main Street: ✉ *www.waynetheatre.com*

★ **Logan** Logan Art Cinema, 795 North Main Street: ✆ 435-753-1900

★ **Salt Lake City** Broadway Centre Cinemas, 111 East Broadway: ✆ 801-321-0310

★ **Salt Lake City** Regency Theatres Trolley Square, 602 East 500 Street: ✆ 801-746-1555

★ **Salt Lake City** Tower Theatre, 876 East 900 South: ✉ *www.towertheatre.com*

Virginia

★ **Buchanan** Buchanan Theatre, 19778 Main Street: ✉ *www.buchanantheatre.com*

★ **Charlottesville** Jefferson Theater, 110 East Main Street: ✉ *www.jeffersontheater.com*

★ **Charlottesville** Vinegar Hill Theatre, 220 West Market Street: ✉ *www.vinegarhilltheatre.com*

★ **Danville** North Theatre, 629 North Main Street: ✉ *www.edanvilleonline.com/Pages/norththeater/index.htm*

★ **Norfolk** Naro Expanded Cinema, 1507 Colley Avenue: ✉ *www.narocinema.com*

★ **Richmond** The Byrd Theatre, 2908 West Cary Street: ✉ *www.byrdtheatre.com*

★ **Richmond** Regal Westhampton Cinema 2, 5706 Grove Avenue: ☎804-288-9068
★ **Roanoke** The Grandin Theatre, 1310 Grandin Road: ✎*www.grandintheatre.com*

FINE DINING

Fear not, hungry Blue Stater. There's more to Red States than Golden Corrals, Sizzlers, and other restaurants-cum-feeding troughs. Just because you're not in civilized civilization doesn't mean you have to develop a taste for hog jowls, corn dogs, and turnip greens.

Mobil Travel Guide has ranked restaurants in North America for a half-century. They've even ventured into the darkest reaches of your Red State, to sniff out four-star and five-star restaurants. And since we're talking about a Red State, three-star places will be included in the following list as well . . . if four- and five-star establishments aren't plentiful. Beggars can't be choosers. Be thankful you've got alternatives to Joe Bob's Brisket Bonanza.

According to Mobil, three stars indicate "good food, warm and skillful service and enjoyable décor." Four-star restaurants provide "professional service, distinctive presentations and wonderful food." And five stars offer a "flawless dining experience."

Alabama Alabama has no four-star or five-star places. But it does have several three-star restaurants.

★ **Birmingham** Highlands, 2011 11th Avenue: ☎205-939-1400
★ **Mobile** The Pillars, 1757 Government Street: ☎251-471-3411
★ **Mobile** Ruth's Chris Steak House, 271 Glenwood Street: ☎251-476-0516
★ **Montgomery** Vintage Year, 405 Cloverdale Road: ☎334-264-8463
★ **Point Clear** The Grand Dining Room, One Grand Boulevard: ☎251-928-9201

Alaska Alaska has no four-star or five-star places. But it has more than twenty three-star restaurants. A selected list follows.

- ★ **Anchorage** Club Paris, 417 West 5th Avenue: ☎907-277-6332
- ★ **Denali National Park and Preserve** Nenana View Grill, George Parks Highway, mile 238.9: ☎907-683-8200
- ★ **Fairbanks** Pike's Landing, 4438 Airport Way: ☎907-479-6500
- ★ **Girdwood** Katsura Teppenyaki, 1000 Arlberg Avenue: ☎907-754-2237
- ★ **Homer** The Homestead, East End Road, mile 8.2: ☎907-235-8723
- ★ **Juneau** Chinook's Restaurant, 51 Egan Drive: ☎907-586-5123
- ★ **Ketchikan** Heen Kahidi, 800 Venetia Way: ☎907-225-8001
- ★ **Talkeetna** Foraker Restaurant, Talkeetna Spur Road, mile 12.5: ☎907-733-9509
- ★ **Valdez** The Rose Cache, 321 Egan Street: ☎907-835-8383

Arizona Arizona has four four-star restaurants. Better hope you're moving to or near Scottsdale.

- ★ **Scottsdale** Acacia, 10600 East Crescent Moon Drive: ☎480-515-5700
- ★ **Scottsdale** Mary Elaine's, 6000 East Camelback Road: ☎480-423-2444
- ★ **Scottsdale** Vu, 7500 East Doubletree Road: ☎480-483-5572
- ★ **Tucson** The Ventana Room, 7000 North Resort Drive: ☎520-299-2020

Arkansas Arkansas has no four-star or five-star places. But it does have two three-star restaurants.

- ★ **Altus** Weinkeller Restaurant, 3324 Swiss Family Drive: ☎479-468-3551
- ★ **Hot Springs** Hamilton House: 130 Van Lyell Trail: ☎501-525-2727

Colorado Colorado has five four-star restaurants.

- ★ **Aspen** Montagna, 675 East Durant Avenue: ☎970-920-6313
- ★ **Beaver Creek** Mirabelle at Beaver Creek, 55 Village Road: ☎970-949-7728
- ★ **Boulder** Flagstaff House Restaurant, 1138 Flagstaff Road: ☎303-442-4640

* **Colorado Springs** Penrose Room, 1 Lake Avenue: ✆719-577-5773
* **Denver** Restaurant Kevin Taylor, 1106 14th Street: ✆303-820-2600

Florida Florida has fifteen four-star restaurants. A selected list follows.

* **Amelia Island** The Grill, 4750 Amelia Island Parkway: ✆904-277-1100
* **Coral Gables** La Palme d'Or, 1200 Anastasia Avenue: ✆305-913-3201
* **Jacksonville** Matthew's, 2107 Hendricks Avenue: ✆904-396-9922
* **Lake Buena Vista** Victoria and Albert's, 4401 Floridian Way:
  ✆407-824-1089
* **Manalapan** The Grill, 100 South Ocean Boulevard: ✆561-533-6000
* **Miami:** Azul, 500 Brickel Key Drive: ✆305-913-8254
* **Miami Beach** Blue Door, 1685 Collins Avenue: ✆305-674-6400
* **Naples** The Dining Room, 280 Vanderbilt Beach Road: ✆239-598-6644
* **Orlando** Norman's, 4012 Central Florida Parkway: ✆407-393-4333
* **Palm Beach** Café Boulud, 301 Australian Avenue: ✆561-655-6060
* **Sarasota** Vernona Restaurant, 1111 Ritz-Carlton Drive: ✆941-309-2008

Georgia Georgia has two five-star and two four-star restaurants. Better hope you're living in or near Atlanta, though.

* **Atlanta** The Dining Room (5 stars), 3434 Peachtree Road NE: ✆404-237-2700
* **Atlanta** Seeger's (5 stars), 111 West Paces Ferry Road: ✆404-846-9779
* **Atlanta** Bacchanalia (4 stars), 1198 Howell Mill Road, Suite 100:
  ✆404-365-8020
* **Atlanta** Park 75 at the Four Seasons (4 stars), 75 14th Street NE:
  ✆404-253-3840

Idaho Idaho has no four-star or five-star places. But it does have two three-star restaurants.

* **Coeur d'Alene** Beverly's, 115 South 2nd Street: ✆208-765-4000
* **Sun Valley** Gretchen's, Sun Valley Road: ✆208-622-2144

Indiana Indiana has no four-star or five-star places. But it does have seven three-star restaurants.

★ **Gary** Miller Bakery Café, 555 South Lake Street: ☎219-938-2229
★ **Greencastle** Different Drummer, 2 West Seminary Street: ☎765-653-2761
★ **Indianapolis** Chanteclair, 2501 South High School Road: ☎317-243-1040
★ **Indianapolis** Restaurant at the Canterbury, 123 South Illinois Street: ☎317-634-3000
★ **South Bend** The Carriage House Dining Room, 24460 Adams Road: ☎574-272-9220
★ **South Bend** La Salle Grill, 115 West Colfax: ☎574-288-1155
★ **Valparaiso** Clayton's, 66 West Lincolnway: ☎219-531-0612

Iowa Iowa has no four-star or five-star places. But it does have five three-star restaurants.

★ **Bettendorf** The Lodge, 900 Spruce Hills Drive: ☎563-359-1607
★ **Des Moines** Christopher's, 2816 Beaver Avenue: ☎515-274-3694
★ **Johnston** Greenbrier, 5810 Merle Hay Road: ☎515-253-0124
★ **Le Claire** The Faithful Pilot Café, 117 North Cody Road: ☎563-289-4156
★ **Sioux City** The Victorian Opera Company, 1021 4th Street: ☎712-255-4821

Kansas Kansas doesn't have any four-star or five-star places. But it does have six three-star restaurants.

★ **Abilene** Kirby House, 205 NE 3rd Street: ☎785-263-7336
★ **Leawood** Hereford House, 5001 Town Center Drive: ☎913-327-0800
★ **Overland Park** J. Gilbert's Wood Fired Steaks, 8901 Metcalf Avenue: ☎913-642-8070
★ **Overland Park** Nikko, 10800 Metcalf Road: ☎913-451-8000
★ **Prairie Village** 4603 West 90th Street: ☎913-383-9801
★ **Wichita** Olive Tree, 2949 North Rock Road: ☎316-636-1100

Kentucky Kentucky has no five-star or four-star places. But it has seven three-star restaurants.

★ **Covington** Waterfront, 14 Pete Rose Pier: ✆859-581-1414
★ **Lexington** Mansion at Griffin Gate, 1800 Newtown Pike: ✆859-288-6142
★ **Louisville** English Grill, 335 West Broadway: ✆502-583-1234
★ **Louisville** Kunz's Fourth and Market, 115 South 4th Street: ✆502-585-5555
★ **Louisville** Le Relais, 2817 Taylorsville Road: ✆502-451-9020
★ **Louisville** Lilly's, 1147 Bardstown Road: ✆502-451-0447
★ **Louisville** Vincenzo's, 150 South 5th Street: ✆502-580-1350

Louisiana The New Orleans area has a lock on four-star restaurants in the Bayou State. Louisiana boasts a total of five four-star places.

★ **Lacombe** La Provence, Highway 190 East: ✆985-626-7662
★ **New Orleans** Bayona, 430 Dauphine Street: ✆504-525-4455
★ **New Orleans** Emeril's Delmonico, 1300 St. Charles Avenue: ✆504-525-4937
★ **New Orleans** Emeril's Restaurant, 800 Tchoupitoulas Street: ✆504-528-9393
★ **New Orleans** The Grill Room, 300 Gravier Street: ✆504-522-1992

Mississippi Mississippi has no five-star or four-star places. It has one three-star restaurant.

★ **Biloxi** Mary Mahoney's Old French House, Magnolia and Water Streets: ✆228-374-0163

Missouri Missouri has two four-star restaurants.

★ **Kansas City** American, 200 East 25th Street, Suite 400: ✆816-545-8000
★ **St. Louis** Tony's, 410 Market Street: ✆314-231-7007

Montana Montana has no four-star or five-star places. But it does have nine three-star restaurants.

- ★ **Bigfork** Coyote Riverhouse, 600 Three Eagle Lane: ✆406-837-1233
- ★ **Big Sky** Lone Mountain Ranch Dining Room, 160069 Big Sky: ✆406-995-2782
- ★ **Billings** Juliano's, 2912 North 7th Avenue: ✆406-248-6400
- ★ **Billings** Walker's Grill, 301 North 27th Street: ✆406-245-9291
- ★ **Bozeman** Gallatin Gateway Inn, 76405 Gallatin Road: ✆406-763-4672
- ★ **Butte** Lydia's, 4915 Harrison Avenue: ✆406-494-2000
- ★ **Butte** Uptown Café, 47 East Broadway: ✆406-723-4735
- ★ **Livingston** Chatham's Livingston Bar and Grill, 130 North Main Street: ✆406-222-7909
- ★ **Red Lodge** Arthur's Grill, 2 North Broadway: ✆406-446-0001

Nebraska Nebraska doesn't have any five-star or four-star places. But it does have four three-star restaurants, mostly in Omaha.

- ★ **Norfolk** The Uptown Café, 801 10th Street: ✆402-439-5100
- ★ **Omaha** Café de Paris, 1228 South 6th Street: ✆402-344-0227
- ★ **Omaha** Signature's, 1616 Dodge Street: ✆402-346-7600
- ★ **Omaha** V. Mertz, 1022 Howard Street: ✆402-345-8980

Nevada Nevada has four four-star restaurants, all in Sin City.

- ★ **Las Vegas** Aureole, 3950 Las Vegas Boulevard: ✆702-632-7401
- ★ **Las Vegas** Bradley Ogden, 3570 Las Vegas Boulevard: ✆800-346-4642
- ★ **Las Vegas** Michael Mina, 3600 Las Vegas Boulevard South: ✆702-693-8255
- ★ **Las Vegas** Picasso, 3600 Las Vegas Boulevard South: ✆702-693-7223

New Mexico New Mexico has one four-star restaurant.

- ★ **Santa Fe** Geronimo, 724 Canyon Road: ✆505-982-1500

North Carolina The Tarheel State has two four-star restaurants.

- ★ **Chapel Hill** Carolina Crossroads, 211 Pittsboro Street: ✆919-933-2001

★ **Pittsboro** The Fearrington House Restaurant, 2000 Fearrington Village Center: ☎919-542-2121

North Dakota Sorry, Blue Stater. North Dakota doesn't have any three-star, four-star, or five-star restaurants.

Ohio This key swing state has one five-star restaurant.

★ **Cincinnati** Maisonette, 114 East 6th Street: ☎513-721-2260

Oklahoma Oklahoma has no five-star or four-star places. But it does have nine three-star restaurants.

★ **Oklahoma City** Bellini's, 6305 Waterford Boulevard #1: ☎405-848-1065
★ **Oklahoma City** Coach House, 6437 Avondale Drive: ☎405-842-1000
★ **Oklahoma City** JW's Steakhouse, 3233 Northwest Expressway Street: ☎405-842-6633
★ **Oklahoma City** Keller in the Kastle German Restaurant, 820 North MacArthur: ☎405-942-6133
★ **Tulsa** Atlantic Sea Grill, 8321-A East 61st Street: ☎918-252-7966
★ **Tulsa** Bodean Seafood, 3323 East 51st Street: ☎918-743-3861
★ **Tulsa** Fountains, 6540 South Lewis Avenue: ☎918-749-9916
★ **Tulsa** Polo Grill, 2038 Utica Square: ☎918-744-4280
★ **Tulsa** Warren Duck Club, 6110 South Yale: ☎918-495-1000

South Carolina The Charleston area has two four-star restaurants and one five-star restaurant.

★ **Summerville** The Dining Room at the Woodlands (5 stars), 125 Parsons Road: ☎843-875-2600
★ **Charleston** Charleston Grill (4 stars), 224 King Street: ☎843-577-4522
★ **Charleston** Peninsula Grill (4 stars), 112 North Market Street: ☎843-723-0700

South Dakota South Dakota doesn't have any five-star or four-star places. But it does have three three-star restaurants.

★ **Deadwood** Jake's Atop the Midnight Star, 677 Main Street: ✆ 605-578-1555
★ **Pierre** La Minestra, 106 East Dakota Avenue: ✆ 605-224-8090
★ **Sioux Falls** C.J. Callaway's, 500 East 69th Street: ✆ 605-334-8888

Tennessee The Volunteer State has two four-star restaurants.

★ **Nashville** The Wild Boar, 2014 Broadway: ✆ 615-329-1313
★ **Memphis** Chez Phillipe, 149 Union Avenue: ✆ 901-529-4188

Texas Former Governor George W. Bush's state has six four-star restaurants.

★ **Austin** Café at the Four Seasons, 98 San Jacinto Boulevard: ✆ 512-478-4500
★ **Dallas** Abacus, 4511 McKinney Avenue: ✆ 214-559-3111
★ **Dallas** The French Room, 1321 Commerce Street: ✆ 214-742-8200
★ **Dallas** Restaurant at the Mansion on Turtle Creek, 2821 Turtle Creek Boulevard: ✆ 214-559-2100
★ **Houston** Quattro, 1300 Lamar Street: ✆ 713-652-6250
★ **San Antonio** Le Reve, 152 East Pecan Street: ✆ 210-212-2221

Utah Utah has one four-star restaurant.

★ **Park City** Riverhorse on Main, 540 Main Street: ✆ 435-649-3536

Virginia Virginia has one five-star and one four-star restaurant.

★ **Washington** The Inn at Little Washington (5 stars), 309 Main Street: ✆ 540-675-3800
★ **McLean** Maestro (4 stars), 1700 Tysons Boulevard: ✆ 703-917-5498

West Virginia West Virginia has one four-star restaurant.

★ **White Sulphur Springs** The Tavern Room, 300 West Main Street: ☎304-536-1110

Wyoming Wyoming doesn't have any five-star or four-star restaurants. But it does have eight three-star places.

★ **Jackson** Blue Lion, 160 North Millward Street: ☎307-733-3912
★ **Jackson** Cadillac Grille, 55 North Cache Drive: ☎307-733-3279
★ **Jackson** Snake River Grill, 84 East Broadway: ☎307-733-0557
★ **Jackson** Sweetwater, 85 South King Street: ☎307-733-3553
★ **Moose** Jenny Lake Lodge Dining Room, Inner Loop Road, Box 240: ☎307-543-2811
★ **Teton Village** The Alpenrose in the Alpenhof Lodge, 3255 West Village Drive: ☎307-733-3242
★ **Teton Village** The Westbank Grill at the Four Seasons Resort, 7680 Granite Loop Road: ☎307-734-5040
★ **Wilson** Teton Pines, 3450 North Clubhouse Drive: ☎307-733-1005

CONSERVATIVE SCALAWAGS

Red States cling to double standards like a drunk holds on to the last beer he can afford. It's another state of affairs that will make you feel you've stepped through the looking glass and entered a bizarre world where right and wrong/good and bad are arbitrary labels, depending solely on the political leanings of the do-gooder/do-badder.

The obvious case in point: President Dub-Yuh vs. President Clinton. Bush wages war on Iraq for specious reasons. Conservatives cry: God bless your leadership, Sir! Clinton has oral sex in the Oval Office. Conservatives cry: Off with his head (no pun intended)!

In your new state, you'll run into this double standard regularly. But fear not. The antidote to Red State brainwashing is a quick reminder of the foibles of your new state's beloved leaders and pundits.

Newt Gingrich Newt Gingrich, paper general of the so-called Second American Revolution, enjoyed condemning President Clinton for his lack of character.

But Gingrich has a laundry list of family values-lacking skeletons in his closet: A) Gingrich allegedly pushed his wife to give him a divorce while she was in the hospital for surgery, B) Gingrich allegedly avoided the Vietnam War through a combination of student and family deferments, C) He admitted to using funds from a tax-exempt charitable foundation to fund his televised college course, and D) Gingrich allegedly is a serial adulterer: Callista Bisek, Anne Manning, etc.

William Bennett Drug czar, secretary of education, Chairman of the National Endowment for the Humanities, best-selling author of books on virtues, and—oh yeah—longtime problem gambler, who lost millions of dollars a month . . . money made from being the Conservative Voice Box of Values. William Bennett can put all of these on his curriculum vitae.

Rush Limbaugh Rush Limbaugh, circa 1995: "Too many whites are getting away with drug use . . . We're becoming too tolerant, folks." Rush Limbaugh, circa 2003: "I need to tell you that part of what you have heard and read is correct. I am addicted to prescription pain medication."

And don't hesitate, if cornered, to trot out Limbaugh's "color commentary" during his very brief time on ESPN's *Sunday Night Countdown.* Also Rush Limbaugh, circa 2003: "I think what we've had here is a little social concern in the NFL. The media has been very desirous that a black quarterback do well. There is a little hope invested in McNabb, and he got a lot of credit for the performance of this team that he didn't deserve. The defense carried this team."

Bill O'Reilly Bill O'Reilly was sued for sexual harassment by a female Fox News producer. Allegedly, the brilliant conversationalist attempted to engage her in such diverse topics as phone sex, vibrators, threesomes, masturbation, and sexual fantasies.

Sean Hannity Do you remember that nasty business called the Abu Ghraib prisoner abuse scandal? Well, Red State leaders had nothing to do with it. So there! Infallible font of truth Sean Hannity suggested to America that it was all just one big Democratic National Committee plot to make conservatives look bad. And the fact that no weapons of mass destruction ever turned up in Iraq? Surely, somewhere, Hannity blamed progressives for that, too.

LIBERAL FAITH

Folks in Red States talk about matters of faith the way colleagues in your good ol' Blue State talked about sports or trash TV. The first few times you're asked if you have a "church home," you'll find it quaint. Before long, you'll learn what happens if you answer in the negative. "Well then," your new neighbor/colleague/total stranger will say, "I want to personally invite you to attend my church home, The House of His Everlasting Blood of the Tongues of Flame Holiness Tabernacle."

The best way to shut them up is to say that you do, in fact, have a church home. Then name the local Unitarian Universalist church. To your Red State friends, Unitarians sound a lot like Scientologists. "I don't think I've heard of that one," will be the likely response. Then the questions about faith will stop. You, they've decided, already are surely damned to Hell. So it's best not to get too close to you, in case some of that sin rubs off.

To find the closest Unitarian congregation, contact one of the following district offices.

RED STATE

Eastern Missouri/Upper Western Indiana
★ Central Midwest District of the Unitarian Universalist Association: ☎708-236-0831; ✎*www.cmwd-uua.org*

Florida/Southern Georgia
★ Florida District of the Unitarian Universalist Association: ☎407-894-2119; ✎*www.floridadistrict.org*

Indiana, Kentucky, and Western Ohio
★ Heartland District of the Unitarian Universalist Association: ☎888-948-4883; ✎*www.heartlanduu.org*

Northern Virginia
★ Joseph Priestly District of the Unitarian Universalist Association: ☎302-778-4564; ✎*www.jpduua.org*

Alabama, Northwestern and Central Georgia, Mississippi, the Florida Panhandle, First Unitarian Universalist in Nashville, Tennessee
★ Mid-South District of the Unitarian Universalist Association: ☎662-234-4423; ✎*www.msd.uua.org*

Colorado, Eastern Idaho, Montana, Western Nebraska, New Mexico, Western Texas, Utah, Wyoming
★ Mountain Desert District of the Unitarian Universalist Association: ☎303-756-1378; ✎*www.uua.org/mdd*

West Virginia, Ohio
★ Ohio Meadville District: ☎330-948-2600; ✎*www.omd.uua.org*

Northern Nevada
★ Pacific Central District of the Unitarian Universalist Association: ☎510-601-1437; ✎*www.pcd-uua.org*

Alaska, Idaho
★ Pacific Northwest District of the Unitarian Universalist Association: 800-313-7693; *www.pnwd.org*

Arizona/Southern Nevada
★ Pacific Southwest District of the Unitarian Universalist Association: 818-769-5917; *www.pswd.uua.org*

Iowa, Kansas, Northwestern Missouri, Eastern Nebraska, North Dakota, Eastern South Dakota
★ Prairie Star District of the Unitarian Universalist Association: 612-230-3273; *www.psduua.org*

Arkansas, Louisiana, Southwestern Missouri, Oklahoma, Western Tennessee, Texas
★ Southwest District of the Unitarian Universalist Association: 817-446-0099; *www.swuuc.org*

North Carolina, South Carolina, Eastern Georgia, Eastern and Central Tennessee, Virginia
★ Thomas Jefferson District of the Unitarian Universalist Association: 704-549-0750; *www.uua.org/tjd*

THE DEMOCRATIC PARTY

Yes, it does exist in Red states. Below is a state-by-state list of organizations for you to join. Just think! You'll still be in a backwards-thinking Red State, but you'll be surrounded by people with brains, compassion, and steadfast idealism.

Alabama
★ The Alabama Democratic Party: 334-262-2221; *www.aladems.org*
★ Alabama Federation of Democratic Women: 866-542-2339

★ Alabama Young Democrats: ☎ 256-468-7458
★ Alabama College Democrats: ☎ 205-535-0204; ✉ *www.alabamacollegedemocrats.com*

Alaska
★ Alaska Democratic Party: ☎ 907-258-3050; ✉ *www.alaskademocrats.org*

Arizona
★ Arizona Democratic Party: ☎ 602-298-4200; ✉ *www.azdem.org*

Arkansas
★ The Democratic Party of Arkansas: ☎ 501-374-2361; ✉ *www.arkdems.org*
★ Young Democrats of Arkansas: ✉ *www.ydarkansas.org*
★ Arkansas Democratic Hispanic Caucus: ✉ *www.arkdhc.org*

Colorado
★ Colorado Democratic Party: ☎ 303-623-4762; ✉ *www.coloradodems.org*

Florida
★ Florida Democratic Party: ☎ 850-222-3411; ✉ *www.fladems.com*
★ Florida College Democrats: ✉ *www.donkeysrock.com/CollegeDems.shtml*
★ Democratic Caribbean Caucus of Florida: ✉ *www.dccf.net*
★ Democratic Women's Club of Florida: ✉ *www.democratic-women.org*
★ Florida Democratic Party Small County Coalition: ✉ *www.fdpscc.tripod.com*

Georgia
★ The Democratic Party of Georgia: ☎ 404-870-8201; ✉ *www.georgiaparty.com*
★ Georgia Legislative Democratic Caucus: ☎ 404-656-5035; ✉ *www*
  .gademocraticmajority.com
★ Red Clay Democrats: ✉ *www.redclaydemocrats.org*
★ Young Democrats of Georgia: ✉ *www.georgiayds.org*

Idaho
★ Idaho Democratic Party: ☎ 208-336-1815; ✉ *www.idaho-democrats.org*
★ Idaho Progressive Caucus: ✉ *www.idahoprogressives.org*

Indiana
★ Indiana Democratic Party: ☎317-231-7100; ✎*www.indems.org*

Iowa
★ Iowa Democratic Party: ☎515-244-7292; ✎*www.iowademocrats.org*

Kansas
★ Kansas Democratic Party: ☎785-234-0425; ✎*www.ksdp.org*
★ Democratic Asian Caucus of Kansas: ✎*www.dack.us*
★ Kansas Democratic Lesbian, Gay, Bisexual, Transgendered Caucus: ✎*www.kansaslgbtdemocrats.org*
★ Kansas Progressive Caucus: ✎*www.ksprogressives.org*
★ Kansas Young Democrats: ✎*www.kansasyoungdemocrats.org*

Kentucky
★ Kentucky Democratic Party: ☎502-695-4828; ✎*www.kydemocrat.com*

Louisiana
★ Louisiana Democratic Party: ☎225-336-4155; ✎*www.lademo.org*

Mississippi
★ The Democratic Party of the State of Mississippi: ☎601-969-2913; ✎*www.msdemocrats.net*

Missouri
★ Missouri Democratic Party: ☎573-636-5241; ✎*www.missouridems.org*
★ Heartland Democrats of America: ✎*www.heartlanddemocrats.com*

Montana
★ Montana Democratic Party: ☎406-442-9520; ✎*www.montanademocrats.org*
★ Big Sky Democrats: ✎*www.bigskydemocrats.org*

Nebraska
★ Nebraska Democratic Party: ✎*www.nebraskademocrats.org*

Nevada

★ Nevada State Democratic Party: ✐*www.nvdems.com*

New Mexico

★ New Mexico Democratic Party: ✐*www.nmdemocrats.org*

North Carolina

★ North Carolina Democratic Party: ✆919-821-2777; ✐*www.ncdp.org*
★ African American Caucus of the North Carolina Democratic Party: ✐*www.aac-ncdp.org*
★ Hispanic Democrats of North Carolina: ✐*www.hdnc.org*
★ Young Democrats of North Carolina: ✐*www.ydnc.org*

North Dakota

★ North Dakota Democratic/Non-Partisan League Party: ✆701-222-1371; *www.demnpl.com*

Ohio

★ Ohio Democratic Party: ✆614-221-6563; ✐*www.ohiodems.org*
★ Ohio Democratic Catholic Caucus: ✐*www.catholicdemsoh.org*
★ Federated Democratic Women of Ohio: ✆330-727-2534; ✐*www.ohiofederatedwomen.org*
★ Ohio Legislative Black Caucus: ✐*www.olbc1967.org*
★ Stonewall Democrats of Central Ohio: ✆614-265-7444; ✐*www.stonewalldemocratsohio.org*

Oklahoma

★ Oklahoma Democratic Party: ✆405-427-3366; ✐*www.okdemocrats.org*

South Carolina

★ South Carolina Democratic Party: ✆803-799-7798; ✐*www.scdp.org*
★ Young Democrats of South Carolina: ✐*www.ydsc.org*

South Dakota
★ South Dakota Democratic Party: ☏605-224-1759; ✍*www.sddp.org*

Tennessee
★ Tennessee Democratic Party: ✍*www.tndp.org*
★ Tennessee Federation of College Democrats: ✍*www.tfcd.org*

Texas
★ Texas Democratic Party: ☏512-478-9800; ✍*www.txdemocrats.org*
★ Asian American Democrats of Texas: ✍*www.aadt.org*
★ Texas Coalition of Black Democrats: ✍*www.tcbd.org*
★ Texas Democratic Veterans: ✍*www.geocities.com/texasdemocraticvets/index .html*
★ Texas Democratic Women: ✍*www.tdw.org*
★ Texas Young Democrats: ✍*www.texasyds.org*

Utah
★ Utah Democratic Party: ☏801-328-1212; ✍*www.utdemocrats.org*

Virginia
★ Democratic Party of Virginia: ☏804-644-1966; ✍*www.vademocrats.org*
★ Virginia Young Democrats: ✍*www.vayd.org*

West Virginia
★ West Virginia State Democratic Party: ☏304-342-8121; ✍*www.wvdemocrats .com*

Wyoming
★ Wyoming Democratic Party: ☏307-473-1457; ✍*www.wyomingdemocrats .com*

PART 2

State-by-State Breakdown

ALABAMA

GOVERNOR, SENATORS, CONGRESS MEMBERS

Governor Bob Riley, Republican Riley served in the U.S. House of Representatives before being elected governor in 2002. He's the guy who tried to get rich voters to approve burdensome taxes on them by suggesting that was the Christian thing to do. Riley's proposal was soundly defeated by voters. You can vote him out of office in 2006.
➤ **Contact** 334-242-7100; *www.governor.state.al.us*

Senator Jeff Sessions, Republican Sessions has been a senator since 1997. You can vote him out of office in 2008.
➤ **Contact** 202-224-4124; *www.sessions.senate.gov*

Senator Richard Shelby, Republican Shelby is the senate's only current Red State flip-flopper. He served as a Democratic congressman from 1979 to 1986. He served as a Democratic senator from 1987 to 1992. Shelby switched to the Republican Party in 1992. You can vote him out of office in 2010.
➤ **Committees** Chair, Committee on Banking, Housing, and Urban Affairs
➤ **Contact** 202-224-5744; *www.shelby.senate.gov*

Congress Members, 109th Congress
★ Jo Bonner, Republican: Began serving in 2002. 202-225-4931; *www.bonner.house.gov*
★ Terry Everett, Republican: Began serving in 1992. 202-225-2901; *www.house.gov/everett*
★ Mike Rogers, Republican: Began serving in 2002. 202-225-3261; *www.house.gov/mike-rogers*
★ Robert Aderholt, Republican: Began serving in 1996. 202-225-4876; *www.aderholt.house.gov*
★ Bud Cramer Jr., Democrat: Began serving in 1990. 202-225-4801; *www.cramer.house.gov*

★ Spencer Bachus, Republican: Began serving in 1992. ✆ 202-225-4921; ✐ *www.bachus.house.gov*

★ Artur Davis, Democrat: Began serving in 2002. ✆ 202-225-2665; ✐ *www.house.gov/arturdavis*

PITHY POLITICAL POOP AND SCINTILLATING SCANDAL

The Creek War Alabama and Georgia were born with the death of a thousand Creek Indians. Tired of having their lands encroached on, the Creeks attacked and burned Fort Mims on the Alabama River. They killed about 500 people. That's bad. The Creeks were allies of the British during the French and Indian War. Call that strike two. And finally, the Creeks committed the so-called Fort Mims Massacre in the midst of the War of 1812. Strike three.

Famous Indian hater and future president Andrew Jackson was sent to give the Creeks a friendly warning. He destroyed two villages—Tallasahatchee and future NASCAR hotspot Talladega—in 1813.

Jackson wasn't certain the Creeks got his point, so he pursued them with a 3,000-man army and killed more than 800 Indians, decimating the Creek nation. As a way of saying thanks for destroying us and our civilization, the Creeks ceded 23 million acres to the United States, including half of Alabama and part of southern Georgia.

George Wallace Takes a (Stupid) Stand George Wallace transformed himself from an icon of segregation to one of reconciliation.

He was elected governor of Alabama in 1962, after running on a platform of resistance to federal attempts to end segregation. Wallace became a national figure in 1963, during the so-called "Stand in the Schoolhouse Door." He literally blocked the entrance to a building at the University of Alabama, when federal authorities attempted to enroll two African American students.

Later on, you have Wallace to thank for the election of Richard Nixon. Just as Ross Perot helped ensure Bill Clinton's election in 1992, Wallace's third-party bid for president in 1968 leeched enough votes away from Hubert Humphrey to put Tricky Dick in the White House. Wallace again tried for president in 1972, when he was shot and paralyzed by Arthur Bremer. Wallace's presidential bids were over, but he continued to run for and be elected as governor.

During the late 1970s, Wallace became a born-again Christian and apologized for his racist views. During his last term in office, from 1983 to 1987, he appointed a record number of black Alabamians to government positions.

PEOPLE FROM YOUR NEW STATE
WHO WON'T MAKE YOU FEEL ILL

* Hammerin'Hank Aaron, baseball player, Mobile
* Nat "King"Cole, entertainer, Montgomery
* W. C. Handy, considered founder of the blues, Florence
* Emmylou Harris, country chanteuse, Birmingham
* Coretta Scott King, civil rights leader, Marion
* Rosa Parks, civil rights leader, Tuskegee
* Hank Williams, country music god, Georgiana

ALASKA

GOVERNOR, SENATORS, CONGRESS MEMBERS

Governor Frank Murkowski, Republican Murkowski was a U.S. senator from 1981 to 2002. He's infamous for impeding the efforts of environmentalists who wanted to stop oil drilling in parts of his state.

Murkowski was elected governor in 2002, and his daughter, Lisa Murkowski, was appointed to finish his term. As of 2005, his approval rating hovered around 25 percent. He may have been voted out of office by the time you read this.

➤ **Contact** ✆907-465-3500; ✍*www.gov.state.ak.us*

Senator Lisa Murkowski, Republican Murkowski has served as a senator since 2002, when she was tapped to fill the vacancy caused by the resignation of her father, Senator Frank H. Murkowski. She was elected to the senate in 2004. You can vote her out of office in 2010.

➤ **Contact** ✆202-224-6665; ✍*www.murkowski.senate.gov*

Senator Ted Stevens, Republican Stevens has served as a senator since 1968. You can vote him out of office in 2008.

➤ **Committees** Committee on Commerce, Science, and Technology
➤ **Contact** ✆202-224-6665; ✍*www.stevens.senate.gov*

Congress Member, 109th Congress

★ Don Young, Republican: Began serving in 1972. ✆202-225-5765; ✍*www.donyoung.house.gov*

PITHY POLITICAL POOP
AND SCINTILLATING SCANDAL

Exxon Valdez Enough oil to fill 125 Olympic-sized swimming pools spilled into Prince William Sound on March 24, 1989. The Exxon *Valdez* spill remains one of the worst in American history. For a short time, it even forced Red Staters to think about the environment, as oil-covered birds and sea otters stared mutely from television screens.

The spill occurred because miscommunication among the ship's crew caused the *Valdez* to strike a reef. Captain Joe Hazelwood had alcohol in his blood following the wreck, but he was cleared of drunkenness. He was, however, fined $50,000 for negligent discharge of oil. After the 11-million gallon spill, Congress passed the Oil Pollution Act of 1990, which required the U.S. Coast Guard to toughen regulations on oil tank vessels, owners, and operators. In addition, Congress will require all oil tankers to be double-hulled by 2015.

Mt. What's-Its-Name The renaming of Mt. McKinley to its original Mt. Denali was blocked in 1975 by Ohio Congressman, Representative Ralph Regula.

Regula's hometown of Canton is the birthplace of President William McKinley. Regula blocked a compromise proposed by the Alaska legislature to rename the mountain but leave the national park around it named after McKinley. So the mountain continues to be named after a man who never set eyes on it.

PEOPLE FROM YOUR NEW STATE
WHO WON'T MAKE YOU FEEL ILL

* Irene Bedard, actress, Anchorage
* Hilary Lindh, Olympic medalist, Juneau
* Elizabeth Peratrovich, civil rights activist, Petersburg
* Howard Rock, anti-nuclear activist, Point Hope

ARIZONA

GOVERNOR, SENATORS, CONGRESS MEMBERS

Governor Janet Napolitano, Democrat Napolitano served as Arizona's attorney general before being elected governor in 2002. There was some talk of her being John Kerry's running mate during Kerry's ill-fated 2004 presidential run. If this is your new state, you can breathe easy. Napolitano is for abortion and strongly supports biotechnology projects in the state's university system. You can reelect her in 2006.

➤ **Contact** ✆602-542-3331; ✍*www.governor.state.az.us*

Senator Jon Kyl, Republican Kyl served as a congressman from 1987 to 1994. He has served as a senator since 1995. You can vote him out of office in 2006.

➤ **Committees** Chair, Republican Policy Committee
➤ **Contact** ✆202-224-4521; ✐*www.kyl.senate.gov*

Senator John McCain, Republican McCain served as a congressman from 1983 to 1986. He has served as a senator since 1987. You can vote him out of office in 2010. McCain was unsuccessful in his bid for the 2000 presidency.

➤ **Committees** Chair, Committee on Indian Affairs; Committee on Commerce, Science, and Transportation
➤ **Contact** ✆202-224-2235; ✐*www.mccain.senate.gov*

Congress Members, 109th Congress

★ Rick Renzi, Republican: Began serving in 2002. ✆202-225-2315; ✐*www.house.gov/renzi*
★ Trent Franks, Republican: Began serving in 2002. ✆202-225-4576; ✐*www.house.gov/franks*
★ John Shadegg, Republican: Began serving in 1994. ✆202-225-3361; ✐*www.johnshadegg.house.gov*
★ Ed Pastor, Democrat: Began serving in 1990. ✆202-225-4065; ✐*www.house.gov/pastor*
★ J.D. Hayworth, Republican: Began serving in 1994. ✆202-225-2190; ✐*www.hayworth.house/gov*
★ Jeff Flake, Republican: Began serving in 2000. ✆202-225-2635; ✐*www.house.gov/flake*
★ Raul Grijalva, Democrat: Began serving in 2002. ✆202-225-2435; ✐*www.house.gov/grijalva*
★ Jim Kolbe, Republican: Began serving in 1984. ✆202-225-2542; ✐*www.house.gov/kolbe*

PITHY POLITICAL POOP AND
SCINTILLATING SCANDAL

The "Daisy" Ad   Maybe it's because he was too conservative even for most conservatives, but the most likely reason Arizona's Barry Goldwater lost his 1964 bid for the presidency was a commercial. The so-called "Daisy" ad never mentioned Goldwater by name, but it was understood Goldwater was the target.

The commercial begins with a little girl picking petals off a daisy and counting them. When she gets to ten, a voice-over begins counting back, from ten to one. At one, there's a huge explosion, and a mushroom cloud fills the screen. Then you hear the voice of President Johnson: "These are the stakes—to make a world in which all God's children can live, or to go into the darkness. We must either love each other, or we must die." Johnson's pronouncement is followed by a pitchman's voice telling voters to choose Johnson in November.

The Daisy ad pioneered negative campaign ads, even though it was shown only once as a paid commercial. Fortunately, the media was more than happy to show the commercial over and over on the evening news. Johnson won the November 1964 election with 61 percent of the vote.

PEOPLE FROM YOUR NEW STATE
WHO WON'T MAKE YOU FEEL ILL

* Lynda Carter, actress, Phoenix
* Cochise, Apache Indian chief, Arizona Territory
* Geronimo, Apache Indian chief, Arizona Territory
* Charles Mingus, jazz great, Nogales
* Linda Ronstadt, singer, Tucson

ARKANSAS

GOVERNOR, SENATORS, CONGRESS MEMBERS

Governor Mike Huckabee, Republican Huckabee was a Baptist minister before he turned to politics. Like William Jefferson Clinton, Huckabee was born in a place called Hope. And, in another nod to Clinton, Huckabee first took office due to the resignation of Governor Jim Guy Tucker, who was convicted of a felony related to the Whitewater scandal.

Huckabee is proof that conservative Christians can actually have hearts. He created a health insurance program that treats the working poor's children. He vastly improved the state's aging road system. And he took tobacco settlement money and put it into the state's health-care system, rather than into its general fund.

On the minus side, Huckabee commuted the sentences of convicted felons, including rapists. Huckabee's term as governor ends in 2006. Don't be surprised if he becomes your new senator afterward.

➤ **Contact** ✆501-682-2345; ✑*www.arkansas.gov/governor*

Senator Blanche Lincoln, Democrat Lincoln is one of two Democratic senators from this swing state that went Red in 2004. She served as a congresswoman from 1993 to 1996. She has served as a senator since 1999. You can reelect her in 2010.

➤ **Contact** ✆202-224-4843; ✑*www.lincoln.senate.gov*

Senator Mark Pryor, Democrat Pryor is Arkansas's other Democratic senator. He has served since 2003. You can reelect him in 2008.

➤ **Contact** 202-224-2353; ✑*www.pryor.senate.gov*

Congress Members, 109th Congress

★ Marion Berry, Democrat: Began serving in 1996. ✆202-225-4076; ✑*www.house.gov/berry*

★ Vic Snyder, Democrat: Began serving in 1996. ☎202-225-2506; ✎*www. house.gov/snyder*

★ John Boozman, Republican: Began serving in 2000. ☎202-225-4301; ✎*www.boozman.house.gov*

★ Mike Ross, Democrat: Began serving in 2000. ☎202-225-3772; ✎*www.house.gov/ross*

PITHY POLITICAL POOP AND SCINTILLATING SCANDAL

Bill Clinton Nuff said.

The Little Rock Nine Alabama's governor, George Wallace, was content to stand in a doorway to protest integration. That wasn't enough for Arkansas Governor Orval Faubus. He sent in the National Guard.

In 1954, the Supreme Court handed down its landmark *Brown v. The Board of Education* decision. It said that "separate" schools for blacks and whites are inherently unequal. As a result, nine African American students enrolled at Central High School in Little Rock in 1957. Faubus didn't care for this turn of events, so he sent the National Guard to the school to ban entrance to the new students. In turn, President Eisenhower checkmated Faubus by sending in the 101st Airborne Division to ensure the safety of the group that history calls the Little Rock Nine.

PEOPLE FROM YOUR NEW STATE
WHO WON'T MAKE YOU FEEL ILL

* Maya Angelou, author, Saint Louis
* Johnny Cash, country music legend, Kingsland
* Eldridge Cleaver, activist, Walbaseha
* Bill Clinton, president, Hope
* Scott Joplin, composer, Texarkana

COLORADO

GOVERNOR, SENATORS, CONGRESS MEMBERS

Governor Bill Owens, Republican Owens became governor in 1999. Conservative rag, the *National Review*, named him the country's best governor in 2002. Yikes. Despite that, Owens is a rare breed of conservative: an intellectual. He is an expert on Russian affairs and writes and lectures often on the country. Owens's term will end in 2007. Don't be surprised if he makes a presidential run afterward.

➤ **Contact** ✆ 303-866-2471; ✍ *www.colorado.gov/governor*

Senator Wayne Allard, Republican Allard served as a congressman from 1991 to 1996. He has served as a senator since 1997. You can vote him out of office in 2008.

➤ **Contact** ✆ 202-224-5941; ✍ *www.allard.senate.gov*

Senator Ken Salazar, Democrat Salazar has served as senator since 2005. You can reelect him in 2010. He is the brother of Democratic congressman John Salazar.

➤ **Contact** ✆ 202-224-5941; ✍ *www.salazar.senate.gov*

Congress Members, 109th Congress

★ Diana DeGette, Democrat: Began serving in 1996. ✆ 202-225-4431; ✍ *www.house.gov/degette*
★ Mark Udall, Democrat: Began serving in 1998. ✆ 202-225-2161; ✍ *www.markudall.house.gov*
★ John Salazar, Democrat: Began serving in 2004. ✆ 202-225-4761; ✍ *www.house.gov/salazar*
★ Marilyn Musgrave, Republican: Began serving in 2002. ✆ 202-225-4676; ✍ *www.musgrave.house.gov*
★ Joel Hefley, Republican: Began serving in 1986. ✆ 202-225-4422; ✍ *www.house.gov/hefley*

★ Thomas Tancredo, Republican: Began serving in 1998. ✆202-225-7882; ✉www.tancredo.house.gov

★ Bob Beauprez, Republican: Began serving in 2002. ✆202-225-2645; ✉www.house.gov/beauprez

PITHY POLITICAL POOP AND SCINTILLATING SCANDAL

Tom Tancredo Representative Tom Tancredo set off a fire storm of protest in 2005, thanks to some typical Red State remarks made on a Florida radio program.

When asked by the radio host how the United States should react to terrorists using nuclear weapons within its borders, Tancredo took a moment to open his mouth wide enough to insert both feet.

If the attacks are discovered to be the result of fundamentalist Muslims, Tancredo said, the United States should threaten to bomb Mecca. The remark drew howls of protests, but Tancredo refused to admit it was a dumb thing to say. Not surprisingly, chatter on conservative blogs suggested the Colorado congressman's remarks were justified and that Tancredo's opinion is shared by so-called sane Americans. Just pray you haven't moved next door to any of these "sane" Americans.

PEOPLE FROM YOUR NEW STATE
WHO WON'T MAKE YOU FEEL ILL

* Tim Allen, actor, Denver
* Lon Chaney, actor, Colorado Springs
* Douglas Fairbanks, actor, Denver

FLORIDA

GOVERNOR, SENATORS, CONGRESS MEMBERS

Governor Jeb Bush, Republican Here are some of the ways Jeb Bush is different from his older brother, Dub-Yuh. J-Bush actually was born in Texas. J-Bush has admitted to toking weed during his college days. J-Bush legitimately did not serve in Vietnam. He registered for the draft, but the war ended before his number was called. J-Bush was a successful businessman before he decided to focus on public service. J-Bush is a converted Catholic.

J-Bush first arrived in Florida in 1980 and made a killing in real estate and entrepreneurial ventures. He first ran for governor in 1993 and lost. Before running again in 1998, J-Bush developed nonprofits focused on children's issues and Florida's future.

As governor, he has supported education and environmental issues. He opposed plans to drill for oil in the Everglades. In 2002, Bush became the first Republican in Florida's history to be elected for a consecutive term. After he leaves office in 2006, he could try to follow his brother into the White House or possibly run for the senate. Bottom line: If there has to be a Bush in the White House, better it be Jeb than Dub-Yuh.

➤ **Contact** ☎850-488-7146; ✉*www.myflorida.com*

Senator Mel Martinez, Republican Martinez has served as senator since 2005. You can vote him out of office in 2010. Martinez served in Dub-Yuh's cabinet as the Secretary for the Department of Housing and Urban Development.

➤ **Contact** ☎202-224-3041; ✉*www.martinez.senate.gov*

Senator Bill Nelson, Democrat Nelson served as a congressman from 1979 to 1990. He has served as a senator since 2001. You can reelect him in 2006. Nelson ran unsuccessfully for Florida governor in 1990.

➤ **Contact** ☎202-224-5274; ✉*www.billnelson.senate.gov*

Congress Members, 109th Congress

★ Jeff Miller, Republican: Began serving in 2000. ✆ 202-225-4136; ✐ www.jeffmiller.house.gov

★ Allen Boyd, Democrat: Began serving in 1996. ✆ 202-225-5235; ✐ www.house.gov/boyd

★ Corrine Brown, Democrat: Began serving in 1992. ✆ 202-225-0123; ✐ www.house.gov/corrinebrown

★ Ander Crenshaw, Republican: Began serving in 2000. ✆ 202-225-2501; ✐ www.crenshaw.house.gov

★ Ginny Brown-Waite, Republican: Began serving in 2002. ✆ 202-225-1002; ✐ www.house.gov/brown-waite

★ Cliff Stearns, Republican: Began serving in 1988. ✆ 202-225-5744; ✐ www.house.gov/stearns

★ John Mica, Republican: Began serving in 1992. ✆ 202-225-4035; ✐ www.house.gov/mica

★ Ric Keller, Republican: Began serving in 2000. ✆ 202-225-2176; ✐ www.keller.house.gov

★ Michael Bilirakis, Republican: Began serving in 1982. ✆ 202-225-5755; ✐ www.house.gov/bilirakis

★ C.W. Bill Young, Republican: Began serving in 1970. ✆ 202-225-5961; ✐ www.house.gov/young

★ Jim Davis, Democrat: Began serving in 1996. ✆ 202-225-3376; ✐ www.house.gov/jimdavis

★ Adam Putnam, Republican: Began serving in 2000. ✆ 202-225-1252; ✐ www.house.gov/putnam

★ Katherine Harris, Republican: Began serving in 2002. ✆ 202-225-5015; ✐ www.harris.house.gov

★ Connie Mack, Republican: Began serving in 2004. ✆ 202-225-2536; ✐ www.mack.house.gov

★ Dave Weldon, Republican: Began serving in 1994. ✆ 202-225-3671; ✐ www.weldon.house.gov

★ Mark Foley, Republican: Began serving in 1994. ✆ 202-225-5792; ✐ www.house.gov/foley

- ★ Kendrick Meek, Democrat: Began serving in 2002. ✆202-225-4506; *www.kendrickmeek.house.gov*
- ★ Ileana Ros-Lehtinen, Republican: Began serving in 1988. ✆202-225-3931; *www.house.gov/ros-lehtinen*
- ★ Robert Wexler, Democrat: Began serving in 1996. ✆202-225-3001; *www.wexler.house.gov*
- ★ Debbie Wasserman Schultz, Democrat: Began serving in 2004. ✆202-225-7931; *www.house.gov/schultz*
- ★ Lincoln Diaz-Balart, Republican and brother of Mario Diaz-Balart: Began serving in 1992. ✆202-225-4211; *www.diaz-balart.house.gov*
- ★ E. Clay Shaw Jr., Republican: Began serving in 1980. ✆202-225-3026; *www.shaw.house.gov*
- ★ Alcee Hastings, Democrat: Began serving in 1992. ✆202-225-1313; *www.alceehastings.house.gov*
- ★ Tom Feeney, Republican: Began serving in 2002. ✆202-225-2706; *www.house.gov/feeney*
- ★ Mario Diaz-Balart, Republican and brother of Lincoln Diaz-Balart: Began serving in 2002. ✆202-225-2778; *www.house.gov/mariodiaz-balart*

PITHY POLITICAL POOP AND
SCINTILLATING SCANDAL

Rosewood Alabama, Mississippi, Georgia—heck, even Arkansas—have the dubious distinction of being the states most Americans think about when they think about racially motivated human rights violations. For some reason, Florida is one Deep South state that often gets overlooked in the long, often disturbing history of the civil rights struggle. But the Sunshine State has the distinction of destroying an entire town.

Rosewood was a thriving community, comprised almost entirely of African Americans, until 1923. The week of January 1, Fanny Taylor—a white woman—claimed a black man from Rosewood had assaulted her. Two white men were killed trying to get into the home where they believed Taylor's assailant was hiding. The following day hordes of whites converged on the town and burned every home owned by a black family. Many African Americans were killed. The town was effectively wiped off the face of the Earth.

In 1994, the state enacted the Rosewood Claims Act, which gave scholarships and compensation to descendants of former Rosewood families.

I'm Ready for My Close-Up Representative Katherine Harris, who is probably running for the senate as you read this, is most "famous" nationally for her claims that newspapers have doctored photos of her. Harris suggests they've distorted her makeup job to make Tammy Lee Bakker Messner look demure by contrast. The media have repeatedly said that no photos of Harris have been altered.

PEOPLE FROM YOUR NEW STATE
WHO WON'T MAKE YOU FEEL ILL

* Julian "Cannonball" Aderley, jazz giant, Tampa
* Zora Neale Hurston, author, Eatonville
* Jim Morrison, singer, Melbourne
* Janet Reno, attorney general, Miami

GEORGIA

GOVERNOR, SENATORS, CONGRESS MEMBERS

Governor Sonny Perdue, Republican Perdue took office in 2003. He's the first Republican governor of Georgia since Reconstruction!

Perdue has worked to reduce wasteful government, and he's moved his state out of last place in SAT scores. On the other hand, he was opposed to efforts to change the state's flag when it still

RED STATE

resembled the Confederate Stars 'n' Bars. You can vote him out of office in 2006.

➤ **Contact** 📞404-656-1776; ✎*www.gov.state.ga.us*

Senator Saxby Chambliss, Republican Chambliss served as a congressman from 1995 to 2002. He has served as a senator since 2003. You can vote him out of office in 2008.

➤ **Committees** Chair, Committee on Agriculture, Nutrition, and Forestry
➤ **Contact** 📞202-224-3521; ✎*www.chambliss.senate.gov*

Senator Johnny Isakson, Republican Isakson served as a congressman from 1996 to 2004. He has served as a senator since 2005. You can vote him out of office in 2010. Isakson was Newt Gingrich's replacement, when Gingrich did not take his seat in the 106th Congress. Isakson was elected to congress in 1998.

➤ **Contact** 📞202-224-3643; ✎*www.isakson.senate.gov*

Congress Members, 109th Congress

★ Jack Kingston, Republican: Began serving in 1992. 📞202-225-5831; ✎*www.house.gov/kingston*
★ Sanford Bishop Jr., Democrat: Began serving in 1992. 📞202-225-3631; ✎*www.house.gov/bishop*
★ Jim Marshall, Democrat: Began serving in 2002. 📞202-225-6531; ✎*www.house.gov/marshall*
★ Cynthia McKinney, Democrat: Began serving in 1992. 📞202-225-1605; ✎*www.house.gov/mckinney*
★ John Lewis, Democrat: Began serving in 1986. 📞202-225-3801; ✎*www.house.gov/johnlewis*
★ Tom Price, Republican: Began serving in 2004. 📞202-225-4501; ✎*www.tomprice.house.gov*
★ John Linder, Republican: Began serving in 1992. 📞202-225-4272; ✎*www.linder.house.gov*
★ Lynn Westmoreland, Republican: Began serving in 2004. 📞202-225-5901; ✎*www.house.gov/westmoreland*

★ Charlie Norwood, Republican: Began serving in 1994. ✆202-225-4101; ✉www.house.gov/norwood

★ Nathan Deal, Republican: Began serving in 1992. ✆202-225-5211; ✉www.house.gov/deal

★ Phil Gingrey, Republican: Began serving in 2002. ✆202-225-2931; ✉www.gingrey.house.gov

★ John Barrow, Democrat: Began serving in 2004. ✆202-225-2823; ✉www.barrow.house.gov

★ David Scott, Democrat: Began serving in 2002. ✆202-225-2939; ✉www.davidscott.house.gov

PITHY POLITICAL POOP AND SCINTILLATING SCANDAL

Galphinism President Zachary Taylor, from the Red State of Virginia, died only a little over a year after taking office. But that didn't mean his administration was without scandal.

Taylor's secretary of war was Georgia's George W. Crawford. Crawford earned $95,000—a princely sum now, an ungodly sum in 1850—because of a decision made by two other cabinet members.

Before he became a member of Taylor's cabinet, Crawford was an attorney. He defended his friend, George Galphin, in Galphin's pre-Revolutionary War claim against the government, which amounted to $235,000. Treasury Secretary John Clayton and Attorney General John M. Johnson agreed to pay Galphin's heirs the full amount owed them, plus interest. Part of the settlement included Crawford's $95,000. Taylor did not fire Crawford.

For generations, the term "Galphinism" was synonymous with corruption in the executive branch.

RED STATE

PEOPLE FROM YOUR NEW STATE
WHO WON'T MAKE YOU FEEL ILL

* Jimmy Carter, president, Plains
* Ray Charles, genius of soul, Albany
* Ossie Davis, actor and activist, Cogdell
* Oliver Hardy, comedian, Harlem
* Jasper Johns, artist, Augusta
* Martin Luther King Jr., civil rights activist, Atlanta
* Gladys Knight, singer, Atlanta
* Carson McCullers, author, Columbus
* Otis Redding, singer, Dawson
* Little Richard (Richard Penniman), singer, Macon
* Alice Walker, author, Eatonton

IDAHO

GOVERNOR, SENATORS, CONGRESS MEMBERS

Governor Dirk Kempthorne, Republican Kempthorne was a senator before he was elected governor in 1998. He is about as conservative as a human being can be, despite his having been born in California. Here, for example, is a fine example of one of our nation's most bombastic poetic forms, American Jingoism. It's taken from Kempthorne's Web site: "It is my honor to serve with you, the people of Idaho. This great state, this forty-third star in the galaxy of states that form the greatest nation in the world." His term ends in 2006.

➤ **Contact** 📞208-334-2100; ✏️*www.gov.idaho.gov*

Senator Larry Craig, Republican Craig served as a congressman from 1981 to 1990. He has served as senator since 1991. You can vote him out of office in 2008.

➤ **Committees** Chair, Senate Republican Policy Committee; Special Committee on Aging; Committee on Veterans' Affairs

➤ **Contact** 📞202-224-2752; ✍*www.craig.senate.gov*

Senator Michael Crapo, Republican Crapo served as a congressman from 1993 to 1998. He has served as a senator since 1999. You can vote him out of office in 2010.

➤ **Contact** 📞202-224-6142; ✍*www.crapo.senate.gov*

Congress members, 109th Congress

★ Butch Otter, Republican: Began serving in 2000. 📞202-225-6611; ✍*www.house.gov/otter*

★ Michael Simpson, Republican: Began serving in 1998. 📞202-225-5531; ✍*www.house.gov/simpson*

PITHY POLITICAL POOP AND SCINTILLATING SCANDAL

Governor Steunenberg Has Been Murdered The assassination of Idaho Governor Frank Steunenberg in 1905 mushroomed out of a massive explosion carried along the rails by the "Dynamite Express."

By 1899, all but one of the lead mines in Shoshone County was controlled by local chapters of the Western Federation of Miners. On April 29, 1899, members of these locals got together to send a message to the owner of that mine, the Bunker Hill and Sullivan Company.

About a thousand armed and, in many cases, masked union men hijacked a train and loaded it with 3,000 pounds of stolen dynamite. When they got to the Bunker Hill and Sullivan, the amassed men became a group of rioters, certain that they could destroy the mine and get away with it. The fact that the county's pro-union local sheriff was among the group probably had something to do with their certainty.

By 2:30 p.m., the mine and all of its offices and plants were blown sky high. It wasn't a work day for miners, so no one was killed—except for one of the union men, who died from friendly fire. Two unlucky Bunker Hill and Sullivan workers who happened to be on-hand were kicked, hit, and threatened. One, James Cheyne, was "accidentally" shot—probably by a drunken shooter—and later died of his injury.

The result? Steunenberg appealed to President William McKinley for National Guard forces and declared martial law in Shoshone County. Ultimately, only a handful of union men were jailed for the explosion. National Guard troops stayed in the area until the end of October.

After this incident, Steunenberg repeatedly cracked down on miners' strikes. This was an ironic decision, since many labor unions supported Steunenberg during his 1896 campaign for governor. Steunenberg did not run for reelection in 1900, and five years later, he too was blown sky high by a booby-trapped gate at his home. It was widely believed that the assassination was performed by a professional assassin, hired by the Western Federation of Miners.

PEOPLE FROM YOUR NEW STATE
WHO WON'T MAKE YOU FEEL ILL

* Ezra Pound, poet, Hailey
* Picabo Street, skier, Triumph
* Lana Turner, actress, Wallace

GOVERNOR, SENATORS, CONGRESS MEMBERS

Governor Mitch Daniels, Republican The guy Dub-Yuh nicknamed "My Man Mitch" took office in 2005. Prior to that, Dub-Yuh named him director of the Office of Management and Budget. In an absolutely amazing coincidence, Daniels sold $1.45 million in Indiana Power & Light stock just before the stock's value plummeted. Daniels claimed he sold his stock because of his appointment to the OMB. Didn't Martha Stewart get sent to the pokey for doing something eerily similar? You can vote Daniels out of office in 2008.
➤ **Contact** ✆317-232-4567; ✍*www.in.gov/gov*

Senator Evan Bayh, Democrat Bayh has been a senator since 1999. You can reelect him in 2010. Bayh was governor of Indiana from 1989 to 1997, and he is the son of longtime Indiana senator, Birch Evan Bayh.
➤ **Contact** ✆202-224-5623; ✍*www.bayh.senate.gov*

Senator Richard Lugar, Republican Lugar has been a senator since 1977. You can vote him out of office in 2006.
➤ **Committees** Chair, Republican Senatorial Campaign Committee; Committee on Foreign Relations; Committee on Agriculture, Nutrition, and Forestry
➤ **Contact** ✆202-224-4814; ✍*www.lugar.senate.gov*

Congress Members, 109th Congress
★ Peter Visclosky, Democrat: Began serving in 1984. ✆202-225-2461; ✍*www.house.gov/visclosky*
★ Chris Chocola, Republican: Began serving in 2002. ✆202-225-3915; ✍*www.chocola.house.gov*
★ Mark Souder, Republican: Began serving in 1994. ✆202-225-4436; ✍*www.souder.house.gov*
★ Steve Buyer, Republican: Began serving in 1992. ✆202-225-5037; ✍*www.stevebuyer.house.gov*

★ Dan Burton, Republican: Began serving in 1982. ☎202-225-2276;
  ✍www.house.gov/burton

★ Mike Pence, Republican: Began serving in 2000. ☎202-225-3021;
  ✍www.mikepence.house.gov

★ Julia Carson, Democrat: Began serving in 1996. ☎202-225-4011;
  ✍www.juliacarson.house.gov

★ John Hostettler, Republican: Began serving in 1994. ☎202-225-4636;
  ✍www.house.gov/hostettler

★ Michael Sodrel, Republican: Began serving in 2004. ☎202-225-5315;
  ✍www.sodrel.house.gov

PITHY POLITICAL POOP AND
SCINTILLATING SCANDAL

Mr. "Potatoe" Head Pity Poor J. Danforth Quayle.

He's not the only politician ever to mangle the English language. Heck, his boss, President Bush the Elder, did a pretty good job of it. So, for that matter, does Dub-Yuh.

And Quayle can't possibly be the only adult in America who is unable to spell "potato." But to this day, Quayle is the name you're most likely to get at a dinner party should you ask your friends who, in their opinion, is the dumbest politician of modern times.

Maybe it was that deer-in-the-headlights look Quayle could adopt at a moment's notice. Perhaps it was the fact that he acted like a pre-pubescent when picked for the Veep spot by Bush. Or it could just be that he actually is dumb. Here are some of his classic quotes, courtesy of Quotationspage.com.

> *"I love California. I practically grew up in Phoenix."*
> *"Republicans understand the importance of bondage between a mother and child."*
> *"We have a firm commitment to NATO. We are a part of NATO. We have a firm commitment to Europe. We are a part of Europe."*

"What a waste it is to lose one's mind. Or not to have a mind is being very wasteful. How true that is."

"The Holocaust was an obscene period in our nation's history. I mean in this century's history. But we all lived in this century. I didn't live in this century."

"We're going to have the best-educated American people in the world."

"I stand by all the misstatements that I've made."

PEOPLE FROM YOUR NEW STATE
WHO WON'T MAKE YOU FEEL ILL

* James Dean, actor, Marion
* David Letterman, comedian, Indianapolis
* John Mellencamp, singer, Seymour
* Cole Porter, composer, Peru
* Kurt Vonnegut, author, Indianapolis

IOWA

GOVERNOR, SENATORS, CONGRESS MEMBERS

Governor Tom Vilsack, Democrat Vilsack took office in 1999. Conservative leadership in the state has accused Vilsack of being a tax-and-spend Democrat. Of course, they've also glommed onto Vilsack's triumphs: increasing the number of children covered by health insurance, lowering the price of prescription drugs for seniors, and making efforts to reduce methamphetamine labs in the state.

Iowa has no term limits, so Vilsack will be up for reelection in 2006. He has claimed he won't run for a third term, but don't count on that.

➤ **Contact** ☎ 512-281-5211; *www.governor.state.ia.us*

Senator Chuck Grassley, Republican Grassley served as a congressman from 1975 to 1980. He has been a senator since 1981. You can vote him out of office in 2010.

➤ **Committees** Chair, Special Committee on Aging; Committee on Finance
➤ **Contact** ☎202-224-3744; ✎*www.grassley.senate.gov*

Senator Tom Harkin, Democrat Harkin served as a congressman from 1975 to 1984. He has been a senator since 1985. You can reelect him in 2008.
➤ **Committees** Chair, Committee on Agriculture, Nutrition, and Forestry
➤ **Contact** ☎202-224-3254; ✎*www.harkin.senate.gov*

Congress Members, 109th Congress

★ Jim Nussle, Republican: Began serving in 1990. ☎202-225-2911; ✎*www.nussle.house.gov*
★ James Leach, Republican: Began serving in 1976. ☎202-225-6576; ✎*www.house.gov/leach*
★ Leonard Boswell, Democrat: Began serving in 1996. ☎202-225-3806; ✎*www.house.gov/boswell*
★ Tom Latham, Republican: Began serving in 1994. ☎202-225-5476; ✎*www.tomlatham.house.gov*
★ Steve King, Republican: Began serving in 2002. ☎202-225-4426; ✎*www.house.gov/steveking*

PITHY POLITICAL POOP AND SCINTILLATING SCANDAL

A Chicken in Every Pot...Not! Iowa-born Herbert Hoover entered the White House in 1929 as one of the most popular men in America.

He had served as commerce secretary under Calvin Coolidge and became known for cutting government waste. In fact, people of the time used the word "Hooverism" as a synonym for waste prevention.

Hoover ran for president under the slogan, "A chicken in every pot," and his presidency seemed to promise unlimited prosperity. Hoover began his first and only term in office with a lengthy agenda of government reforms. Then came the stock market crash that plunged the country into the Great Depression.

Hoover wasn't directly responsible for the Depression, of course. The prosperity of the Roaring Twenties had a shaky foundation, but Hoover became the preeminent symbol of the Great Depression. And his name was again borrowed for American slang. The villages of cardboard boxes into which many Americans were forced to move were dubbed "Hoovervilles."

Hoover's approval ratings took a further beating, thanks to his secretary of labor, William Doak. Doak could easily be called the godfather of the Patriot Act. As most of America blamed Hoover and his administration for the Depression, Doak blamed it on illegal aliens. He was a zealous fascist in his alien bashing and harassing, rounding up aliens and imprisoning them for as much as eighteen months without legitimate cause.

And finally, Hoover's unpopularity was not limited solely to the fact that the Great Depression occurred during his watch. After Hoover vetoed a bonus bill for veterans of World War I, a group of veterans protested by marching across the country and forming a Hooverville in Washington. The president dispersed the veterans by sending in Gen. Douglas MacArthur to crack skulls. An eleven-year-old child died from tear gas poisoning during the ensuing onslaught.

PEOPLE FROM YOUR NEW STATE
WHO WON'T MAKE YOU FEEL ILL

* Bix Beiderbecke, jazz great, Davenport
* Johnny Carson, entertainer, Corning
* Ann Landers, columnist, Sioux City
* Glenn Miller, bandleader, Clarinda
* Donna Reed, actress, Denison
* Abigail "Dear Abby" Van Buren, columnist, Sioux City
* Grant Wood, artist, Anamosa

RED STATE

KANSAS

GOVERNOR, SENATORS, CONGRESS MEMBERS

Governor Kathleen Sebelius, Democrat Sebelius was elected governor in 2002. She's the daughter of former Ohio Governor John Gilligan. They are the first father/daughter governor team in American history. Sebelius supports abortion rights and opposes capital punishment. Even better, she became governor because of rifts within the state's Republican Party. You can reelect Sebelius in 2006.

➤ **Contact** ✆877-579-6757; ✎*www.ksgovernor.org*

Senator Sam Brownback, Republican Brownback was elected to the U.S. House of Representatives in 1994. In the middle of his term, he was tapped to fill the seat vacated by Senator Bob Dole, who left the senate for his failed presidential bid. Brownback later was elected to the senate. You can vote him out of office in 2010.

➤ **Contact** ✆202-224-6521; ✎*www.brownback.senate.gov*

Senator Pat Roberts, Republican Roberts served as a congressman from 1981 to 1996. He has been a senator since 1997. You can vote him out of office in 2008.

➤ **Committees** Chair, Select Committee on Ethics; Select Committee on Intelligence
➤ **Contact** ✆202-224-4774; ✎*www.roberts.senate.gov*

Congress Members, 109th Congress
★ Jerry Moran, Republican: Began serving in 1996. ✆202-225-2715; ✎*www.house.gov/moranks01*
★ Jim Ryun, Republican: Began serving in 1994. ✆202-225-6601; ✎*www.ryun.house.gov*
★ Dennis Moore, Democrat: Began serving in 1998. ✆202-225-2865; ✎*www.moore.house.gov*
★ Todd Tiahrt, Republican: Began serving in 1994. ✆202-225-6216; ✎*www.house.gov/tiahrt*

PITHY POLITICAL POOP AND
SCINTILLATING SCANDAL

Bleeding Kansas At least fifty-five people died during the violence now called "Bleeding Kansas." The riots and bloodshed in Kansas were one of the brief pit stops along the highway to the Civil War.

In December 1853, Iowa senator Augustus Dodge introduced a bill that led to organization of the future state of Kansas. There was one problem, though. Southerners were adamant that the new state allow slavery. If it were admitted as a slave state, however, the so-called Missouri Compromise would be violated.

The compromise was an earlier effort to forestall civil war. It forbade slavery above the United States' 36th parallel, and Kansas would be north of that line.

Dodge's bill went to the Committee of the Territories, which was chaired by the Little Giant, Senator Stephen Douglas. Douglas believed wholeheartedly in manifest destiny as well as in popular sovereignty, so he decided to leave the slavery question up to the territory's new settlers. That way, he could placate Southerners by leaving open the possibility for slavery in the new state. And in turn, Douglas would be able to add a new state to the Union.

His solution seems logical, but Douglas didn't count on thousands of pro-slave and pro-free state folks heading for Kansas in an effort to affect the outcome of the territory's slavery vote. As these opposing factions met up, battles erupted and blood flowed. Abolitionist John Brown got into the action, hacking to death five pro-slavery men. Numerous efforts were made to draft a constitution that would bring Kansas into the United States. Some allowed slavery. Some didn't.

Ultimately, Kansas did not join the Union until 1861, after the country's southern states had seceded. It entered as a free state, of course.

PEOPLE FROM YOUR NEW STATE
WHO WON'T MAKE YOU FEEL ILL

* Gwendolyn Brooks, poet, Topeka
* Amelia Earhart, aviator, Atchison
* Dennis Hopper, actor, Dodge City
* Buster Keaton, actor, Piqua
* Stan Kenton, bandleader, Wichita
* Damon Runyon, journalist, Metropolis

KENTUCKY

GOVERNOR, SENATORS, CONGRESS MEMBERS

Governor Ernie Fletcher, Republican Fletcher was a congressman before he was elected governor in 2003. You might remember that Fletcher's plane was nearly shot out of the sky by the U.S. Air Force. While en route to Ronald Reagan's funeral, the governor's plane flew into restricted air space. The Capitol was evacuated.

Back home, Fletcher hasn't been a very popular governor, in part because he raised health insurance costs for state employees. You can vote him out of office in 2007.

➤ **Contact** ✆ 502-564-2611; ✍ *www.governor.ky.gov*

Senator Jim Bunning, Republican Bunning served as a congressman from 1987 to 1998. He has been a senator since 1999. You can try to vote him out of office in 2010.

Bunning was a professional baseball player from 1955 to 1971. He spent most of his career with the Detroit Tigers and Philadelphia Phillies. When he pitched a perfect game in 1964, it was the first time that had been done in the National League since 1880. Bunning was elected to the National Baseball Hall of Fame in 1996.

➤ **Contact** ✆ 202-224-2541; ✍ *www.bunning.senate.gov*

Senator Mitch McConnell, Republican McConnell has been a senator since 1985. You can try to vote him out of office in 2009, should he run for reelection. McConnell is the Republican Party whip.

➤ **Committees** Chair, Select Committee on Ethics; National Republican Senatorial Campaign Committee; Committee on Rules and Administration

➤ **Contact** ☎202-224-2541; ✎*www.mcconnell.senate.gov*

Congress Members, 109th Congress

★ Ed Whitfield, Republican: Began serving in 1994. ☎202-225-3115; ✎*www.house.gov/whitfield*

★ Ron Lewis, Republican: Began serving in 1992. ☎202-225-3501; ✎*www.house.gov/ronlewis*

★ Anne Northup, Republican: Began serving in 1996. ☎202-225-5401; ✎*www.northup.house.gov*

★ Geoff Davis, Republican: Began serving in 2004. ☎202-225-3465; ✎*www.geoffdavis.house.gov*

★ Harold Rogers, Republican: Began serving in 1980. ☎202-225-4601; ✎*www.house.gov/rogers*

★ Ben Chandler, Democrat: Began serving in 2002. ☎202-225-4706; ✎*www.chandler.house.gov*

PITHY POLITICAL POOP AND SCINTILLATING SCANDAL

John C. Breckenridge Congressman John C. Breckenridge of Kentucky was the prototype for such hypocrites as William Bennett and Jimmy Swaggart. And he was one of the "founders" of palimony. It destroyed his hopes for a Victorian-era presidential run.

Breckenridge began an affair with Madeline Pollard when she was just seventeen. Sexual affairs weren't any more unusual in the late nineteenth century than they are today. What set this one apart is that Breckenridge built his reputation as the "silver-tongued orator from Kentucky" by speaking often on the evils of sex. He warned one group of young ladies at an all-girl's school to avoid "useless handshaking, promiscuous kissing, needless touches, and all exposures." To another group, he proudly intoned, "Chastity is the foundation, the cornerstone of human society."

And then he was sued for $50,000 by Pollard, who claimed he had broken his promise to marry her. Breckenridge married a cousin instead, even though he and Pollard had two children together (!). Breckenridge figured he could overcome this exposure of his hypocrisy. He hired six high-powered lawyers and stormed into court with them. Pollard, by contrast, entered the courtroom dressed demurely, accompanied only by a nun (!). The jury found Breckenridge guilty.

He thought he might still be able to overcome the self-spilled stain on his career. Breckenridge ran for re-election and gave a speech that served as a template for Swaggart's, some ninety years later. Wiping a tear, Breckenridge told voters, "I knew the secret sin; I tried to atone for it . . . entangled by weakness, by passion, by sin, in coils which it was almost impossible to break."

It almost worked. But women organized and spoke out against him in droves. Breckenridge lost by a landslide in what became one of the cornerstones of the American suffrage movement.

Practically Neighbors In his outstanding *The Civil War, a Narrative*, Shelby Foote begins his account of the war by pointing out one of its most intriguing ironies.

The two men who would lead the "divided house" that the United States became from 1861 to 1865 were born in the same state, within a year and a hundred miles of each other.

Future Confederacy president, Jefferson Davis, was born in a log cabin in Fairview, Kentucky. Soon after his birth, his family moved south, to Louisiana. Future "Father of the Union" Abraham Lincoln was born in Hodgenville, also in a log cabin. His family soon moved to Indiana.

RED STATE

PEOPLE FROM YOUR NEW STATE
WHO WON'T MAKE YOU FEEL ILL

* Muhammad Ali, boxer, Louisville
* Rosemary Clooney, singer, Maysville
* Casey Jones, engineer, Cayce
* Abraham Lincoln, president, Hodgenville
* Loretta Lynn, country music legend, Butchers Hollow
* Bill Monroe, bluegrass legend, Rosine
* Hunter S. Thompson, gonzo journalist, Louisville

LOUISIANA

GOVERNOR, SENATORS, CONGRESS MEMBERS

Governor Kathleen Blanco, Democrat Blanco was elected in 2003, becoming the state's first female governor. She served formerly as the state's lieutenant governor. She took center stage in the United States in the aftermath of Hurricane Katrina, which devastated New Orleans and many other, smaller communities. Blanco was vocal in her disapproval of how the federal government handled cleanup and assistance efforts in the Pelican State.

Prior to Katrina, Blanco was probably best known for waging a political war with New Orleans Saints owner Tom Benson. She ran hot and cold with her support for the team and improvements to its stadium. If the state loses its football team, Blanco might very well lose her bid for reelection in 2007.

➤ **Contact** ✆866-366-1121; ✎*www.gov.louisiana.gov*

Senator Mary Landrieu, Democrat Landrieu has been a senator since 1997. You can reelect her in 2008. Landrieu ran for governor in 1995 but did not win.

★ **Contact** ✆202-224-5824; ✎*www.landrieu.senate.gov*

Senator David Ritter, Republican Vitter served as a congressman from 1999 to 2004. He became a senator in 2005. You can vote him out of office in 2010.

Vitter was first sent to congress after a special election to fill the seat of Robert Livingston Jr., who resigned. Livingston stepped down from congress after his marital infidelities came to light. He called for Clinton's resignation in the midst of Monica-gate, then resigned, saying he would serve as an example of doing the right thing. Fortunately, Clinton stayed in office.

➤ **Contact** ✆ 202-224-4623; ✐ *www.vitter.senate.gov*

Congress Members, 109th Congress

★ Bobby Jindal, Republican: Began serving in 2004. ✆ 202-225-3015; ✐ *www.jindal.house.gov*

★ William Jefferson, Democrat: Began serving in 1990. ✆ 202-225-6636; ✐ *www.house.gov/jefferson*

★ Charlie Melancon, Democrat: Began serving in 2004. ✆ 202-225-4031; ✐ *www.house.gov/melancon*

★ Jim McCrery, Republican: Began serving in 1986. ✆ 202-225-2777; ✐ *www.mccrery.house.gov*

★ Rodney Alexander, Republican: Began serving in 2002. ✆ 202-225-8490; ✐ *www.house.gov/alexander*

★ Richard Baker, Republican: Began serving in 1986. ✆ 202-225-3901; ✐ *www.baker.house.gov*

★ Charles Boustany Jr., Republican: Began serving in 2004. ✆ 202-225-2031; ✐ *www.boustany.house.gov*

PITHY POLITICAL POOP AND SCINTILLATING SCANDAL

A Tale of Two Hueys Louisiana can tell the tale of two very different Hueys. The first is the story of Huey Long, populist governor and senator and inspiration for Robert Penn Warren's Pulitzer Prize-winning novel, *All the King's Men*. Long was one of the few Southern politicians of his time who did not use race-baiting to get himself elected.

As governor, Long created a ruthless political machine in his home state and advocated programs that effectively took from the haves and redistributed their wealth to the have-nots. Not surprisingly, Louisiana's conservative leaders did everything they could to get him out of office. They impeached him on bribery and misuse of state funds, but Long was acquitted.

As a United States senator, Long continued his "take from the rich and give to the poor" policies. Since most voters in Louisiana were poor, Long was tremendously popular. And since Long's machine pretty much controlled everything in the state, his policies continued to be passed.

Long set his sights on the White House in 1935. But on September 8, 1935, he was shot on the steps of Louisiana's capitol, a capitol he helped get built. Long died from his wounds. To this day, some consider him a martyr, while others feel he got what he deserved.

The second nationally famous Huey from Louisiana is Huey Newton, founder of the Black Panther Party. Newton actually was named after Huey Long. And like Long, Newton also was shot to death. Newton's family moved to Oakland when he was still an infant. He became politicized while studying at Oakland City College. He and friend Bobby Seale organized the Black Panther Party for Self Defense in 1966. Much of the group's effort was focused on protecting blacks from police officers, whom Newton and Seale believed targeted African Americans.

Newton was accused of murdering Oakland police officer John Frey in 1967. He was imprisoned for a short time, but ultimately the state of California dropped the case. After Newton got out of jail, he tempered the Black Panther's rhetoric and transformed the group into a community-building organization. As time went on, Newton became a drug addict. He was shot and killed by a drug dealer on the streets of Oakland in 1989.

RED STATE

PEOPLE FROM YOUR NEW STATE
WHO WON'T MAKE YOU FEEL ILL

* Louis Armstrong, jazz legend, New Orleans
* Truman Capote, author, New Orleans
* Mahalia Jackson, gospel great, New Orleans
* Huey Newton, activist, Monroe
* Cokie Roberts, journalist, New Orleans

MISSISSIPPI

GOVERNOR, SENATOR, CONGRESS MEMBERS

Governor Haley Barbour, Republican Barbour was elected in 2003. He's only the second Republican governor in Mississippi since Reconstruction. Barbour was the Republican National Committee chairman from 1993 to 1997. You can vote him out of office in 2007.

➤ **Contact** ✆601-359-3150; ✉*www.governorbarbour.com*

Senator Thad Cochran, Republican Cochran served as a congressman from 1973 to 1978. He has been a senator since 1979. You can vote him out of office in 2008.

➤ **Committees** Chair, Senate Republican Conference; Committee on Agriculture, Nutrition, and Forestry; Committee on Appropriations

➤ **Contact** ✆202-224-5054; ✉*www.cochran.senate.gov*

Senator Trent Lott, Republican Lott was a congressman from 1973 to 1988. He became a senator in 1989. You can vote him out of office in 2006.

Lott has served as the senate's majority and minority leader, until he said something extremely stupid. At a birthday celebration for Senator Strom Thurmond, Lott suggested Thurmond "had the right idea" during the elder politician's days as a racist Dixiecrat.

Dixiecrats dressed up their racist dogma by referring to it as "state's rights." The only "rights" that concerned the party was the right to keep Southern states segregated. Thurmond ran for president on the Dixiecrat ticket in 1948.

➤ **Committees** Chair, Committee on Rules and Administration
➤ **Contact** ✆202-224-6523; ✎ *www.lott.senate.gov*

Congress Members, 109th Congress

★ Roger Wicker, Republican: Began serving in 1994. ✆202-225-4306; ✎ *www.house.gov/wicker*
★ Bennie Thompson, Democrat: Began serving in 1992. ✆202-225-5876; ✎ *www.benniethompson.house.gov*
★ Chip Pickering, Republican: Began serving in 1996. ✆202-225-5031; ✎ *www.house.gov/pickering*
★ Gene Taylor, Democrat: Began serving in 1988. ✆202-225-5772; ✎ *www.house.gov/genetaylor*

PITHY POLITICAL POOP AND
SCINTILLATING SCANDAL

An Unsung Hero of the South John Prentiss Matthews is one of Mississippi's unsung heroes.

Matthews's family was wealthy and owned slaves, but Matthews fought on the Union side during the Civil War. Afterward, he was elected Copiah County sheriff by an interracial coalition of political leaders. In 1875, Reconstruction essentially ended in the state, due to white racists using violence and threats to keep blacks from the polls. But Copiah County remained loyal to Reconstruction efforts, in no small part due to Matthews, who believed blacks were due the rights held by white Americans. He organized a fusion party of blacks and whites who could outvote local Democrats.

Despite his efforts, it became harder after each subsequent election to hold onto interracial leadership. And on November

6, 1883, Matthews was shot and killed as he tried to vote. He had been warned that he should stay away from the polls, but Matthews refused to be intimidated.

PEOPLE FROM YOUR NEW STATE
WHO WON'T MAKE YOU FEEL ILL

* Jimmy Buffett, singer, Pascagoula
* Bo Diddley (Ellis McDaniel), guitarist and composer, McCombs
* Medgar Evers, civil rights leader, Decatur
* William Faulkner, author, New Albany
* Shelby Foote, historian, Greenville
* Jim Henson, Muppet founder, Greenville
* Elvis Presley, entertainer, Tupelo
* Oprah Winfrey, entertainer, Kosciusko
* Richard Wright, author, Natchez

MISSOURI

GOVERNOR, SENATORS, CONGRESS MEMBERS

Governor Matt Blunt, Republican Blunt was thirty-three when he was elected in 2004, making him one of the youngest people ever elected governor. Blunt served a six-month tour of duty in Operation Enduring Freedom, following the September 11 terrorist attacks. His first budget angered many voters because it sought to cut education and Medicaid programs. You can vote him out of office in 2008.

➤ **Contact** ✆573-751-3222; *www.go.missouri.gov*

Senator Christopher Bond, Republican Bond has served as a senator since 1987. You can vote him out of office in 2011.

➤ **Committees** Chair, Committee on Small Business and Entrepreneurship
➤ **Contact** ✆202-224-5721; *www.bond.senate.gov*

RED STATE

Senator James Talent, Republican Talent was a congressman from 1993 to 2000. He has been a senator since 2001. You can vote him out of office in 2006. Talent was an unsuccessful candidate for governor in 2000.

➤ **Contact** ☎ 202-224-6154; ✎ *www.talent.senate.gov*

Congress Members, 109th Congress

★ William Lacy Clay Jr., Democrat: Began serving in 2000. ☎ 202-225-2406; ✎ *www.house.gov/clay*
★ W. Todd Akin, Republican: Began serving in 2000. ☎ 202-225-2561; ✎ *www.house.gov/akin*
★ Russ Carnahan, Democrat: Began serving in 2004. ☎ 202-225-2671; ✎ *www.house.gov/carnahan*
★ Ike Skelton, Democrat: Began serving in 1976. ☎ 202-225-2876; ✎ *www.house.gov/skelton*
★ Emanuel Cleaver, Democrat: Began serving in 2004. ☎ 202-225-4535; ✎ *www.house.gov/cleaver*
★ Sam Graves, Republican: Began serving in 2000. ☎ 202-225-7041; ✎ *www.house.gov/graves*
★ Roy Blunt, Republican: Began serving in 1996. ☎ 202-225-6536; ✎ *www.blunt.house.gov*
★ Jo Ann Emerson, Republican: Began serving in 1994. ☎ 202-225-4404; ✎ *www.house.gov/emerson*
★ Kenny Hulshof, Republican: Began serving in 1996. ☎ 202-225-2956; ✎ *www.hulshof.house.gov*

PITHY POLITICAL POOP AND SCINTILLATING SCANDAL

Rush Is Nuts Congratulations on your visit to the great state of Missouri! It's the birthplace of many famous authors and even of President Harry S. Truman. Unfortunately, it's also the birthplace of conservative blowhard and prescription drug abuser Rush Limbaugh. Sorry about that.

Madame Governor St. Joseph-born Nellie Tayloe Ross became the first woman in America elected a state governor.

Ross was the wife of popular Wyoming governor, William Ross. He died in office in 1924. Wyoming's secretary of state called for a special election to name Ross's successor.

The state's Democratic Party nominated Nellie Tayloe Ross to complete her husband's term. At first, Ross declined the nomination. But she reconsidered and was elected governor of Wyoming. She served from January 5, 1925, to January 3, 1927, and lost a bid for reelection. Ross died in 1977 at the age of 101.

PEOPLE FROM YOUR NEW STATE
WHO WON'T MAKE YOU FEEL ILL

* Robert Altman, director, Kansas City
* Josephine Baker, singer, St. Louis
* Thomas Hart Benton, painter, Neosho
* William Burroughs, author, St. Louis
* Walter Cronkite, newscaster, St. Joseph
* Langston Hughes, poet, Joplin
* John Huston, director, Nevada
* Harry S. Truman, president, Lamar
* Mark Twain (Samuel Clemens), author, Florida

MONTANA

GOVERNOR, SENATORS, CONGRESS MEMBERS

Governor Brian Schweitzer, Democrat Schweitzer was elected in 2004. He elicited national controversy in 2005 when he suggested his state's National Guard troops be sent back from Iraq to help fight Montana forest fires. You can reelect him in 2008.

➤ **Contact** ✆ 406-444-3111; ✍ *www.governor.mt.gov*

Senator Max Baucus, Democrat Baucus served as a congressman from 1975 to 1978. After he was elected to the senate in 1978, he was appointed to fill the seat left by Senator Paul Hatfield's resignation, so Baucus entered the senate in late 1978. You can vote to reelect him in 2008, should he run for reelection.

➤ **Committees** Chair, Committee on Environment and Public Works; Committee on Finance; Vice Chair, Joint Committee on Taxation

➤ **Contact** ✆ 202-224-2651; ✍ *www.baucus.senate.gov*

Senator Conrad Burns, Republican Burns has been a senator since 1989. You can try to vote him out of office in 2006, should he run for reelection.

➤ **Contact** ✆ 202-224-2644; ✍ *www.burns.senate.gov*

Congress Member, 109th Congress

★ Dennis Rehberg, Republican: Began serving in 2000. ✆ 202-225-3211; ✍ *www.house.gov/rehberg*

PITHY POLITICAL POOP AND SCINTILLATING SCANDAL

Rankin Says No The first woman elected to Congress was Missoula-born Jeannette Rankin. She has the distinction of giving a "no" vote to both world wars.

Rankin was a suffragist and social worker elected to the U.S. House of Representatives in 1916. She was an active legislator, using her position to work for peace and women's rights and against child labor. Rankin also spoke out against America's entry into World War I.

She violated protocol by speaking before offering her vote against U.S. involvement in the war. "I want to stand by my country," she said. "But I cannot vote for war." After war was declared, however, Rankin voted for several pro-war bills. She also opened debate on the so-called Susan B. Anthony

Amendment, which gave women the right to vote. Rankin did not win reelection. She was gerrymandered out of her district. Once that happened, she ran for the senate and lost. But Rankin stayed active after politics.

She worked for peace through the Women's International League for Peace and Freedom and served on the staff of the American Civil Liberties Union. In 1939, Rankin again ran for Congress. This time, she won. And for a second time, she got the opportunity to vote against war.

After Pearl Harbor, Rankin was the sole dissenter in the vote that entered the United States into World War II. Once again, she broke with protocol and offered the reason for her vote. "As a woman I can't go to war," Rankin said, "and I refuse to send anyone else." Rankin narrowly escaped an angry mob that went after her following her "no" vote. Rankin didn't even try to run for reelection in 1943. She died in California in 1973.

PEOPLE FROM YOUR NEW STATE
WHO WON'T MAKE YOU FEEL ILL

* Dana Carvey, comedian, Missoula
* Gary Cooper, actor, Helena
* Evel Knievel, daredevil, Butte
* David Lynch, director, Missoula

NEBRASKA

GOVERNOR, SENATORS, CONGRESS MEMBERS

Governor Dave Heineman, Republican Heineman became governor in 2005. He served as the state's lieutenant governor, until Governor Mike Johanns was tapped to be Dub-Yuh's secretary of agriculture. Heineman plans to run for a full gubernatorial term in 2006, but he's likely to face stiff competition from Tom Osborne, a U.S. congressman and former Nebraska Cornhuskers head coach.

➤ **Contact** ✆402-471-2244; ✑*www.gov.nol.org*

Senator Chuck Hagel, Republican Hagel has been a senator since 1997. You can vote him out of office in 2008. Hagel served as deputy director and chief executive officer of the Economic Summit of Industrialized Nations, or G-7, in 1990.

➤ **Contact** ✆202-224-4224; ✑*www.hagel.senate.gov*

Senator Ben Nelson, Democrat Nelson has been a senator since 2001. You can reelect him in 2006.

➤ **Contact** ✆202-224-6551; ✑*www.bennelson.senate.gov*

Congress Members, 109th Congress

★ Jeff Fortenberry, Republican: Began serving in 2004. ✆202-225-4806; ✑*www.fortenberry.house/gov*

★ Lee Terry, Republican: Began serving in 1998. ✆202-225-4155; ✑*www.leeterry.house.gov*

★ Tom Osborne, Republican: Began serving in 2000. ✆202-225-6435; ✑*www.house.gov/terry*

PITHY POLITICAL POOP AND SCINTILLATING SCANDAL

Checkgate Nebraska has been remarkably free of political scandal. That's probably why folks in the squeaky clean Midwestern state were so shocked in 2003 when "Checkgate" surfaced.

By modern political scandal standards, Checkgate was pretty tame. No interns were groped. No state funds were spent on hookers or on questionable real estate deals.

Here's what happened. State Treasurer Loralee Byrd, a Republican (naturally), was accused of writing twelve checks worth about $300,000 and then hiding them in a safe. Once the legislative session ended, she voided the checks. Why? Byrd allegedly wanted it to appear that she'd spent the money, so her department would avoid budget cuts.

Byrd claimed she simply kept the checks as part of a contingency plan, should Nebraska's newly adopted accounting system fail. If it did, she could use the funds to process the state's child-support checks.

Hmm. Byrd made a deal with the state's attorney general's office, pleading guilty to a misdemeanor charge of official misconduct in office. Byrd then resigned before the new legislative season started.

PEOPLE FROM YOUR NEW STATE
WHO WON'T MAKE YOU FEEL ILL

* Fred Astaire, dancer, Omaha
* Marlon Brando, actor, Omaha
* Warren Buffett, investor, Omaha
* Montgomery Clift, actor, Omaha
* Henry Fonda, actor, Grand Island
* Malcolm X (Malcolm Little), activist, Omaha
* Nick Nolte, actor, Omaha

NEVADA

GOVERNOR, SENATORS, CONGRESS MEMBERS

Governor Kenny Guinn, Republican Guinn was elected in 1998 and reelected in 2002. Guinn spent most of his professional life as an educator, and he's considered moderate for a Republican. His 2002 victory indicated many Democrats voted for him. Guinn's term ends in 2006.

➤ **Contact** ✆775-684-5670; *www.gov.state.nv*

Senator John Ensign, Republican Ensign served as a congressman from 1995 to 1998. He became a senator in 2001. You can vote him out of office in 2006. Ensign was an unsuccessful senatorial candidate in 1998.

➤ **Contact** ☎202-224-6244; ✎*www.ensign.senate.gov*

Senator Harry Reid, Democrat Reid served as a congressman from 1983 to 1986. He has been a senator since 1987. You can reelect him in 2010. Reid became the senate minority leader in 2005.

➤ **Committees** Chair, Committee on Environment and Public Works; Select Committee on Ethics; Co-chair, Senate Democratic Conference, Democratic Policy Committee. Red was the Democratic Party whip from 1999 to 2005.

➤ **Contact** 202-224-3542; ✎*www.reid.senate.gov*

Congress Members, 109th Congress

★ Shelley Berkley, Democrat: Began serving in 1998. ☎202-225-5965; ✎*www.house.gov/berkley*

★ Jim Gibbons, Republican: Began serving in 1996. ☎202-225-6155; ✎*www.house.gov/gibbons*

★ Jon Porter, Republican: Began serving in 2002. ☎202-225-3252; ✎*www.house.gov/porter*

PITHY POLITICAL POOP AND SCINTILLATING SCANDAL

Ground Zero So, you're trying to survive in Nevada. Oh, that's not so bad . . . Vegas baby! Sin City! Oh, you're *where*? Nye County? Uh oh.

Between 1951 and 1962, Nye County was ground zero for nuclear testing in the United States. About 125 above-ground and more than 800 below-ground tests of atomic weapons took place. They became tourist attractions for Sin City visitors, who took time away from their busy gambling schedule to watch rising mushroom clouds off in the distance.

But the tests weren't harmless entertainment for plastered gamblers. Elevated levels of a radioactive isotope from the tests began popping up across the United States and even became a political issue during the 1956 presidential campaign. Protestors demonstrated as early as 1957. One piece of advice: Drink bottled water.

PEOPLE FROM YOUR NEW STATE
WHO WON'T MAKE YOU FEEL ILL

* Andre Agassi, tennis player, Las Vegas
* Jack Kramer, tennis player, Las Vegas

NEW MEXICO

GOVERNOR, SENATORS, CONGRESS MEMBERS

Governor Bill Richardson, Democrat Richardson was a congressman for about fifteen years, and he was elected governor in 2002. Richardson has cut taxes and remained active in foreign affairs. You can reelect him in 2006, but keep in mind that he's already expressed interest in the 2008 presidential election.

Richardson presided over the mishandling of the Wen Ho Lee case. Lee was a Chinese-American computer scientist working in Los Alamos. He was accused of stealing nuclear secrets and giving them to China. The U.S. government changed the classification of data with which Lee worked—but did so after he was charged with multiple felonies. Oops.

Lee looked like he was the target of a witch hunt. And he ultimately was found guilty of the minor charge of improperly downloading classified data.

➤ **Contact** ✆ 505-476-2200; ✍ *www.governor.state.nm.us*

Senator Jeff Bingaman, Democrat Bingaman has been a senator since 1983. You can reelect him in 2006.

➤ **Committees** Chair, Senate Impeachment Trial Committee; Committee on Energy and Natural Resources

➤ **Contact** ✆202-224-5521; ✉*www.bingaman.senate.gov*

Senator Pete Domenici, Republican Domenici has been a senator since 1973. You can try to vote him out of office in 2008, should he run for reelection.

➤ **Committees** Chair, Committee on the Budget; Committee on Energy and Natural Resources

➤ **Contact** ✆202-224-6621; ✉*www.domenici.senate.gov*

Congress Members, 109th Congress

★ Heather Wilson, Republican: Began serving in 1996. ✆202-225-6316; ✉*www.wilson.house.gov*

★ Stevan Pearce, Republican: Began serving in 2002. ✆202-225-2365; ✉*www.pearce.house.gov*

★ Tom Udall, Democrat: Began serving in 1998. ✆202-225-6190; ✉*www.tomudall.house.gov*

PITHY POLITICAL POOP AND SCINTILLATING SCANDAL

Whither Los Alamos? The first atomic bomb was exploded in Los Alamos, about a month before the technology was used to level Hiroshima and Nagasaki. It's sad, but that was the high point of this remote New Mexican town.

Nuclear experiments have continued at the Los Alamos National Laboratory since World War II, but questions about the lab's future have persisted since the end of the Cold War.

One thing critics have looked at is embarrassing incidents at Los Alamos. One incident that became a short-lived tempest in a teacup was 1999's Wen Ho Lee case. That was followed a few years later by the case of the—now they're missing, now they're not—classified computer disks in 2004.

At a cost of approximately $360 million, the lab was closed during a frantic search for two missing disks believed to contain classified information. Then it turned out that the disks weren't missing. In fact, they'd never existed. Sloppy inventory measures were responsible for the SNAFU.

The main reason the Los Alamos lab's future is up in the air is that some members of Congress are questioning the need for the facility's continued existence. Representatives Bart Stupak of Michigan, a Democrat, has been particularly vocal about closing down the lab.

In May 2005, he suggested shuttering the birthplace of the bomb once and for all. Stupak suggested there's nothing being done in Los Alamos that couldn't be done someplace else. "Why do we need Los Alamos?" he asked. It may be a museum by the time you're finished moving into your new New Mexican home.

PEOPLE FROM YOUR NEW STATE
WHO WON'T MAKE YOU FEEL ILL

* William Hanna, animator, Melrose
* Demi Moore, actress, Roswell
* Linda Wertheimer, NPR correspondent, Carlsbad

NORTH CAROLINA

GOVERNOR, SENATORS, CONGRESS MEMBERS

Governor Mike Easley, Democrat Easley served as a district attorney and the state's attorney general before being elected governor in 2000. During his days as an attorney, he was noted nationally for his success in attacking illegal drugs in North Carolina.

As governor, Easley has focused on education, despite being saddled with budget issues left over from previous administrations. He repeatedly pushed for a state lottery, and finally got one approved in the summer of 2005.

Easley's second and last term will end in 2008, and he's likely to run for a U.S. senate seat after that.

➤ **Contact** ☎919-733-4240; 🖥 *www.governor.state.nc.us*

Senator Richard Burr, Republican Burr served as a congressman from 1995 to 2004. He became a senator in 2005. You can vote him out of office in 2010.

➤ **Contact** ☎202-224-3154; 🖥 *www.burr.senate.gov*

Senator Elizabeth Dole, Republican Dole has been a senator since 2003. You can vote her out of office in 2008. Dole is the wife of former Kansas senator and male-enhancement enthusiast, Bob Dole. Elizabeth Dole was secretary of transportation from 1983 to 1987 and secretary of labor from 1989 to 1990. She made an unsuccessful bid for the presidential nomination in 2000.

➤ **Contact** ☎202-224-6342; 🖥 *www.dole.senate.gov*

Congress Members, 109th Congress

★ G. K. Butterfield, Democrat: Began serving in 2002. ☎202-225-3101; 🖥 *www.house.gov/butterfield*

★ Bob Etheridge, Democrat: Began serving in 1996. ☎202-225-4531; 🖥 *www.house.gov/etheridge*

★ Walter Jones, Republican: Began serving in 1994. ☎202-225-3415; 🖥 *www.jones.house.gov*

★ David Price, Democrat: Began serving in 1986. ☎202-225-1784; 🖥 *www.price.house.gov*

★ Virginia Foxx, Republican: Began serving in 2004. ☎202-225-2071; 🖥 *www.foxx.house.gov*

★ Howard Coble, Republican: Began serving in 1984. ☎202-225-3065; 🖥 *www.coble.house.gov*

* Mike McIntyre, Democrat: Began serving in 1996. ☎202-225-2731; ✎*www.house.gov/mcintyre*
* Robin Hayes, Republican: Began serving in 1998. ☎202-225-3715; ✎*www.hayes.house.gov*
* Sue Wilkins Myrick, Republican: Began serving in 1994. ☎202-225-1976; ✎*www.myrick.house.gov*
* Patrick McHenry, Republican: Began serving in 2004. ☎202-225-2576; ✎*www.mchenry.house.gov*
* Charles Taylor, Republican: Began serving in 1990. ☎202-225-6401; ✎*www.house.gov/charlestaylor*
* Melvin Watt, Democrat: Began serving in 1992. ☎202-225-1510; ✎*www.house.gov/watt*
* Brad Miller, Democrat: Began serving in 2002. ☎202-225-3032; ✎*www.house.gov/bradmiller*

PITHY POLITICAL POOP AND SCINTILLATING SCANDAL

Andrew Johnson North Carolina's Andrew Johnson became the first president in American history to be impeached. A strong-willed, hard-headed, Confederate-hating Southerner, Johnson loved making former plantation owners grovel at his feet. He made enemies easily. Johnson interfered often with the enforcement of Reconstruction laws. In 1868, he dismissed Secretary of War Edwin Stanton and tried to gain complete control of the army.

House Republicans charged him with violating the Tenure of Office Act, which required the senate's approval should a president wish to remove from office anyone appointed with senatorial consent. Republicans in congress ultimately charged Johnson with eleven articles of impeachment. Conviction required a two-thirds vote by the senate. That amounted to thirty-six of the senate's fifty-four members. Johnson was found not guilty thanks to one vote, that of Kansas senator Edmund Ross. Ross's brave stand for what he thought was right earned him a place in John

F. Kennedy's *Profiles in Courage*. Johnson, who gained the White House after Lincoln's assassination, was not reelected to the presidency. But just five years later, Johnson was elected to the senate. Supposedly, he was welcomed with open arms by many who had tried to boot him out onto the street just a few years before.

Jesse (shudder) Helms If Dan Quayle was the dumbest senator-cum-vice president of the modern era, then Jesse Helms may very well have been the senate's most mean-spirited member. He represented North Carolina for thirty years, finally retiring in 2003. Along the way, he made pronouncements that were so vitriolic and vituperative that he raised (?) lowered (?) political incorrectness to a new level. Take these quotations, for example:

> *"Homosexuals are weak, morally sick wretches."*
>
> *"The* New York Times *and* Washington Post *are both infested with homosexuals themselves. Just about every person down there is a homosexual or lesbian."*
>
> *After the University of North Carolina, Chapel Hill began admitting black students, Helms took to calling it the "University of Negroes and Communists."*
>
> *In 1951, he drafted an attack ad for Republican Willis Smith against Democrat Frank Graham: "White people, wake up before it is too late. Do you want Negroes working beside you, your wife and your daughters, in your mills and factories? Frank Graham favors mingling of the races."*
>
> *On the thirty-first anniversary of the assassination of John F. Kennedy, Helms told CNN, "Mr. Clinton better watch out if he comes down here. He'd better have a bodyguard."*

PEOPLE FROM YOUR NEW STATE
WHO WON'T MAKE YOU FEEL ILL

★ David Brinkley, journalist, Wilmington
★ John Coltrane, jazz great, Hamlet
★ Dolly Madison, first lady, Guilford County
★ Thelonious Monk, jazz great, Rocky Mount

NORTH DAKOTA

GOVERNOR, SENATORS, CONGRESS MEMBERS

Governor John Hoeven, Republican Hoeven was elected and became governor in 2000. He was a banking executive prior to public service. His fiscal policy has made North Dakota one of the few states with a budget surplus.

On the other hand, Hoeven has been criticized for inactivity. His second term ends in 2008, and North Dakota does not have term limits.

So, you may be able to vote him out of office. But you'll have a fight on your hands. Hoeven's approval ratings are among the highest in the country for a governor.

➤ **Contact** ✆ 701-328-2200; ✉ *www.governor.state.nd.us*

Senator Kent Conrad, Democrat Senator Kent Conrad is the first of this Red State's two Democratic senators.

Conrad has been a senator since 1987. You can reelect him in 2006.

➤ **Committees** Chair, Committee on the Budget
➤ **Contact** ✆ 202-224-2043; ✉ *www.conrad.senate.gov*

Senator Byron Dorgan, Democrat Senator Byron Dorgan is also a Democratic senator, despite living in a Red State. Dorgan was a congressman from 1981 to 1992. He has been a senator since 1993. You can reelect him in 2010.

➤ **Committees** Chair, Democratic Policy Committee and Democratic Conference
➤ **Contact** ✆ 202-224-2551; ✉ *www.dorgan.senate.gov*

Congress Member, 109th Congress

★ Earl Pomeroy, Democrat: Began serving in 1992. ✆ 202-225-2611; ✉ *www.pomeroy.house.gov*

PITHY POLITICAL POOP AND
SCINTILLATING SCANDAL

Unhitched in Fargo Long before Nevada became a divorce Mecca in
the 1940s, the divorce capital of the West was . . . Fargo, North
Dakota? It's true.

In 1866, the Dakota Territory legislature passed a law that
allowed applicants for divorce to begin action as soon as they
arrived within the territory. The law was amended in 1877, requiring a three-month residency.

Since Fargo was the largest city in the Dakotas and was
located along two railroads, it became the location of choice for
future gay divorcees. Many would take the Northern Pacific railroad to Fargo, where the train stopped for ten minutes.

During the stopover, folks would register in local hotels, then
hop back on the train. Three months later, they'd return, their
"residency" established. So many folks did this that locals took
to calling the train's short stop the Ten-Minute Divorce.

Those eager to shed spouses came to Fargo from as far away
as Europe. Local lawyers, hoteliers, and restaurateurs made for-
tunes. But the good citizens of North Dakota didn't want their
state to have the reputation as a divorce mill. So they lobbied to
have North Dakota's loose divorce laws tightened.

State legislators changed the law, requiring a one-year residency period before someone could seek a divorce. Governor
Fred Fancher signed it into law on April 1, 1899. A few decades
later, Nevada became the new divorce capital of the world.

PEOPLE FROM YOUR NEW STATE
WHO WON'T MAKE YOU FEEL ILL

* Angie Dickinson, actress, Kulm
* Phil Jackson, Bulls coach, Deer Lodge
* Peggy Lee, singer, Jamestown

OHIO

GOVERNOR, SENATORS, CONGRESS MEMBERS

Governor Bob Taft, Republican Taft was elected in 1998. He's the great-grandson of president and Supreme Court justice William Howard Taft. Taft also has extremely low approval ratings. Maybe that's because he's distantly related to both Dub-Yuh and Dick Cheney. His term will end in 2007, after which Taft might make a senatorial run.

➤ **Contact** ✆614-466-3555; ✐*www.governor.ohio.gov*

Senator Mike DeWine, Republican DeWine served as a congressman from 1983 to 1990. He has been a senator since 1995. You can try to vote him out of office in 2006. DeWine was lieutenant governor of Ohio from 1991 to 1994.

➤ **Contact** ✆202-224-2315; ✐*www.dewine.senate.gov*

Senator George Voinovich, Republican Voinovich has been a senator since 1999. You can vote him out of office in 2010. Voinovich was governor of Ohio from 1991 to 1998.

➤ **Contact** ✆202-224-3353; ✐*www.voinovich.senate.gov*

Congress Members, 109th Congress

★ Steve Chabot, Republican: Began serving in 1994. ✆202-225-2216; ✐*www.house.gov/chabot*

★ Rob Portman, Republican: Began serving in 1992. Resigned in 2005 to become the United States Trade Representative.

★ Michael Turner, Republican: Began serving in 2002. ✆202-225-6465; ✐*www.house.gov/miketurner*

★ Michael Oxley, Republican: Began serving in 1980. ✆202-225-2676; ✐*www.oxley.house.gov*

★ Paul Gillmor, Republican: Began serving in 1988. ✆202-225-6405; ✐*www.gillmor.house.gov*

★ Ted Strickland, Democrat: Began serving in 1992. ✆202-225-5705; ✐*www.house.gov/strickland*

★ David Hobson, Republican: Began serving in 1990. ✆202-225-4324; ✐*www.house.gov/hobson*

★ John Boehner, Republican: Began serving in 1990. ✆202-225-6205; ✐*www.johnboehner.house.gov*

★ Marcy Kaptur, Democrat: Began serving in 1982. ✆202-225-4146; ✐*www.kaptur.house.gov*

★ Dennis Kucinich, Democrat: Began serving in 1996. ✆202-225-5871; ✐*www.kucinich.house.gov*

★ Stephanie Tubbs Jones, Democrat: Began serving in 1998. ✆202-225-7032; ✐*www.house.gov/tubbsjones*

★ Patrick Tiberi, Republican: Began serving in 2000. ✆202-225-5355; ✐*www.house.gov/tiberi*

★ Sherrod Brown, Democrat: Began serving in 1992. ✆202-225-3401; ✐*www.house.gov/sherrodbrown*

★ Steven LaTourette, Republican: Began serving in 1994. ✆202-225-5731; ✐*www.house.gov/latourette*

★ Deborah Pryce, Republican: Began serving in 1992. ✆202-225-2015; ✐*www.house.gov/pryce*

★ Ralph Regula, Republican: Began serving in 1972. ✆202-225-3876; ✐*www.house.gov/regula*

★ Tim Ryan, Democrat: Began serving in 2002. ✆202-225-5261; ✐*www.timryan.house.gov*

★ Robert Ney, Republican: Began serving in 1994. ✆202-225-6265; ✐*www.ney.house.gov*

PITHY POLITICAL POOP AND
SCINTILLATING SCANDAL

The Land of Misfit Presidents Ohio is the cradle of second-rate, all-but-forgotten, and misfit presidents. Seven American commanders in chief were born there. Only Virginia features more presidential birthplaces.

Virginia boasts of the knee-pants days of George Washington, Thomas Jefferson, and James Madison. Ohio can brag of the birthplaces of such illustrious American leaders as, um, Benjamin Harrison, Warren G. Harding, Rutherford B. Hayes, James Garfield, William McKinley, and William Howard Taft. The best-known of the bunch is Ulysses S. Grant. But he's remembered more for his Civil War leadership and his memoirs than for his scandal-ridden presidency.

President Grant and All His Scandals Point Pleasant's gift to the White House was the incorruptible Civil War hero, Ulysses S. Grant, who served from 1869 to 1877. While his own character was impeccable—save for alleged epic battles with the bottle—his judge of character was asleep at the reins. Grant's administration was one of the most corrupt in American history.

First there was Black Friday, the day that marked the beginning of the Gold Panic of 1869. Two shady speculators, James Fisk and Jay Gould, enlisted Grant's brother-in-law, Abel Corbin, in a scheme to corner the gold market. Corbin arranged a party to give Gould and Fisk an audience with the president, where they pumped him for information about the U.S. Treasury's plans. If the treasury wasn't planning to let go of any of its gold, the speculators would make a killing. They, along with Corbin, managed to convince Grant that selling the treasury's gold was a bad idea. Fisk and Gould bought up huge amounts of gold until Grant, finally realizing he'd been duped, ordered the treasury to sell off $4 million in gold reserves. The gold market plunged, igniting a panic that ruined many legitimate investors.

Later, there was Whiskey-gate. The president's personal secretary, General Orville E. Babcock, took a bribe from General John McDonald, supervisor of the Internal Revenue Bureau in St. Louis. McDonald was using his position to help liquor distillers avoid paying their fair share of taxes. McDonald and his cronies skimmed millions in liquor taxes.

Babcock allegedly talked his boss out of looking into the so-called Whiskey Ring. Grant's Treasury Secretary Benjamin Bristow pursued the ring and had 350 men arrested across the country. When he went to Grant with the news, the president was so naïve that he was shocked to find General McDonald—a man he considered scrupulously honest—was at the center of the scandal.

Finally, there was the Grant administration's version of Halliburton. It involved a company called Credit Mobilier, a construction company established by Union Pacific leaders to profit from governmental support of railroad expansion. But those leaders made huge profits by padding construction budgets and charging Union Pacific exorbitant fees. That was bad enough.

What was worse is that one of Credit Mobilier's leaders was Oakes Ames, a Massachusetts congressman, who voted early and often on railroad bills. Congress finally got wind of Ames's scheme. The scandal became public during Grant's 1872 reelection campaign. One of the first dropped from the ticket because of his involvement with the scandal was Grant's vice president, Schuyler Colfax.

PEOPLE FROM YOUR NEW STATE
WHO WON'T MAKE YOU FEEL ILL

* Ambrose Bierce, writer, Meigs County
* Nancy Cartwright, voice of Bart Simpson, Kettering
* Hart Crane, poet, Garrettsville
* Thomas Edison, inventor, Milan
* John Glenn, astronaut and senator, Cambridge
* Toni Morrison, author, Lorain
* Paul Newman, actor, Cleveland
* Steven Spielberg, director, Cincinnati
* Gloria Steinem, feminist, Cleveland
* Tecumseh, Shawnee chief, Oldtown
* James Thurber, author, Columbus

OKLAHOMA

GOVERNOR, SENATORS, CONGRESS MEMBERS

Governor Brad Henry, Democrat   Henry was elected in 2002, in the midst of a budget crisis. He managed to forge bipartisan support of economic initiatives that protected education and health care from cuts.

He figured in national headlines during the so-called "Texas Ten" controversy. Remember that one? In 2003, ten Texas Democrats left the state so a quorum would not be available to vote for Republican-friendly redistricting. Henry allowed some of them to cross the border into Oklahoma and hide out for a bit. You can reelect him in 2006.

➤ **Contact**   ✆405-521-2342; ✉*www.gov.ok.gov*

Senator Tom Coburn, Republican   Coburn served as a congressman from 1995 to 2000. He became a senator in 2005. You can vote him out of office in 2010. Coburn is a physician by trade.

➤ **Contact**   ✆202-224-5754; ✉*www.coburn.senate.gov*

Senator James Inhofe, Republican   Inhofe served as a congressman from 1987 to 1994. He became a senator in 1994, filling in for the unexpired term of Senator David Boren, who resigned, allegedly for sexual harassment. You can vote Inhofe out of office in 2008.

➤ **Committees**   Chair, Committee on Environment and Public Works
➤ **Contact**   ✆202-224-4721; ✉*www.inhofe.senate.gov*

Congress Members, 109th Congress
★ John Sullivan, Republican: Began serving in 2000. ✆202-225-2211; ✉*www.sullivan.house.gov*
★ Dan Boren, Democrat: Began serving in 2004. ✆202-225-2701; ✉*www.house.gov/boren*
★ Frank Lucas, Republican: Began serving in 1992. ✆202-225-5565; ✉*www.house.gov/lucas*

RED STATE

★ Tom Cole, Republican: Began serving in 2002. ✆202-225-6165; ✍www.house.gov/cole
★ Ernest Istook Jr., Republican: Began serving in 1992. ✆202-225-2132; ✍www.house.gov/istook

PITHY POLITICAL POOP AND SCINTILLATING SCANDAL

Term Limits Red States are known for their jingoism, but they also seem to have an inherent mistrust of the government. In 1990, Oklahoma became the first to set term limits for its state legislators. They cannot serve more than twelve years. Proponents believe limits will make voters more willing to go to the polls, make legislators less susceptible to influence by special interests, and make legislators more determined to pass reforms because their time is restricted. Opponents are primarily the legislators themselves.

Saint Woody The man considered the godfather of protest was a native Oklahoman. Woody Guthrie was born in Okemah in 1912. When droughts transformed the Midwest into the so-called Dust Bowl, Guthrie did like many and headed for California. When he arrived there, he encountered scorn and hatred from the native Californians. Guthrie was changed by these experiences. He became an active supporter of outsider causes and began writing songs that reflected his political bent, such as "I Ain't Got No Home" and "Talking Dust Bowl Blues." By 1939, Guthrie was in New York. He supported causes such as union organization and anti-Fascism. By the late 1940s, Guthrie contracted the degenerative disease, Huntington's chorea. He was hospitalized for the last thirteen years of his life. While in the hospital, Guthrie was visited by a young Minnesotan named Bobby Zimmerman. Zimmerman worshipped Guthrie and wanted his blessing. Zimmerman, who adopted the name Bob Dylan, took the mantle from Guthrie and became the new poet laureate of protest.

RED STATE

PEOPLE FROM YOUR NEW STATE
WHO WON'T MAKE YOU FEEL ILL

* Ralph Ellison, writer, Oklahoma City
* Ron Howard, actor and director, Duncan
* Jennifer Jones, actress, Tulsa
* Mickey Mantle, baseball legend, Spavinaw
* Bill Moyers, journalist, Hugo
* Daniel Patrick Moynihan, senator, Tulsa
* Brad Pitt, actor, Shawnee
* Will Rogers, humorist, Oologah

SOUTH CAROLINA

GOVERNOR, SENATORS, CONGRESS MEMBERS

Governor Mark Sanford, Republican Sanford was elected in 2002. He was a congressman prior to that. Sanford and his state's legislature have a tempestuous relationship. He made national headlines when he let pigs run through the state house chamber to protest pork projects. It's hard to hate a guy like that, even if he is a Republican. He'll be up for reelection in 2006.

➤ **Contact** ✆803-734-2100; *www.scgovernor.com*

Senator Jim DeMint, Republican DeMint served as a congressman from 1999 to 2004. He became a senator in 2005. You can vote him out of office in 2010.

➤ **Contact** ✆202-224-6121; *www.demint.senate.gov*

Senator Lindsey Graham, Republican Graham served as a congressman from 1995 to 2002. He became a senator in 2003. You can vote him out of office in 2008.

➤ **Contact** ✆202-224-5972; *www.lgraham.senate.gov*

Congress Members, 109th Congress

★ Harry Brown Jr., Republican: Began serving in 2000. ☎ 202-225-3176; *✐www.house.gov/henrybrown*

★ Joe Wilson, Republican: Began serving in 2000. ☎ 202-225-2452; *✐www.joewilson.house.gov*

★ J. Gresham Barrett, Republican: Began serving in 2002. ☎ 202-225-5301; *✐www.house.gov/barrett*

★ Bob Inglis, Republican: Began serving in 1992. ☎ 202-225-6030; *✐www.house.gov/inglis*

★ John Spratt Jr., Democrat: Began serving in 1982. ☎ 202-225-5501; *✐www.house.gov/spratt*

★ James Clyburn, Democrat: Began serving in 1992. ☎ 202-225-3315; *✐www.house.gov/clyburn*

PITHY POLITICAL POOP AND SCINTILLATING SCANDAL

A Century of Trouble Even at age 100, the late South Carolina Senator Strom Thurmond remained controversial.

In 2002, then-Senate majority leader Trent Lott of Mississippi made comments that appeared to support the segregationist views once espoused by Thurmond. The occasion was Thurmond's 100th birthday party. Lott was pilloried by the left *and* the right for his words, and he resigned his leadership post. Lott was replaced as majority leader by Senator Bill Frist of Tennessee.

PEOPLE FROM YOUR NEW STATE
WHO WON'T MAKE YOU FEEL ILL

✱ James Brown, Godfather of Soul, Barnwell

✱ Althea Gibson, tennis player, Silver

✱ Dizzy Gillespie, jazz giant, Cheraw

✱ Jesse Jackson, activist, Greenville

✱ Vanna White, television personality, North Myrtle Beach

RED STATE

SOUTH DAKOTA

GOVERNOR, SENATORS, CONGRESS MEMBERS

Governor Mike Rounds, Republican Rounds was elected in 2002. Prior to that, he was the state senate's majority leader. Rounds's victory was a surprise to many. He announced his candidacy late and faced better-known opponents. These front-runners took turns wielding judy-bats and brickbats at each other, and dark-horse Rounds won the election by running a positive campaign. Rounds has increased state funding for education and strengthened early education programs. There's not much to dislike about this guy, except that he's from the wrong political party. You can vote him out of office in 2006.

➤ **Contact** ✆605-773-3212; ✍*www.state.sd.us/governor*

Senator Tim Johnson, Democrat Johnson served as a congressman from 1987 to 1996. He has been a senator since 1997. You can reelect him in 2008.

➤ **Contact** ✆202-224-5842; ✍*www.johnson.senate.gov*

Senator John Thune, Republican Thune served as a congressman from 1997 to 2003. He became a senator in 2005. You can vote him out of office in 2010. Thune ran unsuccessfully for senate in 2002.

➤ **Contact** ✆202-224-2321; ✍*www.thune.senate.gov*

Congress Member, 109th Congress

★ Stephanie Herseth, Democrat: Began serving in 2002. ✆202-225-2801; ✍*www.house.gov/herseth*

PITHY POLITICAL POOP AND SCINTILLATING SCANDAL

The Man Who (Unfortunately) Couldn't Beat Nixon South Dakota Senator George McGovern has gone down in history as one of the worst losers of the twentieth century. Nixon absolutely trounced him during the 1972 election, in large part because he got the South to vote a Republican into the Oval Office for the first time. Nixon basically did this the old-fashioned way . . . by appealing to racist Southerners, still a large voting bloc in 1972. By subtly raising racist specters, he manipulated those who might have voted for George Wallace to cast a Nixon ballot instead.

But McGovern held his head high after his spectacular loss. Right after the defeat, McGovern spoke to America through the pages of *Life* magazine. He talked of fighting the good fight and claimed (probably through gritted teeth) that he wasn't humiliated.

In the same article, however, he made a self-assessment that seemed to reveal his true feelings. "It's certainly nothing new to be told that I am unacceptable," McGovern said.

Even though McGovern's appeal to liberal ideals failed, he made a prediction that is just as accurate today as it was in 1972: "You have to remember that at various times in history the forces of irrationalism and fear have temporarily triumphed. Then the other side has its day." So, don't worry. You're in a Red State. The wrong guy's in office. The Middle East is a morass. The other side will have its day. Big George M. said so!

Hit and Run Outspoken governor and congressman Bill Janklow will probably have regained his license to practice law by the time you read this.

You remember Janklow, don't you? He was convicted of second-degree manslaughter for speeding through a stop sign and killing a motorcyclist in 2003. Janklow stepped down from his congressional seat soon after the conviction and served 100 days in a county jail. Janklow claims he still doesn't remember the accident because it occurred when he was in the midst of a diabetic stupor. That must explain the thirteen traffic citations Janklow received between 1990 and the time of the fatal accident.

RED STATE

PEOPLE FROM YOUR NEW STATE
WHO WON'T MAKE YOU FEEL ILL

★ Tom Brokaw, newscaster, Webster
★ Crazy Horse, Oglala chief
★ George McGovern, politician, Avon
★ Sitting Bull, Hunkpapa Lakota chief
★ Mamie Van Doren, actress, Rowena

TENNESSEE

GOVERNOR, SENATORS, CONGRESS MEMBERS

Governor Phil Bredesen, Democrat Bredesen was elected in 2002. Prior to that, he was mayor of Nashville, during a tremendous growth period for the Country Music Capital of the World.

Bredesen has founded nonprofits that help the homeless and work to preserve farmland from development. He's also an amateur artist who helped transform an empty post office in downtown Nashville into a gallery.

During his professional life, Bredesen created HealthAmerica Corp., a gigantic, publicly traded health-care management company. You can reelect him in 2006.

➤ **Contact** ✆615-741-2001; ✐*www.state.tn.us/governor*

Senator Lamar Alexander, Republican Alexander has been a senator since 2003. You can vote him out of office in 2008. Alexander was governor of Tennessee from 1979 to 1987 and served as the U.S. Secretary of Education from 1991 to 1993.

➤ **Contact** ✆202-224-4944; ✐*www.alexander.senate.gov*

Senator Bill Frist, Republican Frist has been a senator since 1995. You can vote him out of office in 2006. Frist is a heart and lung transplant surgeon by trade. Frist became the senate's majority leader in 2003. He earned the rancor of other Republicans in 2005 when he came out in favor of stem-cell research. Dub-Yuh has been very vocally opposed to the potentially life-saving research.

➤ **Committees** Chair, National Republican Senatorial Committee

➤ **Contact** ✆202-224-3344; ✍*www.frist.senate.gov*

Congress Members, 109th Congress

★ William Jenkins, Republican: Began serving in 1996. ✆202-225-6356; ✍*www.house.gov/jenkins*

★ John Duncan Jr., Republican: Began serving in 1986. ✆202-225-5435; ✍*www.house.gov/duncan*

★ Zach Wamp, Republican: Began serving in 1994. ✆202-225-3271; ✍*www.house.gov/wamp*

★ Lincoln Davis, Democrat: Began serving in 2002. ✆202-225-6831; ✍*www.house.gov/lincolndavis*

★ Jim Cooper, Democrat: Began serving in 1982; served until 1994; unsuccessful bid for senate; reelected to House in 2002. ✆202-225-4311; ✍*www.cooper.house.gov*

★ Bart Gordon, Democrat: Began serving in 1984. ✆202-225-4231; ✍*www.gordon.house.gov*

★ Marsha Blackburn, Republican: Began serving in 2002. ✆202-225-2811; ✍*www.house.gov/blackburn*

★ John Tanner, Democrat: Began serving in 1988. ✆202-225-4714; ✍*www.house.gov/tanner*

★ Harold Ford Jr., Democrat: Began serving in 1996. ✆202-225-3265; ✍*www.house.gov/ford*

PITHY POLITICAL POOP AND
SCINTILLATING SCANDAL

Al Gore It's too depressing to think about Gore, the man who should have become president in 2001. For now, the less said about him, the better.

Petticoat Junction The so-called Petticoat War that marred the early part of Andrew Jackson's presidency began with the death of his beloved wife, Rachel.

Jackson's campaign against John Quincy Adams was a nasty one. It makes anything Karl Rove has done seem like a children's game. Rachel Adams died before her husband's inauguration, and Jackson blamed the campaign's pressure for her death.

After he took office, Jackson began to assemble his cabinet. He made his friend, John Eaton, secretary of war. But there was one problem: Eaton's new wife, Peggy O'Neal Timberlake Eaton.

Peggy was considered of ill repute by the wives of other cabinet members. Many believed she drove her first husband, John Timberlake, to drink himself to death—over an alleged affair with Eaton. As Peggy was scorned by these tongue-waggers, Jackson most likely was reminded of the pressure that drove his own wife to die before her time. Add to that Jackson's fierce loyalty to friends, and you had a recipe for disaster just boiling away.

Other cabinet members urged Jackson to fire Eaton, but Jackson basically said, "Balls to you." The impasse crippled the country, until pro-Peggy Secretary of State Martin Van Buren agreed to resign along with Eaton, if the president would demand the other cabinet secretaries follow suit. Bang. No cabinet. Jackson rewarded Van Buren's loyalty by making him his running mate during Jackson's 1832 reelection campaign.

Remember Fort Pillow Fort Pillow was the site of one of the most deplorable acts of the Civil War, a war with no shortage of deplorable acts.

Union forces captured the fort, along the Mississippi River some forty miles north of Memphis, in 1862. In 1864, Confederate General Nathan Bedford Forrest's cavalry recaptured it. The fort was manned by white and black soldiers, but African American casualties were more than six times those of whites. Why?

Because Forrest's troops slaughtered black soldiers with abandon, whether they were trying to defend the fort or trying to surrender. Some black soldiers were buried alive or crucified by being nailed onto tent frames, which were then set afire. The Confederacy commended Forrest and his men for their "brilliant and successful campaign."

PEOPLE FROM YOUR NEW STATE
WHO WON'T MAKE YOU FEEL ILL

* James Agee, writer, Knoxville
* Jack Carter, inventor of miniature golf, Sweetwater
* Aretha Franklin, Queen of Soul, Memphis
* Morgan Freeman, actor, Memphis
* Dolly Parton, country singer, Sevierville
* Tina Turner, singer, Brownsville

TEXAS

GOVERNOR, SENATORS, CONGRESS MEMBERS

Governor Rick Perry, Republican Perry first took office in 2000, when the state's former governor—what's his name—left to become president. Perry was elected to a full term in 2002.

He's almost as lethal-injection-happy as his predecessor, killing 100 inmates by 2005. And he's a flip-flopper who began his public service a Democrat. On the other hand, he's improved health-care programs. You can vote him out of office in 2006.

➤ **Contact** 512-463-2000; *www.governor.state.tx.us*

Senator John Cornyn, Republican Cornyn has been a senator since 2002. You can vote him out office in 2008.

➤ **Contact** 202-224-2934; *www.cornyn.senate.gov*

Senator Kay Hutchison, Republican Hutchison has been a senator since 1993. You can vote her out of office in 2006. She first came to the senate in a special election to replace longtime senator, Lloyd Bentsen, who resigned. She was Republican Conference vice-chair in 2000 and the deputy permanent chair of the 2004 Republican National Convention.

➤ **Contact** ✆202-224-5922; ✎*www.hutchison.senate.gov*

Congress Members, 109th Congress

★ Louie Gohmert, Republican: Began serving in 2004. ✆202-225-3035; ✎*www.gohmert.house.gov*

★ Ted Poe, Republican: Began serving in 2004. ✆202-225-6565; ✎*www.house.gov/poe*

★ Sam Johnson, Republican: Began serving in 1990. ✆202-225-4201; ✎*www.samjohnson.house.gov*

★ Ralph Hall, Republican: Began serving in 1980. ✆202-225-6673; ✎*www.house.gov/ralphhall*

★ Jeb Hensarling, Republican: Began serving in 2002. ✆202-225-3484; ✎*www.house.gov/hensarling*

★ Joe Barton, Republican: Began serving in 1984. ✆202-225-2002; ✎*www.joebarton.house.gov*

★ John Abney Culberson, Republican: Began serving in 2000. ✆202-225-2571; ✎*www.culberson.house.gov*

★ Kevin Brady, Republican: Began serving in 1996. ✆202-225-4901; ✎*www.house.gov/brady*

★ Al Green, Democrat: Began serving in 2004. ✆202-225-7508; ✎*www.house.gov/algreen*

★ Michael McCaul, Republican: Began serving in 2004. ✆202-225-2401; ✎*www.house.gov/mccaul*

★ K. Michael Conaway, Republican: Began serving in 2004. ✆202-225-3605; ✎*www.conaway.house.gov*

★ Kay Granger, Republican: Began serving in 1996. ✆202-225-5071; ✎*www.kaygranger.house.gov*

- ★ Mac Thornberry, Republican: Began serving in 1994. ☏ 202-225-3706; 🖅 *www.house.gov/thornberry*
- ★ Ron Paul, Republican: Began serving in 1974; unsuccessful senate bid in 1984; reelected to House in 1996. ☏ 202-225-2831; 🖅 *www.house.gov/paul*
- ★ Ruben Hinojosa, Democrat: Began serving in 1996. ☏ 202-225-2531; 🖅 *www.hinojosa.house.gov*
- ★ Silvestre Reyes, Democrat: Began serving in 1996. ☏ 202-225-4831; 🖅 *www.house.gov/reyes*
- ★ Chet Edwards, Democrat: Began serving in 1990. ☏ 202-225-6105; 🖅 *www.edwards.house.gov*
- ★ Sheila Jackson Lee, Democrat: Began serving in 1994. ☏ 202-225-3816; 🖅 *www.jacksonlee.house.gov*
- ★ Randy Neugebauer, Republican: Began serving in 2002. ☏ 202-225-4005; 🖅 *www.randy.house.gov*
- ★ Charles Gonzalez, Democrat: Began serving in 1998. ☏ 202-225-3236; 🖅 *www.gonzalez.house.gov*
- ★ Lamar Smith, Republican: Began serving in 1986. ☏ 202-225-4236; 🖅 *www.lamarsmith.house.gov*
- ★ Tom DeLay, Republican: Began serving in 1984. ☏ 202-225-5951; 🖅 *www.tomdelay.house.gov*
- ★ Henry Bonilla, Republican: Began serving in 1992. ☏ 202-225-4511; 🖅 *www.bonilla.house.gov*
- ★ Kenny Marchant, Republican: Began serving in 2004. ☏ 202-225-6605; 🖅 *www.marchant.house.gov*
- ★ Lloyd Doggett, Democrat: Began serving in 1994. ☏ 202-225-4865; 🖅 *www.house.gov/doggett*
- ★ Michael Burgess, Republican: Began serving in 2002. ☏ 202-225-7772; 🖅 *www.burgess.house.gov*
- ★ Solomon Ortiz, Democrat: Began serving in 1982. ☏ 202-225-7742; 🖅 *www.house.gov/ortiz*
- ★ Henry Cuellar, Democrat: Began serving in 2004. ☏ 202-225-1640; 🖅 *www.house.gov/cuellar*
- ★ Gene Green, Democrat: Began serving in 1992. ☏ 202-225-1688; 🖅 *www.house.gov/green*

★ Eddie Bernice Johnson, Democrat: Began serving in 1992. ☏202-225-8885; ✐*www.house.gov/ebjohnson*

★ John Carter, Republican: Began serving in 2002. ☏202-225-3864; ✐*www.house.gov/carter*

★ Pete Sessions, Republican: Began serving in 1996. ☏202-225-2231; ✐*www.sessions.house.gov*

PITHY POLITICAL POOP AND SCINTILLATING SCANDAL

Will the Real Texas Presidents Please Stand Up? Only two U.S. presidents were actually born in Texas: Dwight Eisenhower and Lyndon Johnson. George H. W. Bush moved to Texas as an adult. His son, Dub-Yuh, was born in New Haven, Connecticut. I'm sorry, Blue Stater, but it's true. If it makes you feel better, Dub-Yuh moved to Odessa when he was only two—nowhere near enough time for Blue State qualities to gain a toehold in his pea-sized brain.

Billy Sol Estes In 1962, Billy Sol Estes was convicted of fraud for swindling millions from the government via a cotton allotments and subsidies scandal. His conviction was overturned by the Supreme Court during President Johnson's administration. Of course, Johnson's position had nothing to do with the Supreme Court considering a case involving his friend. Wink, wink.

John Connally Your new Red State neighbors would have you believe that political flip-flopping began with Massachusetts Senator John Kerry. But he was preceded by Governor John Connally, who switched from the Democratic to the Republican Party. Later, he was involved in a milk-price bribery scandal. And conspiracy nuts, both Blue and Red, continue to whisper about the possibility that Connally was somehow involved in JFK's assassination. Connally was in Kennedy's motorcade on November 22, 1963.

John Tower John Tower was elected four times to the U.S. Senate, the first Republican from Texas to serve in the senate since Reconstruction. After his retirement, he served as chairman of the Tower Commission, which investigated the Iran-Contra Affair.

Tower was touched by scandal in 1989, when the first President Bush wanted to name Tower his secretary of defense. The senate would not confirm his nomination, claiming that Tower was a habitual drunk with too many ties to defense contractors. Apparently, ties to defense contractors make one more suitable for the vice presidency of the nation, rather than for its department of defense.

PEOPLE FROM YOUR NEW STATE
WHO WON'T MAKE YOU FEEL ILL

* Mary Kay Ash, cosmetics entrepreneur, Hot Wells
* Carol Burnett, comedienne, San Antonio
* Larry Hagman, actor, Fort Worth
* Buddy Holly, rock pioneer, Lubbock
* Janis Joplin, singer, Port Arthur
* Sandra Day O'Connor, Supreme Court justice, El Paso
* Robert Rauschenberg, artist, Port Arthur
* Gene Rodenberry, father of *Star Trek,* El Paso
* Babe Didrikson, athlete, Port Arthur

UTAH

GOVERNOR, SENATORS, CONGRESS MEMBERS

Governor Jon Huntsman Jr., Republican Huntsman was elected in 2004. He's the son of the founder of the gigantic chemical company, Huntsman Corporation. Huntsman began his first term at odds with the U.S. Congress, which wants to move nuclear waste to his state. And he speaks fluent Mandarin Chinese. You can vote him out of office in 2008.

➤ **Contact** ☎ 801-538-1000; ✎ *www.utah.gov/governor*

Senator Robert Bennett, Republican Bennett has been a senator since 1993. You can vote him out of office in 2010. Bennett is the son of longtime Utah senator, Wallace Bennett.

➤ **Contact** ☎ 202-224-5444; ✎ *www.bennett.senate.gov*

Senator Orrin Hatch, Republican Hatch has been a senator since 1977. You can vote him out of office in 2006. Hatch is a prolific songwriter, with nearly a dozen albums to his credit. Just the titles alone are enough to stir the hearts of your new Red State neighbors: *How His Glory Shines, America United,* and *Freedom's Light* are among them. Gag.

➤ **Committees** Chair, Committee on Labor and Human Resources; Committee on the Judiciary

➤ **Contact** ☎ 202-224-5251; ✎ *www.hatch.senate.gov*

Congress Members, 109th Congress

★ Rob Bishop, Republican: Began serving in 2002. ☎ 202-225-0453; ✎ *www.house.gov/robbishop*

★ Jim Matheson, Democrat: Began serving in 2000. ☎ 202-225-3011; ✎ *www.house.gov/matheson*

★ Chris Cannon, Republican: Began serving in 1996. ☎ 202-225-7751; ✎ *www.chriscannon.house.gov*

PITHY POLITICAL POOP AND SCINTILLATING SCANDAL

Gary Gilmore Utah's Gary Gilmore became the first person executed in the United States in more than a decade, when he faced a firing squad on January 17, 1977. During part of that execution-free decade, the Supreme Court had ruled the death penalty unconstitutional. Fortunately for lethal injection-happy governors like Dub-Yuh, that ruling was later overturned.

Gilmore spent most of his life in prison. He became a free man for a short time in 1976, during which he killed a gas station attendant and a motel keeper in cold blood. Gilmore was sentenced to death, a death he believed he deserved. He did not appeal the court's ruling and fired his lawyers.

Because executions had been in abeyance for ten years, there was a national outcry to spare Gilmore's life. But Gilmore himself went before the justices of Utah's Supreme Court and asked that his death sentence be carried out. Gilmore's mother requested leniency, but Gilmore wrote a letter to the press, asking her to stop.

Gilmore's last words were, "Let's do it." Since Gilmore's death, executions have practically replaced baseball as America's pastime, especially in Texas. By the time you read this, the number of criminals executed in the United States will probably top 1,000. Gilmore's life and death were the subject of Norman Mailer's "nonfiction novel," *The Executioner's Song*.

PEOPLE FROM YOUR NEW STATE
WHO WON'T MAKE YOU FEEL ILL

* Roseanne Barr, actress, Salt Lake City
* Butch Cassidy, outlaw, Circleville
* James Woods, actor, Vernal

VIRGINIA

GOVERNOR, SENATORS, CONGRESS MEMBERS

Governor Tim Kaine, Democrat Kaine became governor in January of 2006, succeeding Democrat Mark Warner. Warner could not run for reelection due to the state's term limits. Though a Democrat,

Kaine actually made significant spending cuts throughout the state's government, including a 30 percent cut to his own salary.

➤ **Contact** ☎804-786-2211; ✐*www.governor.virginia.com*

Senator George Allen, Republican Allen was a congressman in 1991 and 1992. He became a senator in 2001. You can vote him out of office in 2006. Allen was Virginia's governor from 1994 to 1998.

➤ **Committees** Chair, National Republican Senatorial Committee

➤ **Contact** ☎202-224-4024; ✐*www.allen.senate.gov*

Senator John Warner, Republican Warner has been a senator since 1977. You can vote him out of office in 2008. Warner was Secretary of the U.S. Navy from 1972 to 1974. He served in the U.S. Marine Corps during the Korean conflict.

➤ **Committees** Chair, Committee on Rules and Administration; Committee on Armed Services

➤ **Contact** ☎202-224-2023; ✐*www.warner.senate.gov*

Congress Members, 109th Congress

★ Jo Ann Davis, Republican: Began serving in 2000. ☎202-225-4261; ✐*www.joanndavis.house.gov*

★ Thelma Drake, Republican: Began serving in 2004. ☎202-225-4215; ✐*www.drake.house.gov*

★ Robert Scott, Democrat: Began serving in 1992. ☎202-225-8351; ✐*www.house.gov/scott*

★ J. Randy Forbes, Republican: Began serving in 2000. ☎202-225-6365; ✐*www.house.gov/forbes*

★ Virgil Goode Jr., Republican: Began serving in 1996. ☎202-225-4711; ✐*www.house.gov/goode*

★ Bob Goodlatte, Republican: Began serving in 1992. ☎202-225-5431; ✐*www.house.gov/goodlatte*

★ Eric Cantor, Republican: Began serving in 2000. ☎202-225-2815; ✐*www.cantor.house.gov*

* James Moran, Democrat: Began serving in 1990. ✆202-225-4376; ✎*www.moran.house.gov*
* Rick Boucher, Democrat: Began serving in 1982. ✆202-225-3861; ✎*www.house.gov/boucher*
* Frank Wolf, Republican: Began serving in 1980. ✆202-225-5136; ✎*www.house.gov/wolf*
* Tom Davis, Republican: Began serving in 1994. ✆202-225-1492; ✎*www.tomdavis.house.gov*

PITHY POLITICAL POOP AND
SCINTILLATING SCANDAL

Tippecanoe and Tyler Too Does this sound familiar? A college-educated scion of wealth runs against another wealthy, college-educated opponent. The first man's handlers market him as a plain-spoken, aw-shucks man of the people and paint his opponent as an elite, effete Easterner. In truth, there's barely a whit of difference between the men, at least as far as their backgrounds are concerned. The "just like us" candidate wins handily.

No. This isn't a description of the 2004 presidential election that posited two Ivy League men against each other. It's a summary of the 1840 campaign that pitted Virginian William Henry Harrison against Martin Van Buren. Harrison served only a month before dying of pneumonia, but he holds the place in history of being the first presidential candidate to be touted by his party as a salt-of-the-earth populist when, in fact, he was a man born into privilege and wealth.

Harrison's Whig Party created for their candidate the "Tippecanoe and Tyler too" campaign. First, it played on Harrison's status as a "war hero." He was the victor of the Battle of Tippecanoe, one of our country's many wars against Native Americans. But that part of Harrison's vitae wasn't as important as the candidate's completely bogus qualities. The campaign's focus suggested that Harrison was log-cabin-born and that he enjoyed nothing more than tipping back moonshine. Van Buren, on the other hand, was portrayed as an out-of-touch Easterner. Harrison was put into office on a wave of kitschy campaign ephemera, all of which was dominated by the spurious log cabin and moonshine.

PEOPLE FROM YOUR NEW STATE
WHO WON'T MAKE YOU FEEL ILL

* Arthur Ashe, tennis player, Richmond
* Warren Beatty, actor, Richmond
* Willa Cather, author, Winchester
* Ella Fitzgerald, chanteuse, Newport News
* Patrick Henry, statesman, Hanover City
* Thomas Jefferson, president, Shadwell
* Shirley MacLaine, actress, Richmond
* George Washington, president, Westmoreland
* Tom Wolfe, journalist and author, Richmond

WEST VIRGINIA

GOVERNOR, SENATORS, CONGRESS MEMBERS

Governor Joe Manchin III, Democrat Manchin was elected in 2004. Many members of his family are active in state politics. Manchin is Catholic and thus opposed to abortion. You can reelect him in 2008.
➤ **Contact** ☎888-438-2731; ✐*www.wvgov.org*

Senator Robert Byrd, Democrat Senator Robert Byrd is one of two Democratic senators from this Red State. He is one of our country's longest-serving senators. He's been in office since 1959! And he was a congressman prior to that, from 1953 to 1958! Byrd was Democratic whip from 1971 to 1977. He was majority leader from 1977 to 1980 and again from 1987 to 1988. He was minority leader from 1981 to 1986 and president pro tempore from 1989 to 1995.

➤ **Committees** Chair, Committee on Appropriations
➤ **Contact** ✆202-224-3954; ✉*www.byrd.senate.gov*

Senator John Rockefeller, Democrat Senator John Rockefeller is also a Democrat serving a Red State. He has been a senator since 1985. You can reelect him in 2008. Yes, he's a member of *that* Rockefeller family. Rockefeller was governor of West Virginia from 1977 to 1985.

➤ **Committees** Chair, Committee on Veterans' Affairs; Vice-chair, Select Committee on Intelligence
➤ **Contact** ✆202-224-6472; ✉*www.rockefeller.senate.gov*

Congress Members, 109th Congress
★ Alan Mollohan, Democrat: Began serving in 1982. ✆202-225-4172; ✉*www.house.gov/mollohan*
★ Shelley Moore Capito, Republican: Began serving in 2000. ✆202-225-2711; ✉*www.capito.house.gov*
★ Nick Rahall II, Democrat: Began serving in 1976. ✆202-225-3452; ✉*www.rahall.house.gov*

PITHY POLITICAL POOP AND SCINTILLATING SCANDAL

West Virginia Chooses Senator Kennedy West Virginia was more responsible for putting John F. Kennedy in the White House than any other state. In 1960, the state was 95 percent Protestant. Kennedy knew that if he won West Virginia's primary, he could quell the fears of Democratic convention delegates who worried America would never elect a Catholic president. There was just one problem: West Virginia loved Kennedy's rival for the nomination, Hubert Humphrey. The state's coal miners liked Humphrey's homespun ways and support of unions. Kennedy, they thought, was a patrician blue blood, out of touch with "real" people, *and* a

Catholic besides. Enter the mafia. One of Kennedy's extramarital girlfriends was Judith Campbell Exner, who was also a consort of mob boss Sam Giancana. Kennedy asked Exner to arrange a meeting with Giancana, a truly evil man by anyone's definition. What exactly happened next is debatable.

But chances are, two things convinced Giancana to throw his weight behind Kennedy: money and promises that a Kennedy administration would be mob-friendly. Giancana used his influence to persuade or intimidate West Virginia's leaders to make the state's voters favor Kennedy by any means necessary. Kennedy won the primary and subsequently the presidency.

But the joke was on Giancana. JFK appointed his brother Robert attorney general. RFK already had made his hatred of the mob known during the Kefauver Hearings, one of early television's first great reality shows. As attorney general, RFK continued to hunt down and attack the mob. To this day, conspiracy theorists believe the mafia was behind the assassination of both Kennedy brothers.

PEOPLE FROM YOUR NEW STATE
WHO WON'T MAKE YOU FEEL ILL

* Pearl Buck, author, Hillsboro
* Don Knotts, actor, Morgantown
* Chuck Yeager, test pilot, Myra

WYOMING

GOVERNOR, SENATORS, CONGRESS MEMBERS

Governor Dave Freudenthal, Democrat Freudenthal was elected in 2002, and he has one of the highest approval ratings for any governor. He has focused on the environment, families, and on making sure the state's baby boomers will have enough economic resources after retirement. Per capita, Wyoming will have the country's largest number of retirees in ten years. You can reelect Freudenthal in 2006.

➤ **Contact** ✆307-777-7437; ✍*www.wyoming.gov/governor*

Senator Michael Enzi, Republican　Enzi has been a senator since 1997. You can vote him out of office in 2008.

➤ **Committees**　Chair, Committee on Health, Education, Labor, and Pensions
➤ **Contact** ✆202-224-3424; ✍*www.enzi.senate.gov*

Senator Craig Thomas, Republican　Thomas served as a congressman from 1989 to 1994. He's been a senator since 1995. You can vote him out of office in 2006. Thomas first got to congress by special election, to fill the seat vacated by (cue Darth Vader music) Dick Cheney.

➤ **Contact** ✆202-224-6441; ✍*www.thomas.senate.gov*

Congress Members, 109th Congress
★　Barbara Cubin, Republican: Began serving in 1994. ✆202-225-2311; ✍*www.house.gov/cubin*

PITHY POLITICAL POOP AND SCINTILLATING SCANDAL

We Need Women!　In an effort to draw women to the Wyoming Territory, the territory passed the first law in the United States giving women the right to vote. This took place in 1869, more than fifty years before women's suffrage became the law of the land. When Wyoming entered the Union, it took the motto "Equality State."

James Watt　Remember Ronald Reagan's controversial secretary of the interior, James Watt? Wyoming (not so) proudly can claim him as a native son.

Watt was famous for being the nation's first anti-environmentalist interior secretary. He called environmentalists "a left-wing cult dedicated to bringing down the type of government I believe in." And as that quote suggests, Watt also was famous for saying and doing really dumb things.

He wouldn't let the Beach Boys perform for a July 4 concert on the Washington Mall because he said rock concerts attract bad eggs who don't vote Republican, or something to that effect. Sure, he may have wanted to keep KISS off the Mall, but the Beach Boys? How innocuous and all-American can you get? Wayne Newton, the Midnight Idol, performed the Independence Day show instead.

But Watt's most famous moment of idiocy has to be a statement he made that assessed one of his commissions: "We have every mixture you can have. I have a black. I have a woman, two Jews, and a cripple." That comment led directly to his resignation in 1983.

PEOPLE FROM YOUR NEW STATE
WHO WON'T MAKE YOU FEEL ILL

✱ Jackson Pollock, artist, Cody

Works Cited

Books

Brown, Curtis F. *Star-Spangled Kitsch: An Astounding and Tastelessly Illustrated Exploration of the Bawdy, Gaudy, Shoddy Mass-Art Culture in This Grand Land of Ours*. (New York: Universe Books, 1975).

Epting, Chris. *James Dean Died Here: The Locations of America's Pop Culture Landmarks*. (Santa Monica, Cal.: Santa Monica Press, 2003).

Field Enterprises Educational Corporation. *Presidents of the United States*. (Chicago: World Book Ltd., 1973).

Foote, Shelby. *The Civil War, a Narrative: Fort Sumter to Perryville*. (New York: Vintage Books, 1986).

Garraty, John. *1,001 Things Everyone Should Know about American History*. (New York: Doubleday, 1989).

Heaps, Willard A. *Riots USA: 1765–1970*. (New York: The Seabury Press, 1970).

Loewen, James W. *Lies across America: What Our Historic Sites Get Wrong*. (New York: The New Press, 1999).

Mitchell, Jack. *Executive Privilege: Two Centuries of White House Scandals*. (New York: Hippocrene Books, 1992).

Ross, Shelley. *Fall from Grace: Sex, Scandal, and Corruption in American Politics from 1702 to the Present*. (New York: Ballantine Books, 1988).

Web Sites

Abortion facts, *www.guttmacher.org/pubs/sfaa.html*

Alaskans, notable, *www.dced.state.ak.us/oed/student_info/learn/famousalaskans.htm*

Arizona's environmental record, *www.azdeq.gov*

Banned books, *http://digital.library.upenn.edu/books/banned-books.html*

Banned books, *http://home.nvg.org/~aga/bulletin43.html*

Banned books, *www.beaconforfreedom.org*

Banned books, *www.floyd.edu/academics/library/banned/books.htm*

"Checkgate," *www.cnn.com/2003/US/Central/12/17/nebraska.scandal.ap/*

Colorado's environmental record, *www.cdphe.state.co.us/el/EMS/emspermit/*

"Daisy" ad, *www.eagleton.rutgers.edu/e-gov/e-politicalarchive-1964.htm*

Discrimination law, *www.timesargus.com/apps/pbcs.dll/article?AID=/20050911/NEWS/509110354/1003/NEWS02*

Euthanasia, *http://en.wikipedia.org/wiki/Euthanasia* and *www.longwood.edu/library/suic.htm*

Exxon Valdez, *www.evostc.state.ak.us/*

Fargo divorces, *www.fargo-history.com/early/divorce-capitol.htm*

Gilmore, Gary, *www.thebiographychannel.co.uk/new_site/biography
.php?id=423&showgroup=301*

Gubernatorial term limits, *www.termlimits.org/Current_Info/State_TL/
gubernatorial.html*

Gun laws, *www.nraila.org/GunLaws/Default.aspx#*

Guthrie, Woody, *www.woodyguthrie.org/biography.htm*

Hannity, Sean, on Abu Ghraib, *http://mediamatters.org/items/200409150003*

Helms, Jesse, *http://en.wikipedia.org/wiki/Jesse_Helms*

Kansas, "Bleeding," *www.pbs.org/wgbh/aia/part4/4p2952.html*

Limbaugh, Rush's alleged drug use, *www.fair.org/index.php*

Limbaugh, Rush's allegedly racist comments, *http://espn.go.com/gen/
news/2003/1001/1628537.html*

Lingle, Linda, *www.forbes.com/business/2005/09/09/economics-hawaii-politics_cz_
rk_0909dunce.html*

Lingle, Linda, *www.mercurynews.com/mld/mercurynews/news/politics/12584626.htm*

Long, Huey, *http://louisianahistory.ourfamily.com/kingfish.html*

Los Alamos, *www.cbsnews.com/stories/2005/08/07/sunday/main763673.shtml*

Lott, Trent's allegedly pro-segregation comments, *http://archives.cnn.com/2002/
ALLPOLITICS/12/09/lott.comment/*

Newton, Huey, *www.africawithin.com/bios/huey_newton.htm*

Preemption Act, *www.encyclopedia.com/html/P/Preempti.asp*

Pullman Strike, *www.chipublib.org/004chicago/disasters/pullman_strike.html*

Restaurants, *www.Mobiltravelguide.com*

Ross, Nellie, *http://wyoarchives.state.wy.us/articles/rossbio.htm*

Same-sex marriage, *http://en.wikipedia.org/wiki/Same-sex_marriage_in_the_United_
States* and *http://archives.cnn.com/2000/LAW/05/25/same.sex.marriages/*

Senators, *www.senate.gov*

Sodomy laws, *www.sodomylaws.org/usa/usa.htm*

Texas's environmental record, *www.tceq.state.tx.us/*

Wallace, George, *www.cnn.com/US/9809/14/wallace.obit/*

Watergate, *www.answers.com/main/ntquery;jsessionid=iugllp9us4z1?method=4&dsid
=2222&dekey=Watergate+scandal&gwp=8&curtab=2222_1&sbid=lc05a&linktext=
Watergate%20scandal*

Watt, James, *www.geocities.com/thereaganyears/environment.htm*

Enter At Your
Own Risk

Enter At Your
Own Risk

BLUE STATE

The Confused Citizen's
Guide to Surviving
in the Other America

Justin Cord Hayes

Adams Media
Avon, Massachusetts

Published by Adams Media, an F+W Publications Company
57 Littlefield Street
Avon, MA 02322
www.adamsmedia.com

ISBN: 1-59337-642-1

J I H G F E D C B A

Printed in Canada.

Library of Congress Cataloging-in-Publications Data
Hayes, Justin Cord.
Blue state ; Red state / Justin Cord Hayes.
p.   cm.
Added t.p. title: Red state
Flip book. No collective t.p.; titles transcribed from individual title pages.
Includes bibliographical references and index.
ISBN 1-59337-642-1 (alk. paper)
1. United States—Politics and government—2001—Humor. 2. United States—Social life
and customs—1971—Humor. 3. Conservatism—United States—Humor. 4. Liberalism—
United States—Humor. 5. American wit and humor. I. Title. II. Title: Red state.
E902.H395 2006
973.93102'07—dc22
2006007454

This publication is designed to provide accurate and authoritative information with regard to
the subject matter covered. It is sold with the understanding that the publisher is not engaged
in rendering legal, accounting, or other professional advice. If legal advice or other expert
assistance is required, the services of a competent professional person should be sought.
—From a *Declaration of Principles* jointly adopted by a Committee of the American Bar
Association and a Committee of Publishers and Associations

Many of the designations used by manufacturers and sellers to distinguish their product are
claimed as trademarks. Where those designations appear in this book and Adams Media was
aware of a trademark claim, the designations have been printed with initial capital letters.

The views, policies, and opinions expressed herein do not necessarily state or reflect those of
Adams Media or any part of F+W Publications, Inc.

Interior art ©iStockphoto.com/Emanuele Gnani

This book is available at quantity discounts for bulk purchases.
For information, please call 1-800-872-5627.

Contents

PART 1

Help! I'm
Trapped in a
Blue State!

Introduction

Stuck in a Godless Land of Lattes

JUST TAKE A DEEP BREATH and say over and over to yourself: "It could be worse. I could have been told I've got inoperable cancer or that my teenage son has turned out gay." Instead, you're just stuck surviving in one of those god-hating, abortion-loving, tree-hugging Blue States. Life will go on, even if it's vastly different from before.

Blue States believe all kinds of wacky things. For example, they call abortion a "woman's right to choose." They believe the death penalty is a bad thing. Some Blue States have even legalized such bizarre practices as gay marriage and physician-assisted suicide.

They think our fine Christian president is not very bright. Well, if he isn't, it's no wonder. Didn't he graduate from one of those highfalutin' Blue State schools? Radcliffe, wasn't it? Or something like that. But he's a brilliant man, or he wouldn't be president. And besides, he belongs to the right religion and the by-God right political party.

They're weird in Blue States. But don't despair. What follows is a guide to the way those Blue Staters think. You know they're—at best—misguided and—at worst—minions of Satan, out to do his bidding. You'll learn about Blue State views on issues Blue Staters believe are controversial: capital punishment, gun control, censorship. You know they're not controversial. The right way to feel about every last one of them is in the Bible somewhere. God didn't clone

His Only Son, did He? It was Adam and Eve, not Adam and Steve, right?

After a quick lesson in Blue State thought—if you can call it that—you'll discover where to find beloved pockets of Red State favorites within them. And then you'll learn all about the men and women who serve as your state's governor, senators, and congress members. You'll be pleasantly surprised to find that many leaders—in even the most traditionally liberal of states—actually are conservatives, rather than empty-headed bleeding hearts.

You can survive and even thrive in your new state. But, just to be safe, why not get down on your knees right now and start praying.

A Guide to Blue State Thought

ABORTION

You know that abortion is contrary to God's desires. But Blue Staters usually call abortion something wrong-headed and slick like "a woman's right to choose" or describe themselves as being "pro-choice." Pro choice? That's a good one. Red handbag or black handbag. THAT'S a choice. Steak or shrimp. THAT'S a choice. Playing God? That's not a choice. Here's some stuff you ought to know about the new state you'll call home. Just so you know . . . The average abortion rate for the United States is 21.3 abortions per 1,000 women of child-bearing age.

California California's abortion rate is 31.2, well above the national average. And it's no wonder. California doesn't have any of the major types of abortion restrictions, which include waiting periods, mandated parental involvement, or limitations on publicly funded abortions.

Connecticut Connecticut's rate is 21.1. The state requires a woman to receive state-directed counseling before she can have an abortion.

Delaware Delaware's rate is 31.3, amazingly high for the country's second-smallest state. Delaware's restrictions are: A) Parental

notification for minors, and B) Public funding only in cases of life endangerment, rape, or incest.

Hawaii Hawaii's rate is 22.2. It doesn't have any of the major types of abortion restrictions.

Illinois Illinois's rate is 23.2. The state's only restriction is that abortions are covered in insurance policies for public employees only in the case of life endangerment.

Maine Maine's rate is a respectably low 9.9. God must be smiling on Vacationland. The state's restrictions are: A) Mandatory state-directed counseling, and B) Public funding only in cases of life endangerment, rape, or incest.

Maryland Maryland's rate is 29.0. Its only restriction is parental notification for minors.

Massachusetts Massachusetts's rate is 21.4. The state's restrictions are: A) Parental consent for minors, and B) Partial-birth abortions are covered in insurance policies for public employees only in cases of life endangerment or serious health impairment.

Michigan Michigan's rate is 21.6. Its restrictions are: A) Parental consent for minors, B) Mandatory state-directed counseling followed by a twenty-four-hour waiting period, and C) Public funding only in cases of life endangerment, rape, or incest.

Minnesota Minnesota's rate is 13.5, quite low for a state filled with liberals. The state's restrictions are: A) Parental notification for minors, and B) Mandatory state-directed counseling followed by a twenty-four-hour waiting period.

New Hampshire New Hampshire's rate is 11.2. The state's only restriction is that public funding is available only in cases of life endangerment, rape, or incest.

New Jersey New Jersey's rate is 36.3. It does not have any of the major types of abortion restrictions.

New York New York's rate is 39.1, the highest in the country! What's the matter with the Empire State? Well, for starters, it doesn't have any of the major types of abortion restrictions. And second, Hillary Clinton is one of its senators.

Oregon Oregon's abortion rate is 23.5. It doesn't have any of the major types of abortion restrictions.

Pennsylvania Pennsylvania's rate is 14.3. The state's restrictions are: A) Parental consent for minors, B) Mandatory state-directed counseling followed by a twenty-four-hour waiting period, C) Public funding only in cases of life endangerment, rape, or incest, and D) Abortion is covered in insurance policies for public employees only in cases of life endangerment, rape, or incest.

Rhode Island Rhode Island's rate is 24.1.

Vermont Vermont's abortion rate is 12.7. It does not have any of the major types of abortion restrictions.

Washington Washington's rate is 20.2. It doesn't have any of the major types of abortion restrictions.

Wisconsin Wisconsin's rate is 9.6. The state's restrictions are: A) Parental consent for minors, B) Mandatory state-directed counseling followed by a twenty-four-hour waiting period, and C) Public

funding only in cases of life endangerment, rape, incest, or serious health problems.

CENSORSHIP

You're not for censorship, of course. But you know that some books just shouldn't be available to people of all ages. Bleeding hearts in your new state will try to convince you that any form of censorship is unacceptable. They'll point to the Bill of Rights.

Well, you just need to remind them that they're not the only people in the United States. Just because something doesn't bother them doesn't mean it should be available to everyone. Fortunately, there are some right-thinking folks in Blue States. What follows is a selection of books Blue States have banned or challenged over the years.

California

★ *The Grapes of Wrath,* by John Steinbeck, was challenged because it was considered inappropriate reading for eleventh graders. The book contains vulgar language.

★ *Brave New World,* by Aldous Huxley, was challenged for being anti-family and anti-Christian.

★ *The Color Purple,* by Alice Walker, was challenged because of its controversial ideas about race, religion, and sexuality.

★ At one time, all of Ernest Hemingway's books were banned by school libraries in Riverside.

Connecticut

★ J.K. Rowlings's popular *Harry Potter* series has been challenged in a number of states, including Connecticut. Pat Robertson has said the books promote "heathen, pagan practices."

★ *The Witch of Blackbird Pond,* by Elizabeth George Speare, was challenged for promoting witchcraft and violence.

Illinois

★ *Uncle Tom's Cabin,* by Harriet Beecher Stowe, was challenged in Illinois because it contains the word "nigger."

★ Mem Fox's *Guess What?* was challenged because it contains witches, punk rockers, and a reference that could be interpreted to mean God is dead. Hey, guess what? He isn't.

★ At least three towns in Illinois have challenged Mark Twain's *The Adventures of Huckleberry Finn* for its objectionable language and racial content. The fact that Mark Twain wrote books critical of Our Lord probably factored into those decisions.

Maine

★ *Bridge to Terabithia,* by Katherine Paterson, was challenged in Medway because it contains vulgar language. Apparently, the fine folks of Medway didn't object to the fact that the book also is filled with pagan material like witchcraft, magic, and evil spells.

★ Salem schools removed Dorothy Allison's *Bastard Out of Carolina* from its reading list for obscene language and content deemed inappropriate for fifteen-year-olds.

Maryland

★ C. S. Lewis's *The Lion, the Witch, and the Wardrobe* was challenged in Howard County for its graphic violence, mysticism, and gore.

★ William Faulkner's *As I Lay Dying* was challenged in Carroll County for its coarse language.

Massachusetts

★ *Candide,* by Voltaire, was challenged in Boston because it's French. Not really. It was challenged for obscenity.

★ Also banned in Boston were/are: Aldous Huxley's *Antic Hay*; Eugene O'Neill's *Strange Interlude*; *The Decameron* by Boccaccio; Walt Whitman's *Leaves of Grass*; and William Burroughs's *Naked Lunch*.

★ Ken Kesey's *One Flew Over the Cuckoo's Nest* was removed from school reading lists for its vulgar language.

Michigan

★ Shakespeare's *The Merchant of Venice* was banned in Midland because of its portrayal of the Jewish character, Shylock. Some considered it anti-Semitic.

★ *The Headless Cupid,* by Zilpha Keatley Snyder, was challenged because of scenes depicting the occult.

★ *The Catcher in the Rye,* by J. D. Salinger, was removed from the required reading list in Middleville schools, and it should have been. Kids shouldn't be reading a story that contains vulgar language and sexual content.

New Hampshire

★ Judith Guest's *Ordinary People* was banned temporarily from Merrimack High School for being "obscene" and "depressing." The school also challenged Ken Kesey's *One Flew Over the Cuckoo's Nest.*

New Jersey

★ Alexander Solzhenitsyn's *One Day in the Life of Ivan Denisovich* was challenged in Mahwah for its objectionable language.

New York

★ Stephen King's *Cujo* was removed from a school library in Bradford because it contains vulgar language and sexual situations.

★ *A Farewell to Arms,* by Ernest Hemingway, was challenged because of its sexual situations.

Oregon

★ *Bumps in the Night,* by Harry Allard, was challenged because it contains a scene in which a medium holds a séance.

★ Stephen King's *The Stand* was challenged for demonic characters, sexual language, and violence.

Pennsylvania

★ Arthur Miller's *The Crucible* was challenged by Cumberland Valley High School because it contains "sick words from the mouths of demon-possessed people."

★ Emporium banned Daniel Keyes's *Flowers for Algernon* because it contains sexually explicit love scenes.

★ Judy Blume's *Forever* was challenged in Scranton for its vulgar language and for its talk of masturbation, birth control, and disobedience to parents.

★ John Steinbeck's *Of Mice and Men* was banned in Oil City for its profanity.

★ *The Seduction of Peter S,* by Lawrence Sanders, was burned by Stroudsburg High School for being "blatantly graphic, pornographic, and wholly unacceptable for a high school library."

★ Schools in Harrisburg challenged the Bible . . . yes, God's Holy Word. And why? It was challenged because it "contains language and stories (!) that are inappropriate for children of any age, including tales of incest and murder. There are more than three hundred examples of obscenities (!) in the book." Forgive them Lord, for they know not what they do.

Rhode Island

★ The Providence post office tried to block copies of V. I. Lenin's *State and Revolution* because it is commie propaganda.

★ Anthony Burgess's *A Clockwork Orange* was challenged because of its vulgar language and extreme violence.

Vermont

★ *Carrie,* by Stephen King, was challenged because of its occult overtones and scenes depicting menstruation.

Washington

★ Joseph Heller's *Catch-22* was challenged in Snoqualmie for its vulgar language.

★ Norma Klein's *It's Okay if You Don't Love Me* was removed from the Vancouver School District because it has the temerity to portray young people as having

nothing on their minds but sex. That's probably because they grew up in Blue States and had parents that didn't take them regularly to a house of worship.

Wisconsin

★ *Halloween ABC,* by Eve Merriam, was challenged in Rice Lake for promoting Satanism.

★ Washington Park High School was barred from purchasing Kurt Vonnegut's *Slaughterhouse Five* . . . and with good reason. This book is filled with violent, irreverent, profane, and sexually explicit content. There's no reason young people should read such trash.

DEATH PENALTY

Some of your neighbors will try to convince you that it's wrong for a state to execute criminals. What nonsense! You know the truth. People who commit violent acts deserve to die violent deaths. That's the way the Lord meted out justice in the Bible.

At a dark time when it was overwhelmingly liberal, the Supreme Court pretty much struck down capital punishment, from roughly 1972 to 1976, saying—get this—that it constituted cruel and unusual punishment. What about the victims of violent crime? The Supreme Court must have thought what happened to them was just hunky dory.

And so do a lot of Blue States. A whopping eight of them don't have the death penalty. What follows is a guide to the forms of execution in your new Blue State, if it happens to believe in giving violent criminals a just punishment. In addition, you'll see the frequency with which this tool of justice has been used. Then you'll see the violent crime rates in your new state in 1975—the year before capital punishment was reinstated, 1976—the year it was reinstated, and 2000.

California Since 1976, California has executed eleven death row inmates. The state's death row population is 644, and the minimum age in California for death penalty eligibility is eighteen. The state offers a choice of lethal injection or the gas chamber. California's violent crime rate rose between 1975 and 1976. In 1975, the rate was 138,842. It was 144,041 in 1976. The state's violent crime rate hit a high of 345,624 in 1992. In 2000, California's rate was 210,531.

Connecticut Since 1976, Connecticut has executed only one death row inmate. The state's death row population is a measly nine, and the minimum age in Connecticut for death penalty eligibility is eighteen. The state's execution method is lethal injection. Connecticut's violent crime rate rose between 1975 and 1976. In 1975, the rate was 8,308. It was 8,516 in 1976. The state's violent crime rate hit a high of 18,201 in 1990. In 2000, Connecticut's rate was 11,058.

Delaware Since 1976, Delaware has executed thirteen death row inmates. The state's death row population is nineteen, and the minimum age for death penalty eligibility is sixteen. The state's execution method is lethal injection, but those sentenced before June 1986 can opt for hanging. Delaware's violent crime rate decreased between 1975 and 1976. In 1975, the rate was 2,270. It was 1,872 in 1976. In 2000, the state's violent crime rate was 5,363.

Hawaii Aloha, violent criminals! Hawaii does not have the death penalty.

Illinois Since 1976, Illinois has executed twelve death row inmates. The state's death row population is ten, and the minimum age for death penalty eligibility is eighteen. The state uses lethal injection. Illinois's violent crime rate dropped between 1975 and 1976. In 1975, the rate was 74,699. It was 70,266 in 1976. The state's violent crime rate hit a high of 119,955 in 1991. In 2000, Illinois's rate was 81,567.

BLUE STATE
☆ ☆ ☆

Maine Maine does not have the death penalty.

Maryland Since 1976, Maryland has executed four death row inmates. The state's death row population is nine, and the minimum age for death penalty eligibility is eighteen. The state's execution method is lethal injection, but those sentenced before March 1994 can opt for the gas chamber. Maryland's violent crime rate dropped between 1975 and 1976. In 1975, the rate was 29,087. It was 26,249 in 1976. The state's violent crime rate hit a high of 49,540 in 1993. In 2000, Maryland's rate was 41,663.

Massachusetts Massachusetts does not have the death penalty.

Michigan Michigan does not have the death penalty.

Minnesota Minnesota does not have the death penalty.

New Hampshire New Hampshire has the death penalty but has not executed anyone since 1976. And it doesn't have any death row inmates. Can you say, "Soft on crime?" There, I knew you could. The minimum age for death penalty eligibility in New Hampshire is seventeen. The state's execution methods are lethal injection or hanging, if lethal injection is not possible. New Hampshire's violent crime rate dropped between 1975 and 1976. In 1975, the rate was 816. It was 709 in 1976. In 2000, the state's violent crime rate hit a record high of 2,167.

New Jersey The so-called Garden State has the death penalty but hasn't executed anyone since 1976. The state's death row population is fifteen, and the minimum age for death penalty eligibility is eighteen. The state uses lethal injection. New Jersey's violent crime rate dropped between 1975 and 1976. In 1975, the rate was 30,215. It was 29,107 in 1976. The state's violent crime rate hit a high of 50,057 in 1990. In 2000, New Jersey's rate was 32,298.

18

BLUE STATE
⭐ ⭐ ⭐

New York The Empire State has the death penalty but hasn't executed anyone since 1976. And get this—the state's death row population is two! As if New York weren't the second-most Godless state of the union, after California. The minimum age for death penalty eligibility is eighteen, and the state uses lethal injection. New York's violent crime rate rose between 1975 and 1976. In 1975, the rate was 155,187. It was 156,988 in 1976. The state's violent crime rate hit a high of 212,548 in 1990. In 2000, New York's rate was 124,890.

Oregon Since 1976, Oregon has executed two death row inmates. The state's death row population is thirty-two, and the minimum age for death penalty eligibility is eighteen. The state's execution method is lethal injection. Oregon's violent crime rate rose between 1975 and 1976. In 1975, the rate was 10,034. It was 10,654 in 1976. The state's violent crime rate hit a high of 16,408 in 1995. In 2000, Oregon's rate was 12,000.

Pennsylvania Since 1975, Pennsylvania has executed three death row inmates. The state's death row population is a healthy 230, and the minimum age for death penalty eligibility is sixteen. The state uses lethal injection. Pennsylvania's violent crime rate dropped between 1975 and 1976. In 1975, the rate was 38,933. It was 34,985 in 1976. In 2000, Pennsylvania's rate was 51,584.

Rhode Island Rhode Island does not have the death penalty.

Vermont Vermont does not have the death penalty.

Washington Since 1976, Washington has executed four death row inmates. The state's death row population is eleven, and the minimum age for death penalty eligibility is eighteen. The state offers a choice of lethal injection or hanging. Washington's violent crime rate

rose between 1975 and 1976. In 1975, it was 13,851. It was 14,036 in 1976. In 2000, Washington's rate was 21,788.

Wisconsin Wisconsin does not have the death penalty.

EUTHANASIA

Oregon tries to pretty it up by calling it physician-assisted suicide, but you know it's murder. At present, this Blue State is the only one that actually allows this process to occur. Granted, it's for cases when a patient is terminally ill and in pain. But taking work out of God's hands just isn't the right thing to do in any case. Haven't these people heard of the power of prayer?

In 2003, forty-two people were killed when their doctors gave them a strong barbiturate potion. Other states have considered allowing "physician-assisted suicide," and yes, all of them are Blue States. They are Michigan, California, Washington, and Maine.

GAY MARRIAGE

Massachusetts did the unthinkable in 2004. It legalized gay marriages. Yes, that's right. The state decided it's okay for two men or two women to live as husband and wife . . . or would that be husband and husband or wife and wife?

The decision began as a court case: *Goodridge v. Department of Public Health.* The Massachusetts Supreme Judicial Court voted four to three that a ban on gay marriage was unconstitutional. Can you believe that? The ruling went into effect in May 2004.

But there's good news. Right-thinking people in Massachusetts— yes, there are a few—are working to pass a state constitutional

amendment banning gay marriage. And it's supported by Governor Mitt Romney. If you're lucky, it's already been passed. It could be voted on in 2006. And there's more good news. Other states don't have to recognize gay marriages. What follow are the laws for your new Blue State regarding "gay marriage."

California California voted to recognize same-sex domestic partnerships in 1999. That was bad enough. Then, in August 2005, the state's legislature voted to recognize gay marriages from other states. At least the vote was pretty close. It was twenty-one to fifteen in the senate and forty-one to thirty-five in the lower house. That wasn't the end of it, of course. In September 2005, the state's legislature voted to allow gay couples to marry. The measure was sent to Governor Arnold Schwarzenegger, who vetoed it. Really, how could someone who looks down on "girlie men" support gay marriage?

Connecticut Connecticut voted to recognize same-sex civil unions in April 2005. Shame on the state senate. It voted overwhelmingly in favor of something that's so obviously against the Lord's wishes. The vote was twenty-seven to nine. In the lower house, it was a more respectable eighty-five to sixty-three.

Delaware Delaware may be a small state, but it's a smart one. The state voted in 1996 to prohibit same-sex marriages and to invalidate same-sex unions from other states.

Hawaii Hawaii first brought up the gay-marriage issue in 1996. A vote to recognize same-sex partnerships passed in the senate. Fortunately, it did not pass the lower house, so the measure failed.

But the bleeding hearts wouldn't shut up. In 1997, the state passed a measure granting reciprocal benefits to same-sex partners.

Illinois Illinois voted in 1996 to prohibit same-sex marriages and to invalidate same-sex unions from other states.

BLUE STATE
★ ★ ★

Maine Maine voted to recognize same-sex domestic partnerships in April 2004. The vote was eighteen to fourteen in the senate and eighty-four to fifty-eight in the lower house. So, you might want to think twice before you consider your next trip to Vacationland.

Maryland Maryland's legislature voted in May 2005 to recognize same-sex domestic partnerships. The vote was thirty-one to sixteen in the senate and eighty-three to fifty in the lower house.

But the state's governor, Robert Ehrlich Jr., vetoed the bill. The legislature would need a two-thirds majority to override the veto. In February 2006, Maryland's House of Delegates refused to revive the bill. So it looks like you're safe for the foreseeable future.

Massachusetts Massachusetts. Same-sex marriage okay. Enough said.

Michigan Michigan voted in 1996 to prohibit same-sex marriages and to invalidate same-sex unions from other states.

Minnesota Minnesota voted in 1997 to prohibit same-sex marriages and to invalidate same-sex unions from other states.

New Hampshire Since 1987, New Hampshire's statute has prohibited same-sex unions.

New Jersey The Garden State voted in 2004 to recognize same-sex domestic partnerships.

That couldn't have had anything to do with the fact that the governor, James McGreevey, was gay. After all, he said being gay didn't have any effect on his ability as governor. You believe him, right? That same-sex domestic partnership bill he signed into law several months before he resigned? Oops, he did it again. Anyway, the vote in the senate was twenty-three to nine and forty-one to twenty-eight in the lower house.

22

New York New York's statute does not explicitly ban gay marriage, and several court cases are being considered that could determine the issue's future.

Oregon Oregon's senate voted in July 2005 to recognize same-sex civil unions. The vote was nineteen to ten.

As this book was going to press, a vote on the issue had not been taken in the state's lower house. And with any luck, it won't. House majority leader Wayne Scott, a Republican, was refusing to bring the measure up. But it's possible that enough bleeding hearts will have gotten together to convince Scott to bring the issue to a vote. Start praying it won't happen.

Pennsylvania The Keystone State revised its statute in 1996. It defines marriages as a male-female union and prohibits same-sex marriages regardless of how and where they're performed.

Rhode Island Rhode Island doesn't explicitly ban gay marriages. In 2004, Attorney General Patrick Lynch issued an advisory opinion that Rhode Island would recognize gay marriages performed in other states. Lynch's opinion bears no legal weight, but it does suggest that Rhode Island will smile and be friendly to married gay couples.

Vermont Vermont's legislature voted a resounding NO in 2000 to same-sex marriages. But the bleeding hearts had their day.

Later that year, the state voted to recognize same-sex civil unions. The vote was nineteen to eleven in the senate and seventy-nine to sixty-eight in the lower house.

Washington Washington revised its statute in 1998 to define marriage as a male-female union.

Wisconsin As this book was going to press, Wisconsin was considering a vote to ban gay marriages.

GUN CONTROL

You know the only gun control you need is the ability to aim at something or someone and to pull the trigger.

But Blue States believe gun laws are necessary. It's ironic, really. Your new state is soft on crime. It probably doesn't even have the death penalty. Yet it wants to try to restrict law-abiding citizens from access to the guns they need to protect themselves from wild-eyed and subsequently mollycoddled criminals.

As usual, these liberal Blue State types want it both ways. Consult the following list to see just how many restrictions on guns your new state has. And you can see some of the silly laws the state has on its books to "protect" its citizens.

California In California, you are required to register handguns and so-called assault weapons. And you need a permit to carry a concealed handgun. Get ready to shell out a few more bucks, thanks to bleeding hearts in your new state. Dealers sometimes charge a $1 fee, which goes into the state's firearm safety account.

Connecticut In Connecticut, you'd better hope the criminals loiter a bit before threatening your family or property. The state requires a two-week waiting period before you can purchase a handgun. In addition, you need a permit just to carry a handgun in your new state. And just to make your new neighbors even "safer," you can't carry a loaded rifle or shotgun in a vehicle or snowmobile.

Delaware It may be a tiny state, but at least Delaware has some sense. The state's only restriction is that you've got to have a permit to carry a concealed weapon. But if you're being chased by a criminal, run across the street. It's illegal to shoot across a road in Delaware. Sure, that's bound to stop some evil-doer, bent on your destruction, right?

Hawaii You might as well forget about guns in Hawaii. Maybe you can figure out how to make a lei into a deadly weapon. Here are Hawaii's restrictions: A) Permit to purchase rifles, shotguns, and handguns; B) Registration of rifles, shotguns, and handguns; C) Permit to carry a handgun. The state also makes it illegal to have anything to do with an electric gun.

Illinois You'd think Illinois, a state best known for mob figures like Al Capone, would give law-abiding citizens easy access to firearms. Well, you'd be wrong. Illinois has something called the firearms owner's identification (FOID) card. You have to get one of these before you can look at a gun on television. OK, OK. They don't really go that far, but just about.

You need a FOID card to purchase rifles, shotguns, or handguns and to license a rifle, shotgun, or handgun. You need a FOID card to carry rifles, shotguns, or handguns. And you can't get a permit to carry a concealed handgun under any circumstances. Oh, and don't forget that it's illegal in Illinois to carry or possess any firearm while you're hooded or masked.

Maine Maine's only restriction is that you need a permit to carry a handgun. And it's got a law that makes sense. You can't shoot wild animals or birds on Sunday. That's the Lord's day. You should be in church instead of hunting game.

Maryland In Maryland, the police will record your efforts to purchase, register, or license a handgun. And you need a permit to carry a handgun.

Massachusetts It figures that Massachusetts, the state that brought America such "tough" politicians as John Kerry and Mike Dukakis, would just be overflowing with gun restrictions.

Here they are: A) You need a firearm identification (FID) card to purchase rifles and shotguns, and you need a permit to purchase

handguns; B) You don't have to register a firearm, but the police will record all firearm transfers; C) Licenses are required for rifles, shotguns, and handguns; D) You need a FID card to carry a rifle or shotgun. You need a permit to carry a handgun.

And in Massachusetts, you've got to follow these provisions even if you're just trying to buy your kid a BB gun!

Michigan In Michigan, you need: A) A permit to purchase a handgun; B) To register your handgun; and C) A permit to carry a handgun. And if a criminal runs off with your gun, make sure you tell the police within five days, or YOU'LL be in trouble with the law.

Minnesota Minnesota doesn't even have a state constitutional provision regarding firearms. Can you believe that? Even most other Blue States will pay lip service to the Second Amendment in their constitutions. So it figures Minnesota's got gun restrictions.

You need a permit to purchase a handgun and to carry a concealed handgun. While you may not be fully protected from violent criminals, at least you can rest secure in the knowledge that wild animals get special protection from the state of Minnesota. You can't shoot them from a motor vehicle, airplane, or snowmobile. That helps you sleep soundly at night, now doesn't it?

New Hampshire In New Hampshire, you need a permit to carry a handgun.

New Jersey Oh, great. You're in New Jersey, a state with a reputation for crime, and you're going to have the (Jersey) devil's own time getting your hands on a firearm.

You need a firearms identification card to buy a shotgun or rifle. You need a permit to buy a handgun. You don't have to register a handgun, but the police will record any handgun transfers. You need to be licensed to own a rifle, shotgun, or handgun. You need an ID card to carry a rifle or shotgun, and you need a permit to carry a handgun.

Did you get all of that? Sure wouldn't want you to get in trouble with the law for trying to do something legal like buy a gun. And here's a bonus boneheaded law. It's unlawful to riot with a firearm in New Jersey. So, if you decide to incite a riot, arm yourself with a bagel.

New York Of course New York, liberal capital of the entire world, has tons of gun laws. The state's laws are: A) Permit to purchase handguns. In New York City, you need a permit to purchase rifles and shotguns as well; B) Registration of handguns. You guessed it. In New York City, you also need a permit to carry rifles and shotguns.

Oregon Oregon is another one of those Blue States that has some degree of sense. Its only restriction is that you need a permit to carry a concealed handgun.

Pennsylvania Pennsylvania also believes in allowing its law-abiding citizens easy access to firearms. The state's only restriction is that you need a permit to carry a handgun.

Rhode Island Rhode Island wants to have it both ways. Oh no, you don't need a permit to purchase a rifle or shotgun in our state. But you do have to fill out an application and endure a short waiting period. And we wouldn't dream of making you get a permit to buy a handgun in beautiful Rhode Island. But you've got to take a firearm safety course in addition to filling out an application and enduring a waiting period. In addition, you need a permit to carry a handgun.

Vermont It's too bad Vermont's neighbor New Hampshire lays claim to the motto, "Live free or die" because Vermont is serious about not restricting guns. The state doesn't have any of the most common restrictions on firearms.

Washington In Washington, you don't need a permit to purchase a handgun. But the police will record purchases from dealers. And

you need a permit to carry a concealed handgun. In addition, the governor of Washington has the right to forbid you from carrying a gun outside of your home or business during a state of emergency.

Now, the Father of Our Country believed in a strong, centralized government. But he sure didn't believe in fascism. He must be spinning around in his grave.

Wisconsin Wisconsin only has one restriction on guns, but it's a doozy. The state requires a two-day waiting period before you can purchase a handgun. Wisconsin tries to amend for that by specifically exempting firearms for personal use from personal property taxes.

How to (Almost) Feel at Home in a Blue State

A Red Stater Survival Guide

SOUTHERN BAPTIST CHURCHES

Yes, Blue States allow Southern Baptist churches to plant roots in their Godless soil. In time, perhaps the Word will be loud enough for native Blue Staters to hear. Good Red Staters can only pray for that day to come . . . and soon. What follows is the contact information for the Southern Baptist Convention office in your new state. The office can direct you to churches in your area that love and fear God.

California
★ California Southern Baptist Convention: ☎ 559-229-9533; *www.csbc.com*

Connecticut, Maine, Massachusetts, New Hampshire, Rhode Island, Vermont
★ Baptist Convention of New England: ☎ 508-393-6013; *www.bcne.net*

BLUE STATE
★ ★ ★

Delaware, Maryland
★ Baptist Convention of Maryland-Delaware: ✆410-290-5290; ✍www.yourbcmd.org

Hawaii
★ Hawaii Pacific Baptist Convention: ✆808-946-9581; ✍*www.hpbaptist.net*

Illinois
★ Illinois Baptist State Association: ✆217-786-2600; ✍*www.ibsa.org*

Michigan
★ Baptist State Convention of Michigan: ✆810-714-1907; ✍*www.bscm.org*

Minnesota, Wisconsin
★ Minnesota-Wisconsin Baptist Convention: ✆507-282-3636; ✍*www.mwbc.org*

New Jersey, Pennsylvania
★ Baptist Convention of Pennsylvania-South Jersey: ✆717-652-5856; ✍*www.brnonline.org*

New York
★ Baptist Convention of New York: ✆315-433-1001; ✍*www.bcnysbc.org*

Oregon, Washington
★ Northwest Baptist Convention: ✆360-882-2100; ✍*www.nwbaptist.org*

GUN RANGES

You may have a lot of trouble buying or owning a gun in your state, so what will you do when you finally get to protect your family and property? Well, don't try hunting in most Blue States. Those folks consider your behavior immoral, as though most of them don't shove

filet mignon into the pie-holes under their blue noses. Apparently, it's okay if someone else kills animals. Just don't do it yourself.

But you *can* visit a gun range, and most likely there's one somewhere in your new state. The Web site *www.packing.org* lists ranges across the country. If you decide to go to one, invite one of your Blue State neighbors to go with you. Maybe he'll find he actually likes the feel of cold steel and hot lead.

California California has more than sixty gun ranges. A selection of them follows:

★ **Huntington Beach** Firing-Line Indoor Shooting Range, 17921 Jamestown Lane: ✆714-379-9115; ✍*www.firearms-training.info*
★ **Sacramento** Sacramento Valley Shooting Center, 15501 Meiss Road, Sloughouse: ✆916-354-9668; ✍*www.sacvalley.org*
★ **San Diego** American Shooting Center, 5590 Ruffin Road: ✆858-279-7233; ✍*www.gotammo.com*
★ **South San Francisco** Jackson Arms Indoor Shooting Range, 710 Dubuque Avenue: ✆650-588-4209; ✍*www.jacksonarms.com*
★ **Yuba City** Shooters Paradise, 1407A Colusa Avenue: ✆530-673-4100

Connecticut Connecticut has about fifteen ranges. A selection of them follows.

★ **Bridgeport** Bridgeport Shooting Range, 1918 Stratford Avenue: ✆203-330-9772; ✍*www.bridgeportshootingrange.com*
★ **Guilford** Gunsite Indoor Underground Shooting Range, 2458 Boston Post Road: ✆203-453-1570; ✍*www.gunsitect.com*
★ **Hartford** Hartford Gun Club, 157 South Main Street, East Granby: ✆860-658-1614; ✍*www.hartfordgunclub.com*
★ **Norwalk** Forest & Field Outdoor Specialties Inc., 4 New Canaan Avenue: ✆203-847-4008; ✍*www.forestandfield.com*
★ **Simsbury** Metacon Gun Club, 106 Nod Road: ✆860-658-7101; ✍*www .metacongunclub.com*

BLUE STATE
★ ★ ★

Delaware
★ **Dover** Shooters Choice, 5105 N. DuPont Highway: ✆302-736-5166
★ **Georgetown** J.D. Defense Equipment and Training, 18140 County Seat Highway: ✆302-856-6910
★ **New Castle** Ommelanden Range, 1205 River Road: ✆302-323-5333

Hawaii
★ **Honolulu** Koko Head Shooting Complex, 2015 Kapiolani Boulevard: ✆808-395-2992; ✐*www.khsc.info*

Illinois
★ **Belleville** Belleville Indoor Shooting Range and Gun Shop, 209 N. Illinois Street: ✆618-234-9690
★ **Chillicothe** Chillicothe Sportsmen's Club, Yankee Lane at Route 29: ✆309-274-9988
★ **Dundee** G.A.T. Guns Inc., 14N915 Route 25: ✆847-428-4867; ✐*www.gatguns.com*
★ **Lockport** Rink's Gun and Sport Inc., 14363 S. Archer: ✆815-883-1371
★ **Plainfield** Mega Sports, 23248 W. Lincoln Highway: ✆815-439-4867; ✐*www.megasportsfirearms.com*
★ **Rockford** Pine Tree Pistol Club, 5454 11th Street: ✆815-874-7399

Maine
★ **Hampden** Hampden Rifle and Pistol Club, 286 Meadow Road: ✆207-862-3064
★ **Portland** Falmouth Rod and Gun Club Inc., 89 Auburn Street: ✆207-797-0048; *www.frandg.org*

Maryland
★ **Germantown** Rockville Chapter IWLA Inc., 18301 Waring Station Road: ✆301-972-1645; ✐*www.iwla-rockville.com*
★ **Marriottsville** Associated Gun Clubs of Baltimore, 11518 Marriottsville Road: ✆410-461-8532; ✐*www.associatedgunclubs.org*

★ **Rockville** Gilbert Indoor Range, 14690 Rothgeb Drive: ✆ 301-607-0416; ✉ *www.gilbertindoorrange.com*

★ **Severn** On Target, 2618 Annapolis Road: ✆ 410-551-7777

Massachusetts

★ **Rehoboth** Seekonk Gun Club, 61 Reed Street: ✆ 508-336-7282

Michigan

Michigan has more than thirty ranges. A selection of them follows.

★ **Bay City** Duncan's Outdoor Shop, 501 Salzburg Avenue: ✆ 989-894-6691; ✉ *www.duncansoutdoor.com*

★ **Jeddo** Four Square Sportsman's Association, 6779 Cline Road: ✆ 810-327-6859; ✉ *www.foursquaresportsman.com*

★ **Lapeer** Bald Mountain Gun Range, 2500 Kern Road: ✆ 248-814-9193; ✉ *www.wingsandclays.com/Bald_Mountain/bald_mountain.htm*

★ **Madison Heights** Double Action, 32411 Dequindre Avenue: ✆ 248-588-4488; ✉ *www.doubleactionshooting.com*

★ **Utica** Detroit Sportsmen's Congress, 49800 Dequindre Road: ✆ 586-739-3500; ✉ *www.d-s-c.org*

Minnesota

Minnesota has about fifteen ranges. A selection of them follows.

★ **Burnsville** Burnsville Pistol Range, 14300 Ewing Avenue: ✆ 952-890-6228; ✉ *www.bvpistol.com*

★ **Circle Pines** Armored Fire Gun Shop and Range, 3621 88th Avenue NE: ✆ 763-792-4867

★ **Glencoe** Major Avenue Hunt Club, 11721 Major Avenue: ✆ 320-864-6025; ✉ *www.bvpistol.com*

★ **Prior Lake** Dakotah Sport and Fitness Firing Range, 2100 Trail of Dreams NW: ✆ 952-496-6886

★ **Robbinsdale** Bill's Gun Shop and Range, 4080 W. Broadway: ✆ 763-533-9594; ✉ *www.billsgs.com*

BLUE STATE
★ ★ ★

New Hampshire
★ **Manchester** Manchester Firing Line Range, 50 Gay Street: ☎603-628-7663; ✉*www.gunsnh.com*

New Jersey
New Jersey has more than fifteen ranges. A selection of them follows.

★ **Belle Mead** Hillsborough Outdoor Sports Center, 170 Township Line Road: ☎908-359-0837
★ **Glassboro** Bob's Little Sport Shop, 316 North Delsea Drive: ☎856-881-7575; ✉*www.bobslittlesportshop.com*
★ **Jackson** Central Jersey Rifle and Pistol Club, 168 Stump Tavern Road: ☎800-5GUNFUN; ✉*www.cjrpc.org*
★ **Phillipsburg** Phillipsburg Pistol Club, 25 Howard Street: ☎908-454-1232; ✉*www.phillipsburgpistolclub.com*
★ **Thorofare** Eagle Eye Indoor Range, 700 Crown Point Road: ☎856-251-9099

New York
New York has about thirty ranges. A selection of them follows.

★ **Calverton** Calverton Shooting Range, 395 Nugent Drive: ☎631-727-9881
★ **Staten Island** Colonial Rifle and Pistol Club, 4484 Arthur Kill Road: ☎718-948-9531; ✉*www.colonialrifleandpistolclub.com*
★ **Utica** Deerfield Firearms Training Facility, 6560 Trenton Road North: ☎315-797-2184; ✉*www.dftfrange.net*
★ **Yonkers** Coyne Park Rifle and Pistol Range, 771 McLean Avenue: ☎914-377-6488; ✉*www.coyneparkrange.net*

Oregon
★ **Clackamas** Clackamas Public Safety Training Center, 12700 SE 82nd Avenue: ☎503-353-4644; ✉*www.co.clackamas.or.us/sheriff/pstc/main.htm*

★ **Eugene** The Baron's Den, 86321 College View Road: ☎ 541-744-6229; *✎ www.thebaronsden.com*

★ **Grants Pass** Josephine County Sportsman Park, 7407 Highland Avenue: ☎ 541-476-2040; *✎ www.jcsa-shootingsports.org*

★ **Portland** Johnson Creek Gun Club, 7200 SE Lamphier: ☎ 503-771-5139

★ **Portland** The Place to Shoot, 904 N. Hayden Meadows Drive: ☎ 503-283-1995

★ **Salem** Four Corners Rod and Gun Club, 7695 Babcock Street SE: ☎ 503-581-5214; *✎ www.fourcornersrodandgun.com*

★ **Sherwood** Tri-County Gun Club, 13050 SW Tonquin Road: ☎ 503-625-7318; *✎ www.tcgc.org*

Pennsylvania

Pennsylvania has about forty ranges. A selection of them follows.

★ **Latrobe** Army and Navy Store, 800 Ligonier Street: ☎ 724-537-3861

★ **Philadelphia** Colosimo's Pistol Range, 542 N. Percy Street: ☎ 215-236-9292

★ **Pittsburgh** Bullseye Shooting Ranges Inc., 4499 Campbell's Run Road: ☎ 412-494-2803; *✎ www.bullseyeranges.com*

★ **Southampton** Classic Pistol Indoor Range, 1310 Industrial Boulevard: ☎ 215-953-7264; *✎ www.classicpistol.com*

★ **West Mifflin** Anthony Arms and Accessories: Shooting Center Ltd., 2980 Lebanon Church Road: ☎ 412-469-9992; *✎ www.anthonyarms.com/range.html*

Rhode Island

★ **Middletown** Newport Rifle Club, 360 Wyatt Road: ☎ 401-847-5678; *✎ www.newportrifleclub.org*

Vermont

★ **Morrisville** Lamoille Valley Fish and Game Club, 14 Stafford Avenue: ☎ 802-888-3550; *✎ www.gmps.ws/gmpslvfg.htm*

BLUE STATE
⭐ ⭐ ⭐

Washington

Washington has more than twenty ranges. A selection of them follows.

- ★ **Arlington** Arlington Recreational Shooting and Training Center, 8620 172nd Street NE: ☎ 360-474-0880
- ★ **Bellevue** Bellevue Indoor Range, 13570 Bel-Red Road: ☎ 425-649-5995; *www.wadesguns.com*
- ★ **Littlerock** Capitol City Rifle and Pistol Club, 14318 Littlerock Road: ☎ 360-956-0608; *www.ccrpclub.org*
- ★ **Spokane** Sharp Shooting Indoor Range, 1200 N. Freya: ☎ 509-535-4444; *www.sharpshooting.net*
- ★ **Tacoma** Bullseye Shooter Supply, 414 Puyallup Avenue: ☎ 253-572-6417; *www.bullseyeshooter.com*

Wisconsin

- ★ **Deerfield** Deerfield Pistol and Archery Range, 43 N. Main Street: ☎ 608-764-2040; *www.deerfieldpistol.com*
- ★ **Janesville** Rock County Rifle and Pistol Club, 1029 S. Jackson Street: ☎ 608-755-1640; *www.rcrpc.net*
- ★ **Middleton** Middleton Sportsmen's Club, 7910 Airport Road: ☎ 608-836-1118
- ★ **Milwaukee** Badger Outdoors Inc., 2339 South 43rd Street: ☎ 414-383-0885
- ★ **West Allis** The Shooters Shop, 2465 S. 84th Street: ☎ 414-327-7044; *www.shootersshop.com*
- ★ **Whitewater** Ed's Sports Shop, 7631 Lima Center Road: ☎ 262-473-4678

RUSH LIMBAUGH ON THE RADIO

You won't be able to escape the anti-George W. Bush rhetoric in your new state. You'll hear folks badmouth the commander in chief at work, at restaurants, maybe even at church! Apparently, no place is too sacred to make it free of anti-American speech.

BLUE STATE
★ ★ ★

Thank you, Lord, for inventing the radio. On it, you can tune in the voice of reason each day: Mr. Rush Limbaugh, still going strong, despite liberal smear campaigns. The liberal media is trying to make Limbaugh seem like a common crack head.

You know the truth. He became addicted to prescription pain-killers and has admitted and atoned for his mistakes. Limbaugh is probably available on a radio station near you, even if you're in the most liberal of Blue States.

California

California carries Rush on more than thirty stations. A selection of them follows.

★ **Bakersfield** KZTK-AM 970, 9 A.M. to noon
★ **Los Angeles** KFI-AM 640, 9 A.M. to noon
★ **San Diego** KOGO-AM 600, 9 A.M. to noon
★ **San Francisco** KSFO-AM 560, 9 A.M. to noon
★ **Victorville** KIXW-AM 960, 9 A.M. to noon

Connecticut

★ **Groton** WSUB-AM 980, noon to 3 P.M.
★ **Hartford** WTIC-AM 1080, noon to 3 P.M.
★ **New Haven** WELI-AM 960, noon to 3 P.M.

Delaware

★ **Dover** WDOV-AM 1410, noon to 3 P.M.
★ **Rehoboth** WGMD-FM 92.7, noon to 3 P.M.
★ **Wilmington** WDEL-AM 1150, noon to 3 P.M.

Hawaii

★ **Hilo** KPUA-AM 670, 10 A.M. to 1 P.M.
★ **Honolulu** KHVH-AM 830, 10 A.M. to 1 P.M.
★ **Wailuku** KAOI-AM 1110, 9 A.M. to noon

BLUE STATE
☆ ☆ ☆

Illinois

Illinois carries Rush on nearly twenty stations. A selection of them follows.

★ **Champaign** WDWS-AM 1400, 11 A.M. to 2 P.M.
★ **Chicago** WLS-AM 890, 11 A.M. to 2 P.M.
★ **Galesburg** WGIL-AM 1400, noon to 3 P.M.
★ **Peoria** WMBD-AM 1470, 11 A.M. to 2 P.M.
★ **Springfield** WTAX-AM 1240, noon to 3 P.M.

Maine

★ **Boothbay Harbor** WCME-FM 96.7, noon to 3 P.M.
★ **Howland-Bangor** WVOM-FM 103.9, noon to 3 P.M.
★ **Lewiston** WTME-AM 1240, noon to 3 P.M.
★ **Monticello** WREM-AM 710, noon to 3 P.M.
★ **Portland** WGAN-AM 560, noon to 3 P.M.
★ **Presque Isle** WEGP-AM 1390, noon to 3 P.M.
★ **Waterville** WHQO-FM 107.9, noon to 3 P.M.

Maryland

★ **Baltimore** WBAL-AM 1090, noon to 3 P.M.
★ **Frederick** WFMD-AM 930, noon to 3 P.M.
★ **Frostburg** WFRB-AM 560, noon to 3 P.M.
★ **Lexington Park** WMDM-AM 1690, noon to 3 P.M.
★ **Salisbury** WICO-AM 1320, noon to 3 P.M.

Massachusetts

★ **Boston** WRKO-AM 680, noon to 3 P.M.
★ **Pittsfield** WBEC-AM 1430, noon to 3 P.M.
★ **Springfield** WHYN-AM 560, noon to 3 P.M.
★ **West Yarmouth** WXTK-FM 94.9, noon to 3 P.M.
★ **Worcester** WTAG-AM 580, noon to 3 P.M.

BLUE STATE
☆ ☆ ☆

Michigan

Michigan carries Rush on about thirty stations. A selection of them follows.

★ **Battle Creek** WBCK-AM 930, noon to 3 P.M.
★ **Detroit** WJR-AM 760, noon to 3 P.M.
★ **Grand Rapids** WMUS-AM 1090 and WOOD-AM 1300, noon to 3 P.M.
★ **Kalamazoo** WKMI-AM 1360, noon to 3 P.M.
★ **Lansing** WJIM-AM 1240, noon to 3 P.M.

Minnesota

Minnesota carries Rush on about twenty stations. A selection of them follows.

★ **Duluth** WEBC-AM 560, 11 A.M. to 2 P.M.
★ **Minneapolis** KSTP-AM 1500, noon to 3 P.M.
★ **St. Cloud** KNSI-AM 1450, 11 A.M. to 2 P.M.
★ **Wilmar** KDJS-AM 1540, 11 A.M. to 2 P.M.
★ **Worthington** KWOA-AM 730, 1 P.M. to 4 P.M.

New Hampshire

★ **Exeter** WGIP-AM 1540, noon to 3 P.M.
★ **Hanover** WTSL-AM 1400, noon to 3 P.M.
★ **Keene** WKBK-AM 1220, noon to 3 P.M.
★ **Laconia** WEMJ-AM 1490, noon to 3 P.M.
★ **Lebanon** WTSL-AM 1400, noon to 3 P.M.
★ **Manchester** WGIR-AM 610, noon to 3 P.M.
★ **Rochester** WGIN-AM 930, noon to 3 P.M.

New Jersey

What is the matter with New Jersey? In the entire state, you can only hear the voice of reason on ONE radio station!

★ **Pleasantville** WOND-AM 1400, noon to 3 P.M.

39

BLUE STATE
★ ★ ★

New York

New York carries Rush on about twenty stations. A selection of them follows.

★ **Albany-Schenectady** WGY-AM 810, noon to 3 P.M.
★ **Buffalo** WBEN-AM 930, noon to 3 P.M.
★ **New York** WABC-AM 770, noon to 3 P.M.
★ **Rochester** WHAM-AM 1180, 2 P.M. to 5 P.M.
★ **Syracuse** WSYR-AM 570, 1 P.M. to 4 P.M.

Oregon

Oregon carries Rush on about twenty stations. A selection of them follows.

★ **Eugene** KPNW-AM 1120, 9 A.M. to noon
★ **Klamath Falls** KAGO-AM 1150, 9 A.M. to noon
★ **Medford** KCMX-AM 580 and KMED-AM 1440, 9 A.M. to noon
★ **Portland** KEX-AM 620 and KEX-AM 1190, 9 A.M. to noon
★ **Salem** KYKN-AM 1430, 9 A.M. to noon

Pennsylvania

Pennsylvania carries Rush on more than twenty stations. A selection of them follows.

★ **Allentown** WAEB-AM 790, noon to 3 P.M.
★ **Harrisburg** WHP-AM 580, noon to 3 P.M.
★ **Philadelphia** WPHT-AM 1210, noon to 3 P.M.
★ **Pittsburgh** WPGB-FM 104.7, noon to 3 P.M.
★ **Scranton** WGBI-AM 910, noon to 3 P.M.

Rhode Island

★ **Providence** WPRO-AM 630, 9 A.M. to noon

BLUE STATE
☆ ☆ ☆

Vermont

★ **Barre** WSNO-AM 1450, noon to 3 P.M.
★ **Burlington** WKDR-AM 960, noon to 3 P.M.
★ **Plattsburgh-Burlington** WEAV-AM 960, noon to 3 P.M.
★ **Rutland** WSYB-AM 1380, noon to 3 P.M.

Washington

Washington carries Rush on about fifteen stations. A selection of them follows.

★ **Bellingham** KGMI-AM 790, 9 A.M. to noon
★ **Centralia** KELA-AM 1470, 9 A.M. to noon
★ **Port Angeles** KONP-AM 1450, 9 A.M. to noon
★ **Seattle** KTTH-AM 1770, 9 A.M. to noon
★ **Yakima** KIT-AM 1280, 9 A.M. to noon

Wisconsin

Wisconsin carries Rush on about fifteen stations. A selection of them follows.

★ **Eau Claire-Menomonie** WMEQ-AM 880, 11 A.M. to 2 P.M.
★ **Green Bay** WGEE-AM 1360, 11 A.M. to 2 P.M.
★ **Madison** WIBA-AM 1310, 11 A.M. to 2 P.M.
★ **Milwaukee** WISN-AM 1130, noon to 3 P.M.
★ **Wausau** WSAU-AM 550, 1 P.M. to 4 P.M.

GOLDEN CORRAL

Blue States are rife with five-star restaurants catering to snooty folks who believe snails and squids are a delicacy. No wonder they can eat that stuff . . . they're probably tanked up on "fine" wines and single-malt Scotch.

41

BLUE STATE
★ ★ ★

Apparently, Blue States have forgotten that families like to eat too. But don't despair. Your favorite restaurant, the Golden Corral, is probably close by in your new community. These buffet-style, family-friendly restaurants give you a choice of all-American grub in an environment free from alcohol.

California
California has two Golden Corrals. Agitate for more!

★ **El Centro** 2018 North Imperial Avenue, ☎ 760-336-0009
★ **Tracy** 2850 W. Grantline Road, ☎ 209-834-1420

Connecticut
Start a campaign! Connecticut doesn't have a Golden Corral! And it calls itself a part of the United States?

Delaware
Delaware has two Golden Corrals.

★ **Dover** 391 N. DuPont Highway, ☎ 302-741-2120
★ **Seaford** US 13 North, ☎ 302-629-5768

Hawaii
Hawaii doesn't have a Golden Corral! And it's considered a paradise? Ha!

Illinois
Illinois has the right idea. It has six Golden Corrals.

★ **Alton** 2723 Corner Court, ☎ 618-465-1802
★ **Bolingbrook** 381 Brookview Lane, ☎ 630-771-1777
★ **Carbondale** 2255 Reed Station Parkway, ☎ 618-529-1472
★ **Freeport** 1404 W. Galena Avenue, ☎ 815-235-7036

- ★ **Joliet** 2100 W. Jefferson Street, ☎815-725-8989
- ★ **Washington** 1896 Washington Road, ☎309-444-2349

Maine

Maine doesn't have a Golden Corral! Maybe the state has forgotten that not everyone enjoys weird food like lobster bisque. Vacationland, my foot.

Maryland

Maryland is a veritable haven for Golden Corrals. It has eleven of them!

- ★ **Aberdeen** 991 Beards Hill Road, ☎410-272-0668
- ★ **Baltimore** 7908 Rossville Boulevard, ☎410-665-7405; 7911 Eastern Avenue, ☎410-282-1777
- ★ **Easton** 8451 Ocean Gateway, ☎410-822-9030
- ★ **Elkton** 330 E. Pulaski Highway, ☎410-398-1450
- ★ **Frederick** 5621 Spectrum Drive, ☎301-662-5922
- ★ **Glen Burnie** 6701 Chesapeake Center Drive, ☎410-590-0270
- ★ **Hanover** 7407 Arundel Mills Boulevard, ☎410-799-0959
- ★ **Largo** 1001 Shoppers Way, ☎301-324-6807
- ★ **Salisbury** 301 E. Naylor Mill Road, ☎410-219-5100
- ★ **Waldorf** 2800 Crain Highway, ☎301-893-8790

Massachusetts

Well, of *course* Massachusetts is far too cosmopolitan to have a Golden Corral. Sniff. Isn't that right, Muffy?

Michigan

Michigan only has one Golden Corral. Something must be done.

- ★ **Westland** 37101 Warren Road, ☎734-641-9163

BLUE STATE
★ ★ ★

Minnesota
Minnesota also has only one Golden Corral? What's the matter with the Midwest?

★ **Rochester** 2775 43rd Street NW, ☎ 507-282-2180

New Hampshire
New Hampshire needs to get a clue. It doesn't have a single Golden Corral.

New Jersey
Et tu, New Jersey? No Golden Corral?!?

New York
New York has three Golden Corrals. None in New York City.

★ **Colonie** 1901 Central Avenue, ☎ 518-862-1520
★ **Fulton** 706 S. 4th Street, ☎ 315-593-7737
★ **Saratoga Springs** 15 Old Gick Road, ☎ 518-580-0682

Oregon
Oregon doesn't have a Golden Corral.

Pennsylvania
All right, Pennsylvania! You have seven Golden Corrals. God bless you.

★ **Erie** 7500 Peach Street, ☎ 814-864-3488
★ **Lebanon** 1147 Quentin Road, ☎ 717-277-7013
★ **Monroeville** 3591 William Penn Parkway, ☎ 412-856-8515
★ **Pittsburgh** 900 Park Manor Street, ☎ 412-788-1776
★ **Selinsgrove** Route 4 Box 77C, ☎ 570-743-3666
★ **Uniontown** 129 Matthew Drive, ☎ 724-439-5750
★ **Waynesboro** 1543 E. Main Street, ☎ 717-762-4600

44

BLUE STATE
★ ★ ★

Rhode Island
Rhode Island—and all of New England apparently—is too small to host a single Golden Corral.

Vermont
Nope. Sorry.

Washington
Washington has three Golden Corrals. The Father of Our Country would be proud.

★ **Marysville** 1065 State Street, ☎ 360-659-4035
★ **Moses Lake** 930 N. Stratford Road, ☎ 509-765-0565
★ **Spokane** 7117 N. Division Street, ☎ 509-468-1895

Wisconsin
Wisconsin also has three Golden Corrals.

★ **Appleton** 1169 N. Westhill Boulevard, ☎ 920-739-6093
★ **Kenosha** 6208 75th Street, ☎ 262-942-9396
★ **Waukesha** 1673 Arcadian Avenue, ☎ 262-896-1000

FAMILY CHRISTIAN STORES

Blue Staters laugh at traditional family values, believing it's rude to define families as Mom, Dad, and kids. Let's be inclusive, Blue Staters say. And after you've been in your new state for a while, you may find yourself listening to their rhetoric.

That's why it's so crucial for you to continue to visit a good house of worship, and also why you need to know the location of the nearest Family Christian Stores. This company has over 320 locations in twenty-three states, including many Blue States. The next time your

coworkers have your head spinning about what IS and what most definitely IS NOT acceptable to God, hop in the car, and head to Family Christian. They'll have the cure for what ails you.

California
California has more than thirty Family Christian locations. A selection of them follows.

★ **Fresno** Wine Press Shopping Center, 3072 W. Shaw Avenue, ✆559-277-3217
★ **Palm Springs** Palm Springs Mall, 129 S. Farrell Drive, ✆760-318-2514
★ **San Diego** 3146 Sports Arena Boulevard, Suite 4, ✆619-224-2863
★ **Simi Valley** 2986 Cochran Street, ✆805-579-9590
★ **Whittier** 8401 Pioneer Boulevard, ✆562-463-9195

Connecticut
Connecticut has neither Golden Corrals nor Family Christian Stores. This state has its priorities all screwed up.

Delaware
Delaware has two Family Christian Stores locations.

★ **Newark** 600 Peoples Plaza, ✆302-834-1013
★ **Newark** 1105 Churchmans Road, Suite 1107, ✆302-368-7002

Hawaii
Hawaii is the home of sun, surf, and sin. It doesn't have a Family Christian location.

Illinois
Illinois has about fifteen Family Christian locations. A selection follows.

★ **Alton** Alton Square Shopping Center, 118 Alton Square, ✆618-462-5673
★ **Joliet** 3105 W. Jefferson Street, ✆815-729-2400

BLUE STATE
⭐ ⭐ ⭐

- ★ **Naperville** Fox River Commons, 936 S. State Route 59, ☎630-718-9201
- ★ **Springfield** 3435 Freedom Drive, ☎217-793-2085
- ★ **Wheaton** 79 Danada Square East, ☎630-682-8868

Maine
Sorry, Maine is too busy vacationing to care about God. There are no Family Christian Stores there.

Maryland
Maryland has three Family Christian Stores locations.

- ★ **Gaithersburg** Montgomery Village Plaza, 18302 Contour Road, Unit 3, ☎301-990-6611
- ★ **Laurel** 3386 Fort Meade Road, ☎301-604-2002
- ★ **Waldorf** St. Charles Towne Center, 1110 Mall Circle, Suite 1025, ☎301-705-8199

Massachusetts
You didn't really think Massachusetts would deign to have a place called Family Christian Stores, did you?

Michigan
Michigan has about twenty Family Christian Stores locations. A selection of them follows.

- ★ **Battle Creek** Minges Creek Mall, 5700 Beckley Road, Suite B2, ☎269-979-8020
- ★ **Flint** Genessee Crossing Shop Center, G3577 Miller Road, Suite 5, ☎810-732-6700
- ★ **Grand Rapids** Cornerstone University, 915 E. Beltline Avenue NE, ☎616-957-0002; Southridge Center, 2964 28th Street SE, ☎616-949-8892
- ★ **Kalamazoo** Westnedge Corners Shop Center, 4413 S. Westnedge Avenue, ☎269-381-2230
- ★ **Lansing** Jolly Cedar Plaza, 5132 S. Cedar Street, ☎517-887-0448

BLUE STATE
★ ★ ★

Minnesota
Dear Lord, Minnesota has been naughty. It does not have a single Family Christian Stores location, though its neighboring states have them.

New Hampshire
Apparently, all of New England is Godless. New Hampshire lacks a Family Christian Stores.

New Jersey
New Jersey has two Family Christian Stores locations.

★ **Fairfield** Crown Plaza Shopping Center, 461 U.S. Route 46, ✆973-575-5855
★ **Mountain Lakes** 50 Route 46, ✆973-334-1234

New York
In all of New York, there's only *one* Family Christian Stores? For shame. If there's any state of the union that needs the presence of God, it's New York.

★ **Riverdale** 218 W. 234th Avenue, ✆718-543-1719

Oregon
And only one in Oregon? Tsk. Tsk.

★ **Bend** 815 SE 3rd Street, ✆541-389-9796

Pennsylvania
Pennsylvania has seven Family Christian Stores locations.

★ **Altoona** 120 Byron Avenue, ✆814-943-0531
★ **Bridgeville** Chartiers Valley Shopping Center, 1025 Washington Pike, ✆412-221-3222

BLUE STATE
★ ★ ★

- ★ **Cranberry Township** Cranberry Commons Shopping Center, 1717 Route 228, Suite H, ☎724-779-7082
- ★ **Monroeville** Holiday Centre, 3747 William Penn Highway, Space R, ☎412-372-1610
- ★ **Natrona Heights** 1848 Union Avenue, ☎724-226-3322
- ★ **Pittsburgh** Robinson Towne Centre, 1120 Park Manor, Suite 102, ☎412-788-2775
- ★ **West Mifflin** Century Square, 2365 Mountain View Drive, ☎412-653-3954

Rhode Island
Nope.

Vermont
Ditto.

Washington
Washington has eight Family Christian Stores locations.

- ★ **Bellingham** 3560 Meridian Street, Suite 101, ☎360-676-0490
- ★ **Everett** Crown Center, 811 SE Everett Mall Way, ☎425-353-4256
- ★ **Federal Way** 31835 Pacific Highway South, Suite A, ☎253-839-3920
- ★ **Kirkland** 12602 Totem Lake Boulevard, ☎425-821-1281
- ★ **Lynden** 1712 Front Street, ☎360-354-5960
- ★ **Lynnwood** 5116 196th Street, Suite 203, ☎425-774-9507
- ★ **Olympia** Cooper Point Pavilion, 1520 Cooper Point Road SW, Suite 390, ☎360-352-7777; Olympia Square Shopping Center, 3315 Pacific Avenue SE, Suite B2, ☎360-491-4444

Wisconsin
Wisconsin has six Family Christian Stores locations.

- ★ **Appleton** 1400A W. College Avenue, ☎920-731-5829
- ★ **Eau Claire** 2916 London Road, ☎715-835-1291

BLUE STATE
★ ★ ★

- ★ **Madison** Princeton Club Shopping Center, 1746 Eagan Road, ☎608-249-0532; 6730 Odana Road, ☎608-833-0777
- ★ **Milwaukee** Northwest Fashion Square, 8653 W. Brown Deer Road, ☎414-355-0575
- ★ **Wauwatosa** 2525 N. Mayfair Road, Suite 201, ☎414-453-9662

REPUBLICAN PARTY CONTACTS

Surprise! Surprise! Blue States allow conservatives to organize within their borders. Actually, as you'll see below, many Blue States have conservative governors and national leaders. But you'll still be exposed to bleeding-heart rhetoric in your new state. It will come to you black and white and read all over, or it will be proclaimed in lieu of the Gospel by your new coworkers.

If you want to plug into the Republican Party in your new Blue State, you've got a number of options, depending on your race, age, or interests.

California

- ★ California Republican Party: ☎916-448-9496; ✍www.cagop.org
- ★ Asian and Pacific Islander Coalition: ☎415-386-3544
- ★ Asian American Republican Council: ☎916-391-0227
- ★ California Black Republican Council: ☎951-830-1444; ✍www.cablackgop.org
- ★ California Congress of Republicans: ☎916-359-5741; ✍www.ccrgop.org
- ★ California Federation of Republican Women: ☎626-488-8102; ✍www.cfrw.org
- ★ California Republican Veterans of America: ☎916-929-5438
- ★ California Republican Assembly: ☎626-644-0408
- ★ California Republican League: ☎650-321-4112
- ★ California Young Republicans: ☎650-346-9111; ✍www.cyr.org
- ★ California College Republicans: ☎888-227-7976; ✍www.collegegop.org

50

BLUE STATE
★ ★ ★

- ★ Filipino American Republican Council of California: ☎916-691-6642
- ★ Iranian American Republican Council: ☎310-261-9199
- ★ Republican National Hispanic Assembly: ☎661-978-7153; ✍www.carnha.org
- ★ Republican Jewish Coalition: ☎310-478-0752; ✍www.rjchq.org
- ★ Republican Lawyers Association: ☎949-677-3688; ✍www.californiarepublic
  anlawyers.com
- ★ The Wish List: ☎916-484-1339; ✍www.thewishlist.org
- ★ Vietnamese American Republican Council: ☎310-671-2722
- ★ Young Republican Federation of California: ☎714-536-9989;
  ✍www.yrfc.org

Connecticut
- ★ Connecticut Republican State Central Committee: ☎860-547-0589;
  ✍www.ctgop.org

Delaware
- ★ Republican State Committee of Delaware: ☎302-651-0260; ✍www
  .delawaregop.com

Hawaii
- ★ Hawaii Republican Party: ☎808-593-8180; ✍www.gophawaii.com
- ★ Hawaii County Republican Party: ☎808-895-8653; ✍www.ilhawaii.net/
  ~spencer/higop/Repweb.html
- ★ Maui County Republican Party: ☎808-249-8880; ✍www.gopmaui.com
- ★ Hawaii State Federation of College Republicans: ✍www.crhawaii.org
- ★ Hawaii Young Republicans: ✍www.hawaiiyounggop.com

Illinois
- ★ Illinois Republican Party: ☎312-201-9000; ✍www.ilgop.org
- ★ Illinois House Republican Organization: ☎815-577-1400; ✍www.ilhro.com
- ★ Republican State Senate Campaign Committee: ☎217-527-2615; ✍www
  .ilsenategop.com
- ★ Federation of Illinois Young Republicans: ✍www.illinoisyr.com
- ★ Illinois Federation of Republican Women: ☎630-553-1599; ✍www.ifrw.org

BLUE STATE
★ ★ ★

Maine
★ Maine Republican Party: ☎207-622-6247; ✉*www.mainegop.com*

Maryland
★ Maryland Republican Party: ☎410-269-0113; ✉*www.mdgop.org*
★ Women In Support of the President (WISP): ☎410-279-8606; ✉*www
.gowisp04.org*
★ Hispanic Republicans of Maryland, ☎410-685-3700; ✉*www.hrmd.org*
★ Maryland Irish American Republican Club: ☎301-346-8379; ✉*www
.mdirish.org*
★ Maryland Federation of Republican Women: ✉*www.mfrw.org*
★ Maryland Federation of College Republicans: ✉*www.marylandcr.com*
★ Maryland Teenage Republicans: ☎301-530-8590; ✉*www.mdtars.org*

Massachusetts
★ Massachusetts Republican Party: ☎617-523-5005
★ Massachusetts Federation of Republican Women: ☎978-256-2327;
✉*www.massgop.com*
★ Massachusetts Alliance of College Republicans: ✉*www.ma.collegerepublicans
.org*
★ Asian Republicans of Massachusetts: ☎617-448-1413; ✉*www.asianrepublican.org*

Michigan
★ Michigan Republican Party: ☎517-487-5413; ✉*www.migop.org*
★ Republican Main Street Partnership: ☎517-484-8400; ✉*www.rmsp-mi.org*
★ Michigan Federation of College Republicans: ✉*www.mfcr.org*
★ Michigan Teenage Republicans: ✉*www.michigantars.com*

Minnesota
★ Republican Party of Minnesota: ☎651-222-0022; ✉*www.gop-mn.org*
★ Minnesota College Republicans: ☎651-842-0111; ✉*www.mncr.org*
★ Minnesota Young Republicans: ☎651-222-0022; ✉*www.minnesotayr.com*
★ Minnesota Federation of Republican Women: ☎651-290-0737; ✉*www
.mngopwomen.com*

BLUE STATE
★ ★ ★

New Hampshire
★ New Hampshire Republican State Committee, ☎603-225-9341; ✎*www.nhgop.org*
★ New Hampshire College Republicans: ✎*www.nh.collegerepublicans.org*

New Jersey
★ New Jersey Republican State Committee: ☎609-989-7300; ✎*www.njgop.org*
★ New Jersey Federation of Republican Women: ✎*www.njfrw.org*

New York
★ New York Republican State Committee: ☎518-462-2601; ✎*www.nygop.org*
★ New York State Federation of Republican Women: ✎*www.nfrw.org*
★ New York College Republican State Committee: ✎*www.nycrsc.org*
★ New York State Young Republican Clubs: ✎*www.nysyr.us*

Oregon
★ Oregon Republican Party: ☎503-587-9233; ✎*www.orgop.org*
★ Oregon Federation of College Republicans: ✎*www.or.collegerepublicans.org*
★ Oregon Federation of Republican Women: ✎*www.ofrw.org*
★ Oregon Mainstream Republicans: ☎503-670-9353; ✎*www.orgopmainstream.org*
★ Oregon Young Republicans: ✎*www.oregonyoungrepublicans.com*
★ Oregon Republican Leadership Institute: ✎*www.orli.us*

Pennsylvania
★ Republican State Committee of Pennsylvania: ☎717-234-4901; ✎*www.pagop.org*
★ Winning with Women in Pennsylvania: ☎724-463-5110; ✎*www.pagop4women.org*

Rhode Island
★ Rhode Island Republican Party: ☎401-732-8282; ✎*www.rigop.org*

Vermont
★ Vermont Republican Party: ☎802-223-3411; ✎*www.vtgop.org*

BLUE STATE
★ ★ ★

Washington
★ Washington State Republican Party: ☎206-575-2900; ✍www.wsrp.org

Wisconsin
★ The Republican Party of Wisconsin: ☎608-257-4765; ✍www.wisgop.org
★ Wisconsin Federation of Republican Women: ✍www.wisgop.org
★ Assembly of Teenage Republicans of Wisconsin: ✍www.geocities.com/wisteenagegop
★ Wisconsin Republican Labor Federation: ✍www.unionrepublican.com

PART 2

**State-by-State
Breakdown**

CALIFORNIA

GOVERNORS, SENATORS, CONGRESS MEMBERS

Governor Arnold Schwarzenegger, Republican He may have been born in Austria, but Mr. Schwarzenegger is an all-American, red-blooded conservative. He announced his intention to seek the California governorship on *The Tonight Show.* If you'll recall, he was voted into office in 2003 thanks to a recall election. Former Governor Gray Davis—a Democrat of course—was doing a terrible job. His lack of leadership left California's economy in shambles. Everyone from porn stars to diminutive former *Different Strokes* star Gary Coleman threw his or her hat in the ring. But Schwarzenegger quickly became the front-runner, despite the liberal media's attempt to smear him with allegations of sexual misconduct. As governor, Schwarzenegger has been successful at passing legislation to balance California's budget. But he's been a bit soft on crime, granting clemency for many death row inmates. Come on, Terminator! Other than his shaky stance on crime, Governor Schwarzenegger has done an excellent job.
➤ **Contact** ✆916-445-2841; *www.governor.ca.gov*

Senator Barbara Boxer, Democrat Boxer served in the U.S. House of Representatives from 1983 to 1990. She has served as a senator since 1993. Boxer has called for a boycott of any oil company that tries to drill in parts of Alaska that you probably couldn't even get to in a frost-proof helicopter. Maybe this tree hugger hasn't figured out there's a gas crisis going on. You can vote her out of office in 2010.
➤ **Contact** ✆202-224-3553; *www.boxer.senate.gov*

Senator Dianne Feinstein, Democrat Feinstein has been a senator since 1992. She became mayor of San Francisco in 1978 after the assassination of Mayor George Moscone and Harvey Milk. You can vote her out of office in 2006.
➤ **Contact** ✆202-224-3841; ✒*www.feinstein.senate.gov*

BLUE STATE
★ ★ ★

Members of U.S. House of Representatives, 109th Congress

★ Mike Thompson, Democrat: Began serving in 1999. ☏202-225-3311; ✎*www.mikethompson.house.gov*

★ Wally Herger, Republican: Began serving in 1987. ☏202-225-3076; ✎*www.house.gov/herger*

★ Daniel Lungren, Republican: Served from 1979 to 1988; elected again in 2004. ☏202-225-5716; ✎*www.house.gov/lungren*

★ John Doolittle, Republican: Began serving in 1991. ☏202-225-2511; ✎*www.house.gov/doolittle*

★ Doris Matsui, Democrat: Began serving in 2005. ☏202-225-7163; ✎*www.house.gov/matsui*

★ Lynn Woolsey, Democrat: Began serving in 1993. ☏202-225-5161; ✎*www.woolsey.house.gov*

★ George Miller, Democrat: Began serving in 1975. ☏202-225-2095; ✎*www.house.gov/georgemiller*

★ Nancy Pelosi, Democrat: Began serving in 1987. ☏202-225-4965; ✎*www.house.gov/pelosi*

★ Barbara Lee, Democrat: Began serving in 1997. ☏202-225-2661; ✎*www.house.gov/lee*

★ Ellen Tauscher, Democrat: Began serving in 1997. ☏202-225-1880; ✎*www.house.gov/tauscher*

★ Richard Pombo, Republican: Began serving in 1993. ☏202-225-1947; ✎*www.house.gov/pombo*

★ Tom Lantos, Democrat: Began serving in 1981. ☏202-225-3531; ✎*www.lantos.house.gov*

★ Pete Stark, Democrat: Began serving in 1973. ☏202-225-5065; ✎*www.house.gov/stark*

★ Anna Eshoo, Democrat: Began serving in 1993. ☏202-225-8104; ✎*www.eshoo.house.gov*

★ Michael Honda, Democrat: Began serving in 2001. ☏202-225-2631; ✎*www.honda.house.gov*

★ Zoe Lofgren, Democrat: Began serving in 1995. ☏202-225-3072; ✎*www.house.gov/lofgren*

BLUE STATE
★ ★ ★

- ★ Sam Farr, Democrat: Began serving in 1993. ✆202-225-2861; ✉*www.farr.house.gov*
- ★ Dennis Cardoza, Democrat: Began serving in 2003. ✆202-225-6131; ✉*www.house.gov/cardoza*
- ★ George Radanovich, Republican: Began serving in 1995. ✆202-225-4540; *www.radanovich.house.gov*
- ★ Jim Costa, Democrat: Began serving in 2005. ✆202-225-3341; ✉*www.house.gov/costa*
- ★ Devin Nunes, Republican: Began serving in 2003. ✆202-225-2523; ✉*www.nunes.house.gov*
- ★ Bill Thomas, Republican: Began serving in 1979. ✆202-225-2915; ✉*www.billthomas.house.gov*
- ★ Lois Capps, Democrat: Began serving in 1997. ✆202-225-3601; ✉*www.house.gov/capps*
- ★ Elton Gallegly, Republican: Began serving in 1987. ✆202-225-5811; ✉*www.house.gov/gallegly*
- ★ Buck McKeon, Republican: Began serving in 1993. ✆202-225-1956; ✉*www.mckeon.house.gov*
- ★ David Dreier, Republican: Began serving in 1981. ✆202-225-2305; ✉*www.dreier.house.gov*
- ★ Brad Sherman, Democrat: Began serving in 1997. ✆202-225-5911; ✉*www.house.gov/sherman*
- ★ Howard Berman, Democrat: Began serving in 1983. ✆202-225-4695; ✉*www.house.gov/berman*
- ★ Adam Schiff, Democrat: Began serving in 2001. ✆202-225-4176; ✉*www.schiff.house.gov*
- ★ Henry Waxman, Democrat: Began serving in 1975. ✆202-225-3976; ✉*www.house.gov/waxman*
- ★ Xavier Becerra, Democrat: Began serving in 1993. ✆202-225-6235; ✉*www.becerra.house.gov*
- ★ Hilda Solis, Democrat: Began serving in 2001. ✆202-225-5464; ✉*www.solis.house.gov*
- ★ Diane Watson, Democrat: Began serving in 2001. ✆202-225-7084; ✉*www.house.gov/watson*

BLUE STATE
★ ★ ★

★ Lucille Roybal-Allard, Democrat: Began serving in 1993. ☎202-225-1766; *www.house.gov/roybal-allard*

★ Maxine Waters, Democrat: Began serving in 1991. ☎202-225-2201; *www.house.gov/waters*

★ Jane Harman, Democrat: Began serving in 1993. ☎202-225-8220; *www.house.gov/harman*

★ Juanita Millender-McDonald, Democrat: Began serving in 1995. ☎202-225-7924; *www.house.gov/millender-mcdonald*

★ Grace Napolitano, Democrat: Began serving in 1999. ☎202-225-5256; *www.napolitano.house.gov*

★ Linda Sanchez, Democrat: Began serving in 2003. ☎202-225-6676; *www.lindasanchez.house.gov*

★ Edward Royce, Republican: Began serving in 1993. ☎202-225-4111; *www.royce.house.gov*

★ Jerry Lewis, Republican: Began serving in 1979. ☎202-225-5861; *www.house.gov/jerrylewis*

★ Gary Miller, Republican: Began serving in 1999. ☎202-225-3201; *www.house.gov/garymiller*

★ Joe Baca, Democrat: Began serving in 1999. ☎202-225-6161; *www.house.gov/baca*

★ Ken Calvert, Republican: Began serving in 1993. ☎202-225-1986; *www.calvert.house.gov*

★ Mary Bono, Republican: Began serving in 1997. ☎202-225-5330; *www.house.gov/bono*

★ Dana Rohrabacher, Republican: Began serving in 1989. ☎202-225-2415; *www.rohrabacher.house.gov*

★ Loretta Sanchez, Democrat: Began serving in 1997. ☎202-225-2965; *www.lorettasanchez.house.gov*

★ Christopher Cox, Republican: President Bush tapped Cox to head the Securities Exchange Commission, forcing Cox to resign from congress. As this book went to press, his replacement had not been elected.

★ Darrell Issa, Republican: Began serving in 2001. ☎202-225-3906; *www.issa.house.gov*

BLUE STATE
★ ★ ★

★ Duke Cunningham, Republican: Began serving in 1991. ☎202-225-5452;
  🖑www.cunningham.house.gov
★ Bob Filner, Democrat: Began serving in 1993. ☎202-225-8045;
  🖑www.house.gov/filner
★ Duncan Hunter, Republican: Began serving in 1981. ☎202-225-5672;
  🖑www.house.gov/hunter
★ Susan Davis, Democrat: Began serving in 2001. ☎202-225-2040;
  🖑www.house.gov/susandavis

PITHY POLITICAL POOP AND SCINTILLATING SCANDAL

Robert Kennedy's Assassination Senator Robert Kennedy's White House hopes ended in a burst of gunfire on June 5, 1968, in Los Angeles's Ambassador Hotel.

Kennedy had just won the California primary and seemed well on his way to the presidency. Instead, he was assassinated by a Palestinian named Sirhan Sirhan. To this day, it's unclear why Sirhan shot Kennedy. The New York senator died roughly twenty-four hours after he was shot.

President Richard Nixon and Watergate With Watergate, the liberal media had its finest hour, at the expense of California-born President Richard Nixon.

Although Watergate grabbed headlines for years and continues to resonate in American politics and popular culture, it really amounted to a lot of sound and fury, signifying nothing.

On June 17, 1972, police arrested some men who broke into Democratic Party headquarters in Washington's Watergate Office Building. Two journalists, Bob Woodward and Carl Bernstein, began writing a series of articles about the break-in, suggesting that it was done with Nixon's approval.

The journalists got their information from Turn Coat . . . oops, sorry . . . from Deep Throat, who turned out to be Mark Felt, a

60

high-ranking official with the FBI. At the end of the day, it was never conclusively proved that Nixon had anything substantial to do with Watergate.

The entire affair led America to doubt its government. For liberals, that doubt continues to this day. And Watergate made the media more powerful than it's ever been. Thanks to the liberal media's exploitation of Watergate, patriotism became and remains a dirty word to some. Reporters have become obsessed with "bringing down" public figures—especially if they're conservatives. It's a shame.

Assassination of George Moscone and Harvey Milk San Francisco Mayor George Moscone and city supervisor/gay activist Harvey Milk were assassinated by former city supervisor Dan White on November 27, 1978.

White recently had resigned from the board of supervisors to protest a gay civil rights bill Moscone favored and White opposed. The ultra-liberal and ultra-progressive Moscone was followed by the even-more-ultra-liberal Dianne Feinstein. And Milk's assassination became a landmark in the United States' history of "gay rights."

Assassination Attempts on President Gerald Ford Whew. California certainly isn't lacking in political scandals, is it? Not one, but two attempts on the life of President Gerald Ford took place in the state. The first took place on September 5, 1975, in Sacramento. Lynette "Squeaky" Fromme, a one-time member of the Manson Family, attempted to shoot Ford at point-blank range, but her loaded gun didn't fire. Most likely, she didn't have a round in the chamber. Secret service agents wrestled Fromme to the ground before she could make another attempt to fire her gun.

Just a little over two weeks later, another disturbed woman tried to kill President Ford. This time, Ford was in San Francisco. Sara Jane Moore, a forty-five-year-old radical, shot at Ford from thirty

feet away but missed. Both Moore and Fromme were sentenced to life in prison for their attempts to assassinate the president.

Warren G. Harding's Death   And don't forget the mysterious death of our twenty-ninth president, Warren G. Harding.

Harding died in San Francisco's Palace Hotel. How did he die? That was never clear, but rumors of the time pointed to Harding's wife, Florence.

Harding suffered from Bill Clinton's disease, the inability to keep his zipper in place around young women who were not his wife. Florence Harding refused to allow an autopsy on her husband after his death, which provided circumstantial evidence of her guilt. Officially, Harding died of a stroke. But it seems pretty clear that he really died from his immoral activities.

PEOPLE FROM YOUR NEW STATE
WHO WON'T MAKE YOU FEEL ILL

* Julia Child, chef, Pasadena
* Joe DiMaggio, baseball great, Martinez
* James H. Doolittle, general, Alameda
* George Lucas, director, Modesto
* Richard Nixon, president, Yorba Linda
* George S. Patton, general, San Gabriel
* Eldrick "Tiger" Woods, golfer, Cypress

CONNECTICUT

GOVERNOR, SENATORS, CONGRESS MEMBERS

Governor M. Jodi Rell, Republican   No offense to Ms. Rell, but she is governor of Connecticut only because the liberal media just can't seem to stop playing kindergarten cop. Rell was the state's lieutenant

governor in 2004, when Gov. John Rowland resigned. The press alleged that Rowland had work done to his summer cottage by contractors who also did projects for the state of Connecticut. Rowland didn't pay for the work done to his private home, the liberal media alleged. At first, Rowland denied the charge. Then he admitted that his denials were false. He had in fact had work done gratis by contractors associated with the state.

So, let's see. Rowland didn't kill anyone, molest anyone, or have five mistresses on the side. He was found guilty of "stealing honest service." And for this he deserved a year in prison.

It's about as silly as that character in *Les Miserables* being hunted down all his life for stealing a loaf of bread. Rowland resigned, and on July 1, 2004, Rell became Connecticut's second female governor.

Apparently, she's not aware that she's a Republican. She's in favor of so-called civil unions between people of the same sex. At least she believes marriage should only be between men and women.

In late 2004, Rell underwent surgery for breast cancer.

➤ **Contact** 📞860-566-4840; ✎*www.ct.gov/governorrell*

Senator Christopher Dodd, Democrat Dodd served as a congressman from 1975 to 1980. He has been a senator since 1981. You can vote him out of office in 2010. Dodd had the temerity to call John Bolton, President Bush's choice for U.N. ambassador, "damaged goods." Dodd also said Bolton "lacks credibility." Hmm. Then Dodd must have been speaking "credibly" in April 2004, when he suggested West Virginia Senator Robert Byrd "would have been right during the great conflict of Civil War in this nation."

Byrd, also a Democrat, was a member of the Ku Klux Klan before turning to mainstream politics. Similar statements caused Trent Lott to lose his position as senate majority leader. Apparently, it's okay for Democrats—but not for Republicans—to make racist statements.

➤ **Committees** Committee on Rules and Administration
➤ **Contact** 📞202-224-2823; ✎*www.dodd.senate.gov*

BLUE STATE

★ ★ ★

Senator Joseph Lieberman, Democrat Lieberman has been a senator since 1989. You can vote him out of office in 2006.

Lieberman was an unsuccessful candidate for president in 2004. He was an unsuccessful candidate for vice president in 2000. He was on the ticket with . . . oh shoot, what was that guy's name? The guy who invented the Internet? The sore loser? The one who practically caused the American government to shut down? Anyway, he was on the ticket with that guy.

At least Lieberman was smart enough not to resign his senate seat. He must have known he was second banana to a loser.

➤ **Committees** Committee on Governmental Affairs

➤ **Contact** ☎ 202-224-4041; ✐ *www.lieberman.senate.gov*

Congress Members, 109th Congress

★ John Larson, Democrat: Began serving in 1999. ☎ 202-225-2265; ✐ *www.house.gov/larson*

★ Rob Simmons, Republican: Began serving in 2001. ☎ 202-225-2076; ✐ *www.simmons.house.gov*

★ Rosa DeLauro, Democrat: Began serving in 1991. ☎ 202-225-3661; ✐ *www.house.gov/delauro*

★ Christopher Shays, Republican: Began serving in 1987. ☎ 202-225-5541; ✐ *www.house.gov/shays*

★ Nancy Johnson, Republican: Began serving in 1983. ☎ 202-225-4476; ✐ *www.house.gov/nancyjohnson*

PITHY POLITICAL POOP AND SCINTILLATING SCANDAL

Connecticut's "Sundown Town" Blue State folks would have you think that Red States invented racism and bigotry. But it's not true.

Well into the twentieth century, Darien was an example of a so-called sundown town, a place in which it was understood that anyone not a WASP needed to be on the other side of the town limits before nightfall. In 1948, one of the entrances to Darien

greeted visitors with a sign reading, "Gentiles Only." The Academy Award-winning film, *Gentleman's Agreement,* was based on a novel by Laura Z. Hobson about Darien's unwritten covenant denying home sales to Jews. Oh, and, by the way . . . Blacks? Also not welcome. Catholics? Ditto.

Dr. Spock: Make Babies, Not War Connecticut-born Dr. Benjamin Spock preached a gospel of child-rearing that moral leaders like Vice President Spiro Agnew and *Guideposts* founder, Dr. Norman Vincent Peale, blamed for the permissive behavior of 1960s' youth.

As if Spock's touchy-feely legacy weren't enough, he was a vocal opponent of the Vietnam War. Instead of supporting the country's policy to plant seeds of democracy throughout the world, Spock was convicted and sentenced in Boston for conspiracy to aid, abet, and counsel young men to avoid the draft. The conviction was overturned on appeal.

Spock had the temerity to run for president in 1972. He lost, of course. But liberals—who must have begun their lives as mollycoddled infants—across the United States managed to get him more than 75,000 votes.

PEOPLE FROM YOUR NEW STATE
WHO WON'T MAKE YOU FEEL ILL

* Ethan Allan, patriot, Litchfield
* Henry Ward Beecher, preacher and writer, Litchfield
* Samuel Colt, firearms inventor, Hartford
* Nathan Hale, patriot, Coventry
* J. P. Morgan, financier, Hartford
* Noah Webster, wordsmith, West Hartford

DELAWARE

GOVERNOR, SENATORS, CONGRESS MEMBERS

Governor Ruth Ann Minner, Democrat The only problem with Minner is she belongs to the wrong party. She is the state's first female governor. Her second and final term will end in 2008.

Minner's first husband died when she was thirty-two, leaving her a single mother of three children. Minner had left school as a teenager to help support her family. But after her husband's death, she acquired a GED and went to college while working two jobs to support her children.

As governor, she has been fiscally responsible, keeping her state strong during what some folks in the liberal media called a recession. Minner's a bit of a tree-hugger. She's spent a lot of time focusing on environmental issues. And she's also one of those anti-cigarette Nazis. She ushered through the Clean Indoor Air Act, which outlaws smoking in almost every public place in the state.

➤ **Contact** ✆302-577-8229; *www.state.de.us/governor*

Senator Joseph Biden, Democrat Biden has been a senator since 1973. You can vote him out of office in 2008.

Biden has been very critical of President Bush's handling of the obviously justified war in Iraq. It's probably just sour grapes.

Biden's presidential hopes were dashed in 1988, when it came to light that he is a serial plagiarist. One of his campaign speeches was cribbed largely from a British Labor Party leader.

The media, in one of its rare attacks on a liberal, uncovered another serious plagiarism incident from Biden's law school years and found that many of his speeches were sprinkled with unattributed lines from other Democratic politicians.

➤ **Committees** Committee on the Judiciary, Committee on Foreign Relations
➤ **Contact** ✆202-224-5042; ✉*www.biden.senate.gov*

BLUE STATE
★ ★ ★

Senator Thomas Carper, Democrat Carper served as a congressman from 1983 to 1992. He served two terms as Delaware's governor before being elected to the senate in 2001. You can vote him out of office in 2006.

Don't despair, transplanted Red Stater. Carper has proven himself to be remarkably nonpartisan for a Democrat.

➤ **Contact** ✆202-224-2441; ✍*www.carper.senate.gov*

Congress Member, 109th Congress
★ Michael Castle, Republican: Began serving in 1993. ✆202-225-4165; ✍*www.house.gov/castle*

PITHY POLITICAL POOP AND
SCINTILLATING SCANDAL

Abramoff-Reed Indian Gambling Scandal The Diamond State figures prominently in the recent Abramoff-Reed Indian gambling scandal. Lobbyists Jack Abramoff, Grover Norquist, Michael Scanlon, and Ralph Reed Jr. stand accused of illegal lobbying practices and of bribing several prominent Republicans.

It can't be true, though. Reed was the first executive director of the Christian Coalition! The liberal media is probably behind this because they've always hated Reed, and they're always eager to besmirch the good names of Republican leaders.

Supposedly, here's what happened. The lobbyists allegedly conspired together to bilk Indian casinos for millions. Abramoff and his partner Scanlon allegedly had their friends Reed and Norquist lobby against Indian gaming, so tribal leaders would seek out pro-gaming lobbyists Abramoff and Scanlon and pay them handsomely. Often Scanlon and Abramoff would urge tribal leaders to pacify anti-gaming lobbyists by giving large sums to Christian Coalition chapters.

Here's where Delaware enters the mix. Some of the money spent by tribes went to an organization called the American

International Center, which billed itself as a think tank headed by David Grosh. The problem was that the center was bogus. Grosh was a Delaware lifeguard with no qualifications for policy research who ran the "think tank" out of his beach house.

In the midst of all of this alleged double-dealing, the lobbyists supposedly bribed Republican politicians in return for their votes. Some politicians implicated in the scandal thus far are Ohio Congressman Bob Ney, Texas Senator Tom DeLay, and Montana Senator Conrad Burns. The fallout from this scandal was undetermined at the time this book was written.

County Executive Tom Gordon Former New Castle County Executive Tom Gordon was implicated in one of the biggest scandals to hit the First State in recent years.

As this book was going to press, Gordon—along with his chief administrative officer, Sherry Freebery—were under federal indictment for alleged corruption. The two are accused of ordering county workers to perform thousands of hours of personal and political tasks on taxpayer time. Freebery also was accused of accepting a $2.7 million loan from a developer, in exchange for treating a golf course project favorably. Sniff. Sniff. Smells like the liberal media again. Gosh, that stinks!

PEOPLE FROM YOUR NEW STATE
WHO WON'T MAKE YOU FEEL ILL

* E. I. DuPont, businessman, Wilmington
* Henry Heimlich, inventor of the maneuver that bears his name, Wilmington
* Howard Pyle, artist and illustrator, Wilmington
* Caesar Rodney, patriot, Dover

BLUE STATE
☆ ☆ ☆

HAWAII

GOVERNOR, SENATORS, CONGRESS MEMBERS

Governor Linda Lingle, Republican Lingle was elected to her first term in 2001. She is the first female governor of the state of Hawaii. For a Republican, she's sometimes a little too cozy with Democrats and especially with one Democrat's bleeding-heart personal project.

U.S. Senator Daniel Akaka (see below) of Hawaii wants to give "native" status to anyone in Hawaii with so much as a single drop of native Hawaiian blood. These new "natives" would get all sorts of perks and probably try to open gambling casinos.

Shockingly, the Republican Lingle supports these efforts, which led *Forbes* to name her a "Dunce of the Week" in September 2005. Lingle's favorable stance on granting native Hawaiian status even has led some in the U.S. Senate to fear that she's in favor of having the Aloha State secede from the union!

"That's a ridiculous claim and a ridiculous argument," Lingle said in response. "We have over 500 recognized Indian tribes in America. They don't secede. They simply get a federal recognition."

Yes, but those other states aren't islands, hours from the mainland, Governor Lingle.

➤ **Contact** ☎808-586-0034; ✉*www.gov.state.hi.us*

Senator Daniel Akaka, Democrat Akaka served as a congressman from 1977 to 1988. He has been a senator since 1989. You can vote him out of office in 2006.

Akaka introduced legislation to grant federal recognition to native Hawaiians, giving them a status similar to Indians and native Alaskans.

The so-called Akaka Bill created a schism in Hawaii between native Hawaiians and non-natives. Natives believe the legislation will give natives the right to create a form of self-governance, while non-natives fear granting federal recognition will open the door to

casino gambling in Hawaii and affect land values in some parts of the state.

➤ **Contact** ☎202-224-6361; ✍ *www.akaka.senate.gov*

Senator Daniel Inouye, Democrat Inouye served as a congressman from 1959 to 1962. He has been a senator since 1963. You can vote him out of office in 2010.

Inouye has served Hawaii since it became a state in 1959. His longtime public service should be lauded. What isn't so laudatory, though, is the fact that he was among the senators who urged President Bush to release his full military records during the 2000 campaign.

Bush did not, but so what? He's proven his mettle since terrorists attacked the United States in 2001. In addition, Inouye was on the senate committee that tried to place the so-called Iran-Contra Scandal solely on the shoulders of President Ronald Reagan.

➤ **Committees** Select Committee on Intelligence, Committee on Indian Affairs, Select Committee on Secret Military to Iran and the Nicaraguan Opposition

➤ **Contact** ☎202-224-3934; ✍ *www.inouye.senate.gov*

Congress Members, 109th Congress

★ Neil Abercrombie, Democrat: First served 1985 to 1986, began serving again in 1991. ☎202-225-2726; *www.house.gov/abercrombie*

★ Ed Case, Democrat: Began serving in 2001. ☎202-225-4906; ✍ *www.house.gov/case*

PITHY POLITICAL POOP AND SCINTILLATING SCANDAL

Grover Cleveland, Bleeding Heart Hawaii could have become a United States territory five years earlier than it did, if not for the actions of one of the few bleeding-heart liberals to occupy the White House in the waning years of the nineteenth century.

BLUE STATE

☆ ☆ ☆

Sugar cane production linked Hawaii's economy with the United States. American sugar plantation owners dominated the islands' economy and politics . . . as well they should have.

Queen Liliuokalani had the temerity to try to establish a stronger monarchy in Hawaii. Americans, under the leadership of Samuel Dole, deposed her in 1893. The business owners' hope was annexation, which they believed would decrease tariffs on the sugar they produced.

President Benjamin Harrison—a Republican, of course—encouraged the takeover. Then Harrison lost his reelection bid in 1892, and bleeding-heart Grover Cleveland—a Democrat, of course—was back in office. He felt the takeover of Hawaii was wrong and even moved to restore Queen Liliuokalani to the throne.

Yes. An American president supported a monarchy near our own shores. A few years later, the Spanish-American War created a healthy burst of patriotism, which led to the United States' annexation of Hawaii in 1898.

Hawaii's Campaign Donation Scandal A campaign donation scandal began to rock the Aloha State in 2002.

Robert Watada, head of the state's Campaign Spending Commission, and his staff exposed a scandal that caused state business leaders to get slapped with community-service sentences. And it led to the resignation of Honolulu's police commissioner.

Allegedly, well-known and respected architects and engineers illegally made campaign contributions in the names of their employees, wives, and children. The goal? To win government contracts.

Hawaiian law allows a maximum of $6,000 in donations to gubernatorial candidates and $4,000 to mayoral candidates. Some business leaders circumvented the law by making donations appear to come from others.

Watada was modest about uncovering the scandal. "It's what I get paid for," he said. "I believe our system requires all of us in the democracy in which we live to follow the laws."

PEOPLE FROM YOUR NEW STATE
WHO WON'T MAKE YOU FEEL ILL

* Tia Carrere, actress, Honolulu
* Senator Hiram Fong, Honolulu
* Don Ho, entertainer, Honolulu
* Don Stroud, actor, Honolulu

ILLINOIS

GOVERNOR, SENATORS, CONGRESS MEMBERS

Governor Rod Blagojevich, Democrat Blagojevich was elected to his first term in 2002. He's frequently touted by Democrats as a potential candidate for president in 2008.

Blagojevich managed not to raise taxes, even as he increased funding for health and education. But he did so at the expense of state workers.

Blagojevich "borrowed" $1.2 billion from the state employees' pension fund to make his budget in 2005. That's just like a liberal to play the good guy now while leaving the future in shambles.

In addition, Blagojevich may have showed yellow-dog Democrat roots when he signed a bill prohibiting discrimination based on sexual orientation in employment, housing, public accommodations, and credit.

Blagojevich's feud with his father-in-law kept Chicago tongues wagging throughout 2005.

Playing tree-hugger, Blagojevich shut down a landfill owned by a distant relative of his in-laws. Allegedly, Blagojevich's father-in-law—

powerful Chicago alderman Richard Mell—told the landfill owner not to worry about fixing environmental problems at the site. Mell supposedly said he could get the governor to look the other way, since he's a family member.

Blagojevich, who must have been suffering from a bleeding heart, closed the landfill instead. So much for putting one's family first. Since then, Blagojevich and his father-in-law have bickered back and forth. Some believe the whole situation is an elaborate scam to distance Blagojevich from the insular world of Chicago politics in order to make him more popular in other portions of Illinois.

➤ **Contact** 217-782-0244; *www.illinois.gov/gov*

Senator Richard Durbin, Democrat Durbin served as a congressman from 1983 to 1996. He's been a senator since 1997. You can vote him out of office in 2008.

In 2005, Durbin displayed a shocking lack of support for America's fight against terror. He read an FBI report about the treatment of a detainee at Guantanamo Bay. The report indicated the detainee had been subjected to cruel and unusual punishment.

Durbin then said, "If I read this to you and did not tell you that it was an FBI agent describing what Americans had done to prisoners in their control, you would most certainly believe this must have been done by Nazis, Soviets in their Gulags, or some mad regime . . . that had no concern for human beings."

So, America's military is made up of fascists, Mr. Durbin? Most would disagree with you. And besides, you may not be aware there's a war on terror going on.

➤ **Contact** ✆202-224-2152; ✍*www.durbin.senate.gov*

Barack Obama, Democrat Obama has been a senator since 2005. You can vote him out of office in 2010. Obama was the keynote speaker at the Democratic National Convention in 2004. He is considered a rising star of the Democratic party.

➤ **Contact** ✆202-224-2854; ✍*www.obama.senate.gov*

BLUE STATE
★ ★ ★

Congress Members, 109th Congress

★ Bobby Rush, Democrat: Began serving in 1993. ☎202-225-4372; ✍*www.house.gov/rush*

★ Jesse Jackson Jr., Democrat: Began serving in 1995. ☎202-225-0773; ✍*www.house.gov/jackson*

★ Daniel Lipinski, Democrat: Began serving in 2005. ☎202-225-5701; ✍*www.house.gov/lipinski*

★ Luis Gutierrez, Democrat: Began serving in 1993. ☎202-225-8203; ✍*www.luisgutierrez.house.gov*

★ Rahm Emanuel, Democrat: Began serving in 2003. ☎202-225-4061; ✍*www.house.gov/emanuel*

★ Henry Hyde, Republican: Began serving in 1975. ☎202-225-4561; ✍*www.house.gov/hyde*

★ Danny Davis, Democrat: Began serving in 1997. ☎202-225-5006; ✍*www.house.gov/davis*

★ Melissa Bean, Democrat: Began serving in 2005. ☎202-225-3711; ✍*www.house.gov/bean*

★ Janice Schakowsky, Democrat: Began serving in 1999. ☎202-225-2111; ✍*www.house.gov/schakowsky*

★ Mark Steven Kirk, Republican: Began serving in 2001. ☎202-225-4835; ✍*www.house.gov/kirk*

★ Jerry Weller, Republican: Began serving in 1995. ☎202-225-3635; ✍*www.weller.house.gov*

★ Jerry Costello, Democrat: Began serving in 1987. ☎202-225-5661; ✍*www.house.gov/costello*

★ Judy Biggert, Republican: Began serving in 1999. ☎202-225-3515; ✍*www.judybiggert.house.gov*

★ Dennis Hastert, Republican: Began serving in 1987. ☎202-225-2976; ✍*www.house.gov/hastert*

★ Timothy Johnson, Republican: Began serving in 2001. ☎202-225-2371; ✍*www.house.gov/timjohnson*

★ Donald Manzullo, Republican: Began serving in 1993. ☎202-225-5676; ✍*www.manzullo.house.gov*

- ★ Lane Evans, Democrat: Began serving in 1983. ☎202-225-5905; ✉*www.house.gov/evans*
- ★ Ray LaHood, Republican: Began serving in 1995. ☎202-225-6201; ✉*www.house.gov/lahood*
- ★ John Shimkus, Republican: Began serving in 1997. ☎202-225-5271; ✉*www.house.gov/shimkus*

PITHY POLITICAL POOP AND SCINTILLATING SCANDAL

The Preemption Act Illinois—as well as Blue Midwestern States Minnesota and Wisconsin—owe their early lives to a Red State politician.

Virginia's John Tyler oversaw passage of the Preemption Act of 1841. It allowed a settler to claim 160 acres of land by building a cabin on the property. The Preemption Act was replaced twenty years later by the Homestead Act. But for twenty years, Preemption sped the settling of at least three Midwestern states.

So Blue Staters in Illinois, Minnesota, and Wisconsin should think twice before they criticize any Red States.

The Pullman Strike The Pullman Strike of Chicago left thirteen dead and fifty-three seriously wounded in 1894.

Pullmans were sleeping cars found on practically all passenger trains around the turn of the last century. In the late 1880s, founder George Pullman built the company town of Pullman near Chicago to house his employees. The company owned all buildings in town and leased them to workers, churches, and stores.

In response to nationwide economic conditions, Pullman's company cut its workers' wages repeatedly in the 1880s and 1890s. But it didn't lower the rent for workers living in company housing.

Workers struck on May 11, 1894. A couple of months later, sympathetic railway workers agreed to boycott trains that contained Pullman cars. President Grover Cleveland sent federal troops to Chicago, to keep trains moving and break the strike. Violence ensued. But the strike collapsed after its leaders were arrested.

Chicago's 1919 Race Riot Southern blacks emigrated north in huge numbers following World War I. This fueled racial tension that erupted in many towns and cities, but one of the worst riots took place in 1919 in Chicago.

The riot started with the drowning of an African American child, Eugene Williams. Williams, enjoying a swim on a hot July day, strayed onto a beach tacitly understood to be for whites only.

A white boy threw rocks at Williams, causing him to drown. Police refused to arrest the white youth, arresting a black one instead. That was the match that lit the powder keg.

The ensuing riots lasted five days and left dead twenty-three blacks and fifteen whites. Nearly 300 people of both races were wounded.

Leopold and Loeb There is no such thing as the perfect crime. That was a lesson learned the hard way in 1924 by Nathan Leopold and Richard Loeb.

The two wealthy teens, who were attending the University of Chicago, decided they were above the law and order that the rest of us respect. For months, they plotted a "perfect crime," which resulted in the kidnapping and murder of fourteen-year-old Bobby Franks.

The pair lured Franks into a car, bludgeoned him to death with a chisel, used acid to obscure his features, and then hid him in a culvert under a railroad track near Chicago. Afterward,

Leopold and Loeb sent a ransom note to Franks's family, demanding $10,000.

But by the time the note arrived, police already had discovered Franks's body. That's when the pair's "perfect crime" fell apart. A pair of glasses found with the body was traced to Leopold, and police determined the ransom note was written on a typewriter Leopold used with a law-student study group.

When pressed, Leopold and Loeb confessed—both saying the other masterminded the crime. The pair should have been hanged, but they were defended by Clarence Darrow, a bleeding heart who was against the death penalty.

He had his clients plead guilty. Then he argued that they committed the crime because they were exposed in college to Nietzsche's "superman" philosophy. A judge bought it, and Leopold and Loeb got away with nothing more than lengthy jail sentences. Loeb later was killed in prison. But Leopold was released in 1958. He moved to Puerto Rico and died of a heart attack in 1971.

Mayor Anton Cermak's Assassination An attempt on Franklin Roosevelt's life led instead to the death of a Chicago mayor.

The president-elect was in Miami on February 15, 1933. As he waved to a large and welcoming crowd, Guiseppe Zangara fired at him. Native Italian Zangara was having a difficult time enduring the Great Depression. Maybe he should have stayed in Italy, huh? Anyway, he developed a burning hatred for President Herbert Hoover. But after Roosevelt defeated Hoover, Zangara turned his hatred toward the president-to-be.

Zangara encountered Roosevelt during the president-elect's visit to Miami's Bayfront Park. There was one problem for Zangara. The diminutive Italian was only five feet tall. He had trouble seeing his target over the heads of the packed crowd. Zangara stood on a chair and fired some shots, none of which hit Roosevelt.

One did, however, hit Chicago Mayor Anton Cermak, who was with Roosevelt. About a month later, Cermak died from complications that resulted from his abdominal gunshot wound. Zangara was sentenced to Florida's electric chair.

Showing his true (commie red) colors, the immigrant had this to say as he was led to the chair: "You give me electric chair! I no afraid of that chair! You're one of capitalists. You is crook man too. Put me in electric chair. I no care!" Well, they did. And he fried. God rest his crooked little soul.

Arms for Hostages and Iran-Contra The liberal media had a field day with two "scandals" that rocked Illinois native Ronald Reagan's second presidential term. The media had labeled him the "Teflon President" because no matter how hard they tried to besmirch his name, the public continued to love and idealize the Great Communicator.

Ronald Reagan's heart was in the right place in 1986 when he sold arms to Iran in hopes of gaining freedom for Americans being held by pro-Iranian terrorists in Lebanon.

Reagan had always said that he would never make concessions to terrorists, and the liberal media decided that he went against his word when he okayed the arms deal.

The next year, the liberal media was at it again. This time, they claimed that the money obtained by selling arms to Iran had been used to supply weapons to anti-Communist Nicaraguan troops called Contras. Congress had banned such transactions from taking place.

Regan said the sale to the Contras was done by members of his staff, without his knowledge. That wasn't good enough for the liberal press, which lambasted Reagan until the end of his term. They tried to make it seem that the crooked actions of others suggested the president was either lying or incompetent. What nonsense.

PEOPLE FROM YOUR NEW STATE
WHO WON'T MAKE YOU FEEL ILL

* Gillian Anderson, actress, Chicago
* Jack Benny, entertainer, Chicago
* Ray Bradbury, author, Waukegan
* William Jennings Bryan, politician, Salem
* Walt Disney, illustrator, Chicago
* Benny Goodman, musician, Chicago
* Dorothy Hamill, ice skater, Chicago
* Ernest Hemingway, author, Oak Park
* Charlton Heston, actor/NRA president, Evanston
* Bob Newhart, actor, Chicago
* Ronald Reagan, president, Tampico

MAINE

GOVERNOR, SENATORS, CONGRESS MEMBERS

Governor John Baldacci, Democrat By the time you read this, the good, God-fearing folks of Maine may have overturned a piece of gay-rights legislation signed into law by Baldacci. He was elected to his first term in 2002. Hopefully, he won't have another one.

In 2005, the Maine state legislature passed and Baldacci signed a bill that prohibits discrimination based on sexual orientation. The law makes it illegal to discriminate in employment, credit, education, and accommodations.

Church groups throughout the state lobbied for a referendum, which will give state residents the chance to repeal the law. The Christian Civic League and other groups got enough signatures to get the issue on the November 2005 ballot. But the bleeding hearts ruled the day. The repeal was voted down. At least it was close, 55 percent to 45 percent.

➤ **Contact** ☏ 207-287-3531; ✐ *www.maine.gov/governor/baldacci*

BLUE STATE

⭐ ⭐ ⭐

Senator Susan Collins, Republican Collins has been a senator since 1997. You can reelect her in 2008. As chair of the Governmental Affairs Committee, Collins has been at the forefront of the sexual assault scandal plaguing the U.S. Air Force Academy.

Collins requested a survey of female cadets, which indicated that nearly 25 percent had been sexually assaulted at the academy. In a statement, Collins said she was "shocked and saddened" by the survey's results.

➤ **Committees** Chair, Committee on Governmental Affairs; Committee on Homeland Security and Governmental Affairs

➤ **Contact** ✆ 202-224-2523; ✐ *www.collins.senate.gov*

Senator Olympia Snowe, Republican This Blue State's other Republican senator served as a congresswoman from 1979 to 1994. She became a senator in 1995. You can reelect her in 2006. Snowe is a moderate. Thus, she has an important vote in a senate that has close to a fifty-fifty split between Democrats and Republicans. In 1995, Snowe was one of the so-called "Gang of Fourteen." This group of senatorial moderates forged a compromise that limits Democrats' ability to filibuster judicial nominees. Way to go, Ms. Snowe!

➤ **Committees** Committee on Small Business and Entrepreneurship

➤ **Contact** ✆ 202-224-5344; ✐ *www.snowe.senate.gov*

Congress Members, 109th Congress

★ Thomas Allen, Democrat: Began serving in 1997. ✆ 202-225-6116; ✐ *www.tomallen.house.gov*

★ Michael Michaud, Democrat: Began serving in 2003. ✆ 202-225-6306; ✐ *www.michaud.house.gov*

PITHY POLITICAL POOP AND SCINTILLATING SCANDAL

The Aroostook War In 1840, Maine nearly caused the United States to enter into a third war with Britain. The cause was lumber.

BLUE STATE

★ ★ ★

Maine and neighboring Canadian province New Brunswick both claimed timber-rich land, the ownership of which was unclear. When Canadian lumberjacks began working in the area, Maine authorities raised troops to dispel them. In return, New Brunswick asked Britain for troops, and full-scale warfare seemed imminent. Swift action by President Martin Van Buren and General Winfield Scott headed off trouble before a single shot was fired, and the so-called Aroostook War ended before it began.

Ownership of the disputed land was decided by the Webster-Ashburton Treaty of 1842. The 7,000 square miles of land went to America, but waterways within it were free for use by both the United States and Canada. The Webster-Ashburton Treaty also settled the disputed position of the U.S.-Canada border in the Great Lakes region.

Blaine to Christians: Drop Dead You can thank Maine congressman and senator James G. Blaine for the fact that most states have laws that don't allow public money to go to religious schools . . . not even Christian ones. No wonder he was the first Republican after the Civil War to lose the race for the presidency!

In 1875, while speaker of the house of representatives, Blaine pushed to add an amendment to the U.S. Constitution that would forbid taxpayer money from going to educational institutions with a religious affiliation. What a boneheaded move. Why does something like that need to be added to the Constitution, anyway? Amendments should be saved for important things like keeping our flag from being burned or for ensuring that the sacred bonds of matrimony entwine only heterosexual couples.

Anyway, Blaine's move passed almost unanimously in the house. But it did not receive enough votes in the senate to pass. Apparently, senators in those days were god-fearing men. States that supported Blaine's efforts added "Blaine Amendments" to many of their own constitutions, however. All but eleven states have bans on public funds going to religious schools.

The Republican Party nominated Blaine for the 1884 presidential election, but Blaine lost to New Jersey's Grover Cleveland, the only president in history to serve two nonconsecutive terms.

Cleveland was the first Democrat elected to the White House after the Civil War.

PEOPLE FROM YOUR NEW STATE
WHO WON'T MAKE YOU FEEL ILL

* John Ford, director, Cape Elizabeth
* Henry Wadsworth Longfellow, poet, Portland
* Stephen King, author, Portland
* Edward Arlington Robinson, poet, Head Tide

MARYLAND

GOVERNOR, SENATORS, CONGRESS MEMBERS

Governor Robert Ehrlich Jr., Republican Ehrlich served as a U.S. congressman before being elected mayor in 2002. His election proves that Maryland is headed in the right direction because he's the first Republican governor the state has had in forty years.

Ehrlich has made education and health care a priority. His wife, Kendal Ehrlich, made national headlines when she said she'd like to shoot pop idol Britney Spears because Mrs. Ehrlich considers her a bad influence on girls and young women.

The liberal media jumped all over Mrs. Ehrlich, but what's wrong with her expressing an opinion? Ehrlich didn't say she was going to kill Spears, just that she had a fantasy about shooting the performer of such trash as "Oops I Did It Again" and "Baby One More Time." What proponent of traditional family values wouldn't harbor ill will toward Ms. Spears?

If there's one problem with Governor Ehrlich, it's that he believes slot machines are the way to fix his state's economy. Gambling is immoral, and it's likely to attract only the poor who believe in get-rich-quick schemes. Ehrlich pushed for slots in 2005, but the measure was defeated. He has vowed to continue to bring up the issue.

➤ **Contact** ☎410-974-3901; *www.gov.state.md.us*

Senator Barbara Mikulski, Democrat Mikulski served as a congresswoman from 1977 to 1986. She has been a senator since 1987. You can vote her out of office in 2010.

Mikulski was the senate's staunchest supporter of the Hubble Space Telescope. Proof, once again, that liberals don't have their priorities straight. A telescope that never worked properly? Hello! Ms. Mikulski? There's a war on terror going on!

➤ **Contact** ☎202-224-4654; *www.mikulski.senate.gov*

Senator Paul Sarbanes, Democrat Sarbanes served as a congressman from 1971 to 1976. He's been a senator since 1977. In 2005, he announced his intention to retire when his current term ends in 2007. Democrats have come out of the woodwork to throw their hats in the ring and take over for the long-serving senator.

Though a Democrat, Sarbanes seemed to understand the concept of money. After the collapse of Enron, he created legislation to bring more oversight to the corporate world.

On the other hand, he was quick to become a member of the vast left-wing conspiracy that often has plagued the country's legislative branch.

In 1974, Sarbanes made national headlines in the liberal media when he introduced the first article of impeachment against President Richard Nixon. Sarbanes was, at that time, a congressman serving on the judiciary committee that investigated Watergate.

Even worse, Sarbanes helped pass the ridiculous Panama Canal treaty in 1976. Apparently, Sarbanes is a fan of policies allowing the United States to give away some of its hard-fought territory.

➤ **Committees** Chair, Joint Economic Committee; Committee on Banking, Housing, and Urban Affairs

➤ **Contact** ☎ 202-224-4524; ✎ *www.sarbanes.senate.gov*

Congress Members, 109th Congress

★ Wayne Gilchrest, Republican: Began serving in 1991. ☎ 202-225-5311; ✎ *www.gilchrest.house.gov*

★ Dutch Ruppersberger, Democrat: Began serving in 2003. ☎ 202-225-3061; ✎ *www.dutch.house.gov*

★ Benjamin Cardin, Democrat: Began serving in 1987. ☎ 202-225-4016; ✎ *www.cardin.house.gov*

★ Albert Russell Wynn, Democrat: Began serving in 1993. ☎ 202-225-8699; ✎ *www.wynn.house.gov*

★ Stener Hoyer, Democrat: Began serving in 1981. ☎ 202-225-4131; ✎ *www.hoyer.house.gov*

★ Roscoe Bartlett, Republican: Began serving in 1993. ☎ 202-225-2721; ✎ *www.bartlett.house.gov*

★ Elijah Cummings, Democrat: Began serving in 1995. ☎ 202-225-4741; ✎ *www.house.gov/cummings*

★ Chris Van Hollen, Democrat: Began serving in 2003. ☎ 202-225-5341; ✎ *www.house.gov/vanhollen*

PITHY POLITICAL POOP AND SCINTILLATING SCANDAL

The Attempted Assassination of George Wallace George Wallace's hopes for the presidency ended in Laurel on May 15, 1972. The staunch segregationist who later renounced his views was shot and paralyzed by Arthur Bremer.

Bremer intended to kill either President Richard Nixon or George Wallace, and not for political reasons. The disturbed twenty-one-year-old simply wanted to do something "big" that would get people, especially young women, to notice him. Bremer attended Nixon rallies but never got a chance to try to kill him.

Security was too tight. Wallace was more accessible, so Bremer turned his attention to the Alabama governor. Bremer shot Wallace five times. One of the shots turned Wallace into a paraplegic. Partly due to the incident, Wallace found God and renounced the evils of racism. Wallace was reelected to the Alabama governorship in 1982, with support from black voters. He died in 1998. Bremer remains in prison, due to be released in 2025.

Welcome to The Jungle Baltimore-born Upton Sinclair wrote a novel in the early part of the twentieth century that turned the stomachs of thousands, including President Theodore Roosevelt.

The Jungle depicted life in Chicago's meat-packing plants. It was not a happy life. But what really got America retching was scenes such as easily distracted government inspectors feeling the guts of newly slaughtered hogs for tell-tale signs of tuberculosis.

When Roosevelt read *The Jungle*, he immediately called for an investigation of the meat-packing industry. Roosevelt objected and rightly so to Sinclair's Socialist tone throughout his novel, but the president realized that the nation's health could be in danger due to the industry's lackadaisical inspections.

Roosevelt oversaw the passage of the Pure Food and Drugs Act and the Meat Inspection Act. Inspections of slaughterhouses were turned over to agents who belonged to the country's Department of Agriculture. But neither these agents, nor anyone else, ever has been able to determine just what exactly is in SPAM.

PEOPLE FROM YOUR NEW STATE
WHO WON'T MAKE YOU FEEL ILL

* Spiro Agnew, Baltimore
* Frederick Douglass, Tuckahoe
* Billie Holiday, Baltimore
* Francis Scott Key, Carroll County
* Babe Ruth, Baltimore

GOVERNOR, SENATORS, CONGRESS MEMBERS

Governor Mitt Romney, Republican Romney was elected to his first gubernatorial term in 2002. He has been effective in balancing the state's budget, and he's got the right idea about important issues.

For example, he has sought to block the Massachusetts Supreme Court's November 2003 ruling legalizing gay marriage. Romney has worked tirelessly to get an amendment passed in his state that would ban the practice. He also has worked to get the death penalty reinstated in Massachusetts. And finally, he has made it clear that he opposes abortion.

All of these stances are pretty gutsy in a state that appears in dictionaries beside the terms "bleeding heart" and "liberal." Romney's liberal critics have pilloried him for appearing to care more about his future political ambitions than for focusing on the business of Massachusetts. But that's just sour grapes.

In September 2005, Romney postponed a trip to Israel, saying he had to focus on his home state. If Romney does try for the White House in 2008, he'll face one hurdle with middle America: He's a Mormon. No Mormon has ever been elected president.

➤ **Contact** ☎617-725-4005; 🖈*www.mass.gov*

Senator Edward Kennedy, Democrat Kennedy has been a senator for far too long. Seriously, he has served since 1961, when he took over for his brother, John. Please vote Edward Kennedy out of office in 2006.

Kennedy doesn't have a conservative bone in his body.

Of course, on July 19, 1969, he also proved he doesn't have an honorable bone in his body. That's the date of the infamous Chappaquiddick incident.

Kennedy, probably tanked well beyond the legal limit, left a party with Mary Jo Kopechne, a twenty-nine-year-old secretary for his brother, Robert Kennedy. Edward Kennedy drove off a bridge.

86

BLUE STATE
★ ★ ★

He surfaced. Kopechne did not. Kennedy did nothing to try to save her. Kopechne drowned.

Kennedy later said he was in shock. But he wasn't so shocked that he couldn't spend hours after the incident trying to cover up his involvement with it. The tragedy had only one positive consequence: It assured the United States that it would never have to endure Edward Kennedy in the White House.

➤ **Committees** Chair, Committee on the Judiciary; Committee on Labor and Human Resources; Committee on Health, Education, Labor, and Pensions

➤ **Contact** ✆202-224-4543; ✉www.kennedy.senate.gov

Senator John Kerry, Democrat Ha! Ha! Ha! The less said about this loser, the better. But just for your edification, Kerry has been (an emphasis on "has been") a senator since 1985. Please vote him out of office in 2008.

➤ **Committees** Chair, Democratic Senatorial Campaign Committee; Committee on Small Business

➤ **Contact** ✆202-224-2742; ✉www.kerry.senate.gov

Congress Members, 109th Congress

★ John Olver, Democrat: Began serving in 1991. ✆202-225-5335; ✉www.house.gov/olver
★ Richard Neal, Democrat: Began serving in 1989. ✆202-225-5601; ✉www.house.gov/neal
★ James McGovern, Democrat: Began serving in 1997. ✆202-225-6101; ✉www.house.gov/mcgovern
★ Barney Frank, Democrat: Began serving in 1981. ✆202-225-5931; ✉www.house.gov/frank
★ Martin Meehan, Democrat: Began serving in 1993. ✆202-225-3411; ✉www.house.gov/meehan
★ John Tierney, Democrat: Began serving in 1997. ✆202-225-8020; ✉www.house.gov/tierney
★ Edward Markey, Democrat: Began serving in 1975. ✆202-225-2836; ✉www.house.gov/markey

BLUE STATE
★ ★ ★

- ★ Michael Capuano, Democrat: Began serving in 1999. ☏ 202-225-5111; ✎ www.house.gov/capuano
- ★ Stephen Lynch, Democrat: Began serving in 2001. ☏ 202-225-8273; ✎ www.house.gov/lynch
- ★ William Delahunt, Democrat: Began serving in 1997. ☏ 202-225-3111; ✎ www.house.gov/delahunt

PITHY POLITICAL POOP AND SCINTILLATING SCANDAL

The Godfather of the Boston Tea Party Only one person other than King George III gets a major pen-lashing in Thomas Jefferson's immortal Declaration of Independence: Massachusetts Colonial Governor Thomas Hutchinson, whose support of England and attempts to quash patriot rebellion led to the Boston Tea Party and the start of the American Revolution.

The Corrupt Bargain John Quincy Adams was one of the participants in a scandal known as the Corrupt Bargain.

The hotly contested presidential election of 1824 came down to two men: Adams and Andrew Jackson. The election was so close that the decision had to be made by the U.S. House of Representatives. Adams's victory was sealed when powerful Kentucky Senator Henry Clay gave him his support.

Accusations arose—but were never proven—that Clay supported Adams because Adams promised, if elected, to name Clay secretary of state. Adams got elected, and you'll never guess whom he named secretary of state.

The Yuppie Murderer A crime that turned a spotlight on racism in America took place in Boston in 1989. Soon after leaving a childbirth class, Charles Stuart called police from his cellular phone and claimed he and his wife had been shot by a black man. Carol Stuart and the couple's unborn child died from the incident.

88

Police began a manhunt in Roxbury, a predominantly black neighborhood. But no black man was involved in the deaths of Stuart's wife and child. Stuart, a white yuppie, did the shooting himself and hid behind a smokescreen of racism.

To their credit, police quickly shifted their focus to Stuart. On January 3, 1990, Stuart checked into a hotel in nearby Braintree. The next day, he drove his car to the middle of Boston's Tobin Bridge. He stopped his car, got out, and jumped to his death from the bridge.

Shays's Rebellion One of the first challenges to the newly formed nation took place in Massachusetts, the same state in which the American Revolution began.

Massachusetts farmer and Revolutionary War veteran Daniel Shays gathered a group of compatriots and marched on Springfield. The group was protesting poor economic conditions. It sought to stop foreclosures and to obtain new paper money from the state. Shays hoped to seize a government arsenal, but he and his followers were defeated by militia units. Shays fled the state.

Shays's Rebellion is considered an important landmark in the creation of the Constitution of the United States, which strengthened our country's central government.

Far from being concerned about Shays's actions, future president—and opponent of centralized government—Thomas Jefferson wrote the following in a letter to friend (and future president) James Madison:

"I hold it, that a little rebellion, now and then, is a good thing, and as necessary in the political world as storms are in the physical."

And this was from one of the fathers of our country!

Gerrymandering A Massachusetts governor lent his name to a dirty political practice.

BLUE STATE
★ ★ ★

Governor Elbridge Gerry wanted to ensure he would be reelected, so he redrew voting boundaries in such a way that one district would be filled with his supporters. The problem is that the newly drawn district had a very distorted shape. It actually looked sort of like a salamander.

One of Gerry's critics took to calling the distorted shape a Gerrymander. The name stuck. It is still used to describe the practice of redrawing election districts in order to maximize the number of seats controlled by the dominant party.

PEOPLE FROM YOUR NEW STATE
WHO WON'T MAKE YOU FEEL ILL

* John Adams, president, Braintree
* John Quincy Adams, president, Braintree
* Samuel Adams, patriot, Boston
* Horatio Alger, author, Revere
* George H. W. Bush, president, Milton
* Cecil B. DeMille, director, Ashfield
* Benjamin Franklin, patriot and inventor, Boston
* John Hancock, patriot, Braintree
* Cotton Mather, pastor and author, Boston
* Leonard Nimoy, actor, Boston
* Edgar Allan Poe, author, Boston
* Paul Revere, patriot, Boston
* Theodore "Dr. Seuss" Geisel, author, Springfield

MICHIGAN

GOVERNOR, SENATORS, CONGRESS MEMBERS

Governor Jennifer Granholm, Democrat Granholm was elected governor in 2002. She will probably run for reelection in 2006. She is Michigan's

90

first female governor. Granholm has publicly supported gay rights, despite the fact that Michigan has passed a ban on gay marriage. Apparently, she doesn't think the opinions of her legislature and constituents mean all that much. At least Granholm did take the right stand on an issue affecting young people.

She signed into a law a measure that makes it illegal to sell video games rated "mature" to anyone under the age of seventeen. Greedy software companies pass these games off as harmless "entertainment." But they aren't, of course.

"These are not just harmless games," Granholm said. "The child becomes the protagonist."

Those same greedy companies were flooding Granholm with lawsuits as this book went to press.

➤ **Contact** ✆517-373-3400; *www.michigan.gov/gov*

Senator Carl Levin, Democrat Levin has been a senator since 1979. You can vote him out of office in 2008.

Levin was particularly harsh during the Senate Armed Services Committee's hearings on Abu Ghraib. He had the temerity to question Secretary of Defense Donald Rumsfeld's interpretation of the Geneva Conventions. Apparently, Levin thinks people who try to kill American forces should be lodged in five-star hotels, rather than be treated like prisoners.

➤ **Committees** Chair, Committee on Armed Services
➤ **Contact** ✆202-224-6221; *www.levin.senate.gov*

Senator Debbie Stabenow, Democrat Stabenow served as a congresswoman from 1997 to 2000. She has been a senator since 2001. You can vote her out of office in 2006.

Stabenow won her senatorial seat in a 2000 squeaker against Republican incumbent Spencer Abraham, whom President Bush tapped to be U.S. Secretary of Energy.

Stabenow is a liberal of whom to be wary. Her Democratic senatorial colleagues elected her secretary of the Democratic caucus

in 2004. This makes her the third most powerful Democrat in the senate . . . a very high honor for a freshman senator.

➤ **Contact** ✆ 202-224-4822; *www.stabenow.senate.gov*

Congress Members, 109th Congress

★ Bart Stupak, Democrat: Began serving in 1993. ✆ 202-225-4735; *www.house.gov/stupak*

★ Peter Hoekstra, Republican: Began serving in 1993. ✆ 202-225-4401; *www.hoekstra.house.gov*

★ Vernon Ehlers, Republican: Began serving in 1993. ✆ 202-225-3831; *www.house.gov/ehlers*

★ Dave Camp, Republican: Began serving in 1991. ✆ 202-225-3561; *www.house.gov/camp*

★ Dale Kildee, Democrat: Began serving in 1977. ✆ 202-225-3611; *www.house.gov/kildee*

★ Fred Upton, Republican: Began serving in 1987. ✆ 202-225-3761; *www.house.gov/upton*

★ Joe Schwarz, Republican: Began serving in 2005. ✆ 202-225-6276; *www.schwarz.house.gov*

★ Mike Rogers, Republican: Began serving in 2001. ✆ 202-225-4872; *www.mikerogers.house.gov*

★ Joe Knollenberg, Republican: Began serving in 1993. ✆ 202-225-5802; *www.house.gov/knollenberg*

★ Candice Miller, Republican: Began serving in 2003. ✆ 202-225-2106; *www.candicemiller.house.gov*

★ Thaddeus McCotter, Republican: Began serving in 2003. ✆ 202-225-8171; *www.mccotter.house.gov*

★ Sander Levin, Democrat: Began serving in 1983. ✆ 202-225-4961; *www.house.gov/levin*

★ Carolyn Kilpatrick, Democrat: Began serving in 1997. ✆ 202-225-2261; *www.house.gov/kilpatrick*

★ John Conyers Jr., Democrat: Began serving in 1965. ✆ 202-225-5126; *www.house.gov/conyers*

BLUE STATE
☆ ☆ ☆

★ John Dingell, Democrat: Began serving in 1955. ✆ 202-225-4071;
  🖘 *www.house.gov/dingell*

PITHY POLITICAL POOP AND
SCINTILLATING SCANDAL

Dearborn Mayor Orville Hubbard The next time one of your new Blue State neighbors cracks wise on someone like Jesse Helms or Strom Thurmond, just smile and remind them of long-time Dearborn Mayor Orville Hubbard. He was possibly the most outspoken segregationist north of the Mason-Dixon Line, according to his biographer, David L. Good.

Hubbard served from 1942 to 1978. He supported a 1948 campaign to defeat a rental housing development. The campaign carried the charming slogan, "Keep negroes out of Dearborn." In 1967, he told the *Detroit News,* "I just don't believe in integration. When that happens, along comes socializing with the whites, intermarriage and then mongrelization."

Jimmy Hoffa: Last Seen Alive If your new home is in or near Bloomfield Hills, you can visit the last spot Jimmy Hoffa was seen alive. The former Teamsters president announced plans in 1975 to regain the top spot in the organization. On July 30 of that year, he told friends and family he was on his way to a meeting. The meeting was with figures alleged to be part of Detroit's organized crime families. Hoffa was last seen outside the Machus Red Fox Restaurant on Telegraph Road.

Thirty years later, Hoffa remains the most famous missing body in America.

Romney Gets "Brainwashed" Michigan governor, George Romney, made a disastrous attempt to reach the White House in 1968. He campaigned as an anti-Vietnam War candidate. That's bad enough. The bigger problem, though, is that Romney made clear

his support of the war during an inspection trip in 1965. Romney's explanation for the flip-flop was a howler.

He claimed that, during the tour, he had been subjected to "the greatest brainwashing that anybody can get." The "brainwashers" were the American military and diplomatic personnel. Romney's ridiculous explanation made both hawks and doves turn their backs on him.

Romney looked either indecisive, naïve, or just plain nuts. He made Kerry's later flip-flopping seem almost benign.

PEOPLE FROM YOUR NEW STATE
WHO WON'T MAKE YOU FEEL ILL

* Henry Ford, inventor, Dearborn
* William Hewlett, businessman, Ann Arbor
* Charles Lindbergh, aviator, Detroit
* Ted Nugent, rocker, Detroit
* Steven Seagal, actor, Lansing
* Bob Seger, rocker, Detroit
* Danny Thomas, entertainer, Deerfield

MINNESOTA

GOVERNOR, SENATORS, CONGRESS MEMBERS

Governor Tim Pawlenty, Republican Pawlenty was elected in 2002 and plans to run for reelection in 2006.

Pawlenty managed to balance a $4.3-billion deficit without raising taxes. But liberals caused a government shutdown that forced him in 2005 to institute a seventy-five cent "health impact fee" on cigarettes to balance a $404-million deficit. While some conservatives attacked him for this action, liberals left Pawlenty little choice but to do what he did.

He has made a misstep in his support of gambling in Minnesota. Not only is gambling immoral, but it's likely that the folks who would gamble away their money are the very ones Pawlenty hopes to help.

Some of his constituents complain that the governor spends too much time outside the state, trying to broaden his appeal for his future political ambitions. But he's done a good job of making education a priority during tough economic times. If Pawlenty does run for the White House in 2008, he would be a fine choice.

➤ **Contact** ✆651-296-3391; ✍*www.governor.state.mn.us*

Senator Norm Coleman, Republican Coleman has been a senator since 2003. You can reelect him in 2008.

Coleman became a senator by defeating former vice president Walter Mondale. An election was necessary due to the death of ultra-liberal Minnesota senator Paul Wellstone.

Coleman is a fine young man. His senatorial votes mesh with President Bush's desires about 98 percent of the time. And he's shown that he's willing to accept the error of his ways. During his campaign, Coleman spoke against drilling for oil in Alaskan wildlife refuges, but he changed his position later, voting for a bill to allow drilling. Coleman understands there's an energy crisis.

➤ **Contact** ✆202-224-5641; ✍*www.coleman.senate.gov*

Senator Mark Dayton, Democrat Dayton has been a senator since 2001. You can vote him out of office in 2006. Dayton made a name for himself during the 9/11 Commission. It's too bad he wasn't in office before the terrorist attacks because some of his comments indicate he would have done a much, much, much better job than anyone else in the American government to ensure the country's safety.

He called the government's response to 9/11 "unbelievable negligence" and accused many agencies of lacking "common sense." A liberal, freshman senator playing armchair quarterback? Gosh, how unusual.

➤ **Contact** ✆202-224-3244; ✍*www.dayton.senate.gov*

BLUE STATE

★ ★ ★

Congress Members, 109th Congress

★ Gil Gutknecht, Republican: Began serving in 1995. ☎202-225-2472; ✎*www.gil.house.gov*

★ John Kline, Republican: Began serving in 2003. ☎202-225-2271; ✎*www.house.gov/kline*

★ Jim Ramstad, Republican: Began serving in 1991. ☎202-225-2871; ✎*www.house.gov/ramstad*

★ Betty McCollum, Democrat: Began serving in 2001. ☎202-225-6631; ✎*www.mccollum.house.gov*

★ Martin Olav Sabo, Democrat: Began serving in 1979. ☎202-225-4755; ✎*www.sabo.house.gov*

★ Mark Kennedy, Republican: Began serving in 2001. ☎202-225-2331; ✎*www.markkennedy.house.gov*

★ Collin Peterson, Democrat: Began serving in 1991. ☎202-225-2165; ✎*www.collinpeterson.house.gov*

★ James Oberstar, Democrat: Began serving in 1975. ☎202-225-6211; ✎*www.oberstar.house.gov*

PITHY POLITICAL POOP AND SCINTILLATING SCANDAL

Minnesota Shuts Down Well, it's just like a Blue State to let gridlock ruin people's livelihood. Minnesota's government shut down for the first time in history on July 1, 2005, after lawmakers failed to pass a temporary spending plan. Their inability to be responsible left 9,000 state employees out of work.

Minnesota isn't the only state to fail to approve a new budget before the old one has run out. But it's the only state without a law that automatically extends spending past the fiscal year if a new budget isn't approved.

The situation was, of course, the fault of Democrats. Governor Tim Pawlenty, a Republican, believed yellow-dog liberals were out to shut the government down in order to embarrass him and thwart his 2006 reelection.

BLUE STATE
★ ★ ★

"The Democrats turned and left tonight when Minnesota needed them most," Pawlenty said, at a news conference following the shutdown. The shutdown lasted nearly three weeks.

PEOPLE FROM YOUR NEW STATE
WHO WON'T MAKE YOU FEEL ILL

* The Andrews Sisters, entertainers, Minneapolis
* F. Scott Fitzgerald, author, St. Paul
* Judy Garland, entertainer, Grand Rapids
* J. Paul Getty, industrialist, Minneapolis
* John Madden, sports personality, Austin
* Roger Maris, baseball player, Hibbing
* Charles Mayo, physician, Rochester
* Jane Russell, actress, Bemidji
* Charles Schulz, cartoonist, Minneapolis

NEW HAMPSHIRE

GOVERNOR, SENATORS, CONGRESS MEMBERS

Governor John Lynch, Democrat Lynch took office in 2005. We have the media to blame for putting a liberal in New Hampshire's highest office.

When Lynch won the 2004 gubernatorial election, he did so by defeating incumbent Craig Benson, a Republican. Benson became the first New Hampshire governor in nearly eighty years to lose his bid for a second term. He spent that term mired in overblown controversy, dredged up by the liberal media. They must have gotten tired of besmirching the name of our commander in chief and decided to turn to state rabble rousing.

Benson, a multimillionaire, decided to hire some staff members and pay them out of his own pocket. Instead of lauding him for

saving taxpayer money, the media flayed him instead. Since Benson was paying them with his own money, these workers technically were volunteers. And since he was paying their salaries, he didn't have to explain what they did for the State of New Hampshire.

The state's Democratic Party with help from its friends, the media, wouldn't leave the issue alone. The Democrats took Benson to court under the right-to-know law and won. According to the media, some of these volunteers weren't really qualified to serve in leadership positions. For example, Benson made Angela Blaisdell the state's homeland security liaison. According to the media, her only qualification for that post was the fact that her relationship with Benson went back many years. Other "scandals" followed, and Benson lost his reelection bid, turning the state over to liberals like Lynch.

➤ **Contact** ✆ 603-271-2121; ✉ *www.state.nh.us/governor*

Senator Judd Gregg, Republican Gregg served as a congressman from 1981 to 1988. He has been a senator since 1993. Gregg served two terms as New Hampshire's governor between his stints in congress and the senate. You can reelect him in 2010.

Gregg has shown his support for American soldiers by calling a spade a spade. In speeches, he has echoed our commander in chief and pinned the blame for the September 11 terrorist attacks on Islamic fundamentalists. Some left-winger bleeding hearts feel such rhetoric smacks of racism. But, um, the guys who attacked America on that terrible day in 2001 . . . they *were* Islamic fundamentalists, right?

➤ **Committees** Chair, Committee on Health, Education, Labor, and Pensions; Committee on the Budget

➤ **Contact** ✆ 202-224-3324; ✉ *www.gregg.senate.gov*

Senator John Sununu, Republican Sununu served as a congressman from 1997 to 2002. He has been a senator since 2003. You can reelect him in 2008.

Sununu is the son of former White House Chief of Staff, John Sununu. The elder Sununu was fired by President George H. W.

Bush for the misuse of government aircraft. It was one of those silly "scandals" dredged up by a liberal media playing "watchdog." Don't they have anything more important to do?

➤ **Contact** ✆202-224-2841; ✑*www.sununu.senate.gov*

Congress Members, 109th Congress

★ Jeb Bradley, Republican: Began serving in 2003. ✆202-225-5456; ✑*www.house.gov/bradley*

★ Charles Bass, Republican: Began serving in 1995. ✆202-225-5206; ✑*www.house.gov/bass*

PITHY POLITICAL POOP AND SCINTILLATING SCANDAL

To Die For Derry was the site of a particularly heinous crime in 1990, which made national headlines and was the basis for the Nicole Kidman film, *To Die For.*

Gregory Smart, twenty-four, was killed at his home in what at first appeared to be a botched robbery. The truth was much more lurid. Smart's wife, Elizabeth, was sentenced to life in prison for her husband's murder.

Elizabeth Smart was a librarian at Winnacunnet High School. She allegedly seduced a fifteen-year-old boy named Billy Flynn and convinced him to kill her husband. Flynn, with the help of a few friends, did as he was told. He shot Smart execution style at point-blank range.

The Rise and Fall of Franklin Pierce New Hampshire's Franklin Pierce was both built up and torn down by American expansionism.

He oversaw the Gadsden Purchase in 1853, which settled the border between the United States and Mexico and helped give the United States a southern railroad route to the Pacific. The Gadsden Purchase brought parts of Arizona and New Mexico into the union. For this, Pierce was lauded. But one year later,

the so-called Ostend Manifesto caused his approval ratings to plummet. The manifesto, signed by several members of Pierce's cabinet, suggested the United States take Cuba by force.

For Americans north of the Mason-Dixon Line, this was bad. Civil War loomed, and northerners believed the acquisition of Cuba was a thinly veiled attempt to spread slavery beyond U.S. borders. The positive outcome of this situation is that it severely weakened the Democratic Party for a long time to come.

Treaty of Portsmouth In 1905, New Hampshire played a significant role in making President Theodore Roosevelt the first American to win a Nobel Prize. He helped end the Russo-Japanese War by bringing together Russian and Japanese representatives.

Roosevelt held the historic meeting at the Portsmouth Naval Shipyard. He served as mediator of the ensuing peace talks, which led to the Treaty of Portsmouth. The treaty acknowledged Japan, in effect, as in charge of Korea. Both Russia and Japan agreed to evacuate Manchuria and return its sovereignty to China.

Roosevelt's important role in the peace talks earned him the Nobel Prize for peace the following year. There was a less auspicious result of the talks, however.

During negotiations, Roosevelt opposed Japan's demand for compensation payments from Russia. This angered not only the Japanese but also Japanese Americans. Crybabies. Maybe Roosevelt just needed to take his celebrated "big stick" to them to stop their caterwauling.

PEOPLE FROM YOUR NEW STATE
WHO WON'T MAKE YOU FEEL ILL

* Horace Greeley, journalist, Amherst
* Franklin Pierce, president, Hillsboro
* Alan Shepard, astronaut, East Derry
* Daniel Webster, statesman, Salisbury

BLUE STATE
★ ★ ★

NEW JERSEY

GOVERNOR, SENATORS, CONGRESS MEMBERS

Governor Jon Corzine, Democrat Corzine was a senator before he was elected governor in 2005. During his campaign, Corzine battled allegations that he plays funny with the money. According to reports, Corzine loaned $470,000 to former girlfriend and president of the Communications Workers of America Local 1034, Carla Katz. The loan was made in 2002 but not disclosed until media reports started trickling out about the situation.

Corzine later made the loan a gift, claiming he'd done nothing illegal. Hmm. Well, maybe not technically. But in his gubernatorial race, Corzine received the endorsement of the Communications Workers of America Local 1034 . . . just slightly before he forgave the loan. Sniff. Sniff. What's that smell? There's something rotten in the state of New Jersey.

The Senate Ethics Committee slapped Corzine with an ethics complaint in September of 2005.

➤ **Contact** ✆609-292-6000; ✐*www.state.nj.us/governor*

Senator Robert Menendez, Democrat Menendez was appointed senator early in 2006 when then-senator Jon Corzine was elected New Jersey governor. Menendez served previously in the U.S. House of Representatives. His term will end in 2007.

➤ **Contact** ✆202-224-4744; ✐*www.menendez.senate.gov*

Senator Frank Lautenberg, Democrat Lautenberg has been a senator since 1981. You can vote him out of office in 2008. Lautenberg loves to cast slings and arrows at conservatives for his own political gain.

He was very vocal in his criticism of the Bush administration's response to Hurricane Katrina relief efforts. Lautenberg also was outspoken during the ridiculous Columnists-gate "scandal," in which President Bush was accused of paying columnists to make

favorable statements about his administration. All of this from a flip-flopper who "retired" from politics in 2000, only to jump back into politics two years later.

➤ **Contact** 📞202-224-3224; 🖎*www.lautenberg.senate.gov*

Congress Members, 109th Congress

★ Robert Andrews, Democrat: Began serving in 1989. 📞202-225-6501; 🖎*www.house.gov/andrews*

★ Frank LoBiondo, Republican: Began serving in 1995. 📞202-225-6572; 🖎*www.house.gov/lobiondo*

★ Jim Saxton, Republican: Began serving in 1983. 📞202-225-4765; 🖎*www.house.gov/saxton*

★ Christopher Smith, Republican: Began serving in 1981. 📞202-225-3765; 🖎*www.house.gov/chrissmith*

★ Scott Garrett, Republican: Began serving in 2003. 📞202-225-4465; 🖎*www.garrett.house.gov*

★ Frank Pallone Jr., Democrat: Began serving in 1987. 📞202-225-4671; 🖎*www.house.gov/pallone*

★ Mike Ferguson, Republican: Began serving in 2001. 📞202-225-5361; 🖎*www.house.gov/ferguson*

★ Bill Pascrell Jr., Democrat: Began serving in 1997. 📞202-225-5751; 🖎*www.pascrell.house.gov*

★ Steven Rothman, Democrat: Began serving in 1997. 📞202-225-5061; 🖎*www.rothman.house.gov*

★ Donald Payne, Democrat: Began serving in 1989. 📞202-225-3436; 🖎*www.house.gov/payne*

★ Rodney Frelinghuysen, Republican: Began serving in 1995. 📞202-225-5034; 🖎*www.frelinghuysen.house.gov*

★ Rush Holt, Democrat: Began serving in 1999. 📞202-225-5801; 🖎*www.holt.house.gov*

★ Robert Menendez, Democrat: Began serving in 1993. 📞202-225-7919; 🖎*www.menendez.house.gov*

PITHY POLITICAL POOP AND
SCINTILLATING SCANDAL

I Am a Gay American Former New Jersey governor, James McGreevey, abdicated the governorship in 2004 in a particularly lurid way. Though married twice and a father, McGreevey is gay. Before an extramarital affair with another man could be made public, McGreevey gave a speech in which he admitted, "I am a gay American." He took responsibility for his actions and apologized to his wife and family.

You can certainly find fault with McGreevey for claiming, "It makes little difference as governor that I am gay." But you can't fault him for having the guts to do the right thing and resign as governor.

Don't you talk about my wife, buck-o! Richard Codey served as New Jersey's acting governor for a short time after McGreevey's resignation. He announced that he would not run for a full term. Some believe that's because of an altercation Codey had with a New Jersey radio personality. Codey is an outspoken advocate of mental health awareness. He and his wife, Mary Jo, have talked openly about Mary Jo Codey's postpartum depression. In early 2005, talk radio host Craig Carton criticized Mary Jo Codey's mental health on the air. Richard Codey called in and threatened Carton.

It's hard to criticize a man who's defending his wife, even if he *is* a Democrat.

President Garfield Is Dead The second American president to be assassinated died in Elberon, more than two months after he was shot. James A. Garfield, a Republican, was the last president to be born in a log cabin. His was near Orange, Ohio. Garfield was a dark horse candidate during the election of 1880. He did little of import in office during his first six months as president.

103

On July 2, 1881, Garfield was getting ready to leave Washington to attend a college reunion. As he stood in the railroad station, a man stepped out of the crowd and fired two shots at him. The killer was a psychopath named Charles Guiteau.

Guiteau claimed he shot Garfield because the president refused to make him a United States consul in Paris. But really, the assassin acted because he was four bricks shy of a load. Fortunately, the government believed in punishing its criminals in those days, and Guiteau was hanged in 1882.

Garfield lingered on until September 19, 1881. He spent most of his time in a seaside cottage in Elberon. The fatal shot was one that would hardly have been life-threatening just a few decades later. But in the days before X-rays and antiseptics, Garfield was doomed. He is buried in the swing state of Ohio.

Grover Cleveland: The Anti-Veteran President New Jersey-born President Grover Cleveland is proof that Democrats don't support the armed forces.

He opposed many pension measures, defying many veterans' pressure groups. Granted, pension fraud was rampant in the late 1800s. Many able-bodied veterans claimed they were unfit for work and lived off the fat of the land. But they earned the right to take a rest! They served their country valiantly.

But with accusations of corruption ringing in his ears, Cleveland vetoed hundreds of supposedly dishonest claims. The last laugh was on the veterans, though.

Cleveland vetoed the Dependent Pension Bill. It would have extended coverage to all disabled veterans, whether or not their disability stemmed from military service. Cleveland's veto of the pension bill is one of the reasons he did not get reelected in 1888.

His successor, Benjamin Harrison, passed the bill. The irony is that, despite the fact that Cleveland did not support veterans, he was elected president a second time. He succeeded Harrison.

PEOPLE FROM YOUR NEW STATE
WHO WON'T MAKE YOU FEEL ILL

* Bud Abbott, comedian, Asbury Park
* Edwin "Buzz" Aldrin, astronaut, Montclair
* William "Count" Basie, composer, Red Bank
* Ernie Kovacs, entertainer, Trenton
* Jerry Lewis, entertainer Newark
* Norman Schwarzkopf, general, Trenton
* Frank Sinatra, entertainer, Hoboken
* William Henry Vanderbilt, businessman, New Brunswick

NEW YORK

GOVERNOR, SENATORS, CONGRESS MEMBERS

Governor George Pataki, Republican Pataki has been in office since 1995. New York does not have gubernatorial term limits, so he was elected to his third term in 2002.

Pataki is the first conservative Republican governor in New York history. Surprise! Surprise! He's taken the messes left him by bleeding-heart liberals, and he has made New York stronger than ever since the 2001 terrorist attacks.

Pataki ushered through $100 billion in tax cuts and brought more than 500,000 new jobs to the Empire State. He's taken a tough stance on crime. And he's even done some tree-hugging, to appease his bleeding-heart constituents. He protected nearly a million acres of open space during his first ten years in office. Pataki has occasionally gone overboard in courting those liberals, though. He continues to support abortion rights and even gay rights. Pataki may very well have his eyes on the White House. He announced in July 2005 that he does not intend to run for a fourth gubernatorial term.

➤ **Contact** ✆ 518-474-8390; *www.state.ny.us/governor*

Senator Hillary Rodham Clinton, Democrat Clinton has been a senator since 2001. Please, please, please, please vote her out of office in 2006.

Well, what can be said about this native New Yorker . . . What? She isn't? Chicago?!? You mean she *never* lived in New York prior to running for the senate in the state? Back during Reconstruction, they called these folks "carpetbaggers."

Well, we can say Clinton's got a passion for the Yankees . . . What? She doesn't? She wouldn't know the House That Ruth Built from a single-wide trailer in the Whitewater development?

Okay, but Clinton did an excellent job overhauling the nation's health-care system . . . What? She didn't? Her efforts were a dismal failure? She kept medical professionals out of those discussions? You're kidding, right?

In her defense, Clinton has been willing to forge relationships with conservatives to get legislation passed. She's expressed her intention to run for reelection, but (snort, giggle) she may not be in the senate long since she's (choke, snort) being talked about for the White House in 2008. Um, good luck.

➤ **Contact** ✆202-224-4451; ✐*www.clinton.senate.gov*

Senator Charles Schumer, Democrat Schumer served as a congressman from 1981 to 1998. He has been a senator since 1999. You can vote him out of office in 2010.

Schumer has been particularly vocal in his opposition to President Bush's choices for Supreme Court nominees. To paraphrase Shakespeare: Schumer is an idiot, full of sound and fury, signifying nothing.

➤ **Contact** ✆202-224-6542; ✐*www.schumer.senate.gov*

Congress Members, 109th Congress
★ Timothy Bishop, Democrat: Began serving in 2003. ✆202-225-3826; ✐*www.house.gov/timbishop*
★ Steve Israel, Democrat: Began serving in 2001. ✆202-225-3335; ✐*www.house.gov/israel*

BLUE STATE

★★★

- ★ Peter King, Republican: Began serving in 1993. ☏202-225-7896; *www.peteking.house.gov*
- ★ Carolyn McCarthy, Democrat: Began serving in 1997. ☏202-225-5516; *www.carolynmccarthy.house.gov*
- ★ Gary Ackerman, Democrat: Began serving in 1983. ☏202-225-2601; *www.house.gov/ackerman*
- ★ Gregory Meeks, Democrat: Began serving in 1997. ☏202-225-3461; *www.house.gov/meeks*
- ★ Joseph Crowley, Democrat: Began serving in 1999. ☏202-225-3965; *www.crowley.house.gov*
- ★ Jerrold Nadler, Democrat: Began serving in 1991. ☏202-225-5635; *www.house.gov/nadler*
- ★ Anthony Weiner, Democrat: Began serving in 1999. ☏202-225-6616; *www.house.gov/weiner*
- ★ Edolphus Towns, Democrat: Began serving in 1983. ☏202-225-5936; *www.house.gov/towns*
- ★ Major Owens, Democrat: Began serving in 1983. ☏202-225-6231; *www.house.gov/owens*
- ★ Nydia Velazquez, Democrat: Began serving in 1993. ☏202-225-2361; *www.house.gov/velazquez*
- ★ Vito Fossella, Republican: Began serving in 1997. ☏202-225-3371; *www.house.gov/fossella*
- ★ Carolyn Maloney, Democrat: Began serving in 1993. ☏202-225-7944; *www.house.gov/maloney*
- ★ Charles Rangel, Democrat: Began serving in 1971. ☏202-225-4365; *www.house.gov/rangel*
- ★ Jose Serrano, Democrat: Began serving in 1989. ☏202-225-4361; *www.house.gov/serrano*
- ★ Eliot Engel, Democrat: Began serving in 1989. ☏202-225-2464; *www.house.gov/engel*
- ★ Nita Lowey, Democrat: Began serving in 1989. ☏202-225-6506; *www.house.gov/lowey*
- ★ Sue Kelly, Republican: Began serving in 1995. ☏202-225-5441; *www.suekelly.house.gov*

BLUE STATE
★ ★ ★

- ★ John Sweeney, Republican: Began serving in 1999. ☎202-225-5614; ✐*www.house.gov/sweeney*
- ★ Michael McNulty, Democrat: Began serving in 1989. ☎202-225-5076; ✐*www.house.gov/mcnulty*
- ★ Maurice Hinchey, Democrat: Began serving in 1993. ☎202-225-6335; ✐*www.house.gov/hinchey*
- ★ John McHugh, Republican: Began serving in 1993. ☎202-225-4611; ✐*www.mchugh.house.gov*
- ★ Sherwood Boehlert, Republican: Began serving in 1983. ☎202-225-3665; ✐*www.house.gov/boehlert*
- ★ James Walsh, Republican: Began serving in 1989. ☎202-225-3701; ✐*www.house.gov/walsh*
- ★ Thomas Reynolds, Republican: Began serving in 1999. ☎202-225-5265; ✐*www.house.gov/reynolds*
- ★ Brian Higgins, Democrat: Began serving in 2005. ☎202-225-3306; ✐*www.house.gov/higgins*
- ★ Louise McIntosh Slaughter, Democrat: Began serving in 1987. ☎202-225-3615; ✐*www.slaughter.house.gov*
- ★ Randy Kuhl Jr., Republican: Began serving in 2005. ☎202-225-3161; ✐*www.kuhl.house.gov*

PITHY POLITICAL POOP AND SCINTILLATING SCANDAL

Dr. Jekyll and Mrs. Hyde In colonial times Edward Hyde, or Lord Cornbury, governor-general of New York, preferred to address the New York Assembly in drag.

He claimed it made him better able to represent the British Queen Anne, who also was his first cousin. This was considered scandalous at the time, and it of course would be unseemly today. As if it weren't bad enough for Cornbury to live what your new neighbors euphemistically call an "alternative lifestyle," he also sold large land grants to his friends for cash. How large? One grant was larger than Connecticut.

The last straw for the colonists took place at Lady Cornbury's funeral. Her grieving husband showed up for the funeral . . . in drag, of course. Eventually, even his cousin, Queen Anne, couldn't defend him any longer. Cornbury wound up in a debtor's prison for a short time. After his father died, however, Cornbury inherited a large sum that allowed him to cancel his debts. He moved back to England.

The Stonewall Riots So-called alternative lifestyles got another "boost" in New York on June 27, 1969. This is the date of the so-called "Stonewall Rebellion," which led liberals to begin embracing "gay rights." Here's what happened.

Police officers, doing their moral duty, went to New York City's Stonewall Bar and Club and threw out people they believed were practicing homosexuals. At one point, a cross-dressing woman was roughed up, and the growing crowd outside the club began throwing cobblestones and bottles at police officers.

To protect themselves, officers turned a fire hose on the crowd, and order was restored. But skirmishes between police and homosexuals continued for a few nights after the initial confrontation.

The unfortunate outcome of the Stonewall Rebellion was that homosexuals began to organize themselves politically. Traditional family values have taken a beating ever since.

Love Canal President Jimmy Carter declared a federal emergency at New York's Love Canal in 1978.

The Niagara Falls neighborhood had been sold by the Hooker Chemical Company to the city's school board for a dollar. The offer was not exactly generous, though.

The chemical company had used the property as a hazardous waste landfill and then covered it over with a layer of earth. Chemicals began leaking out of the ground right away, and many health problems resulted.

Love Canal is a chained-off ghost town today. Carter's focus on Love Canal is one of the few things he did right during his dismal four-year presidency.

President McKinley Has Been Shot President William McKinley was shot on September 6, 1901, in Buffalo. He was in town to visit the Pan-American Exposition. As he greeted citizens outside the Temple of Music pavilion, McKinley was shot by anarchist Leon Czolgosz. McKinley died eight days later.

The Rosenbergs New York also was the site of the execution of Julius and Ethel Rosenberg. The two were found guilty of selling atomic weapon secrets to the Soviet Union. To this day, bleeding hearts will say the evidence to convict the Rosenbergs was slim. But there was plenty of evidence that this pair was commie to the bone.

Julius once lost a job with the U.S. Army because he was linked to communist activities. In addition, both were known radicals. The Rosenbergs went to the electric chair on June 19, 1953, at Ossining's Sing Sing Prison.

Too Many People The United States could have used the Patriot Act in the early years of the twentieth century.

The immigrant-processing point Ellis Island admitted 1.3 million aliens for the 1907 fiscal year. This created serious domestic problems, and it wasn't until the years following World War I that the government finally decided to stem the tide of immigration and make America again the home of Americans.

PEOPLE FROM YOUR NEW STATE
WHO WON'T MAKE YOU FEEL ILL

* Lucille Ball, entertainer, Jamestown
* Humphrey Bogart, actor, New York City

* James Cagney, actor, New York City
* Aaron Copland, composer, Brooklyn
* Sammy Davis Jr., entertainer, New York City
* Lou Gehrig, baseball player, New York City
* George Gershwin, composer, Brooklyn
* Jackie Gleason, entertainer, Brooklyn
* Julia Ward Howe, songwriter, New York City
* Michael Jordan, basketball player, Brooklyn
* Vince Lombardi, coach, New York City
* Christopher Reeve, actor, Manhattan
* Louis Comfort Tiffany, designer, New York City
* Mae West, entertainer, Brooklyn

OREGON

GOVERNOR, SENATORS, CONGRESS MEMBERS

Governor Ted Kulongoski, Democrat Kulongoski was elected governor in 2002. He served previously as the state's attorney general and as a member of the Oregon Supreme Court.

When he took office, Oregon had a massive deficit, high unemployment, and a flawed public employees' pension system. Gosh, you'd never know that Kulongoski is the latest in a line of Democratic Party governors, now would you? Even though he is one, Kulongoski seems to recognize that longtime liberal leadership has left Oregon in poor condition.

He has pledged to cut government waste without cutting his favorite bleeding-heart services. In September 2005, car dealers and members of the state's Republican leadership filed a lawsuit against Kulongoski. The governor, in tree-hugger mode, had used a line-item veto to try to inaugurate tougher vehicle emissions standards. The suit alleged he did not have the power to do that.

➤ **Contact** ☎ 503-378-4582; ✐ *www.governor.state.or.us*

BLUE STATE
☆ ☆ ☆

Senator Gordon Smith, Republican Smith has been a senator since 1997. You can reelect him in 2008.

Smith is perhaps best known for introducing a youth suicide prevention bill, named after his son, Garrett Lee Smith. Garrett Smith took his life at the age of twenty-one. He was suffering from undiagnosed depression.

President Bush signed the bill into law in 2004. The law provides $82 million in grants to colleges, universities, and Indian organizations for the development of suicide prevention programs.

➤ **Committees** Special Committee on Aging
➤ **Contact** ✆ 202-224-3753; ✎ *www.gsmith.senate.gov*

Senator Ron Wyden, Democrat Wyden served as a congressman from 1981 to 1996. He has been a senator since 1996. He completed the term of Senator Bob Packwood, who resigned from the senate after the liberal media drummed up some nonsense about sexual misconduct (see below). You can vote Wyden out of office in 2010.

He was only too happy to put words in the mouth of John Roberts, soon after President Bush tapped Roberts as a Supreme Court nominee. The ultra-liberal and none-too-trustworthy *New York Times* reported in 2005 that Wyden had a "courtesy meeting" with Roberts. Some courtesy. The liberal rag used Wyden's recollections of the meeting, without checking with Roberts on the accuracy of those recollections. Not surprisingly, Wyden's memories did not paint Roberts in a flattering light.

➤ **Contact** ✆ 202-224-5244; ✎ *www.wyden.senate.gov*

Congress Members, 109th Congress

★ David Wu, Democrat: Began serving in 1999. ✆ 202-225-0855; ✎ *www.house.gov/wu*
★ Greg Walden, Republican: Began serving in 1999. ✆ 202-225-6730; ✎ *www.walden.house.gov*
★ Earl Blumenauer, Democrat: Began serving in 1995. ✆ 202-225-4811; ✎ *www.blumenauer.house.gov*

★ Peter DeFazio, Democrat: Began serving in 1987. ✆202-225-6416; ✐*www.house.gov/defazio*

★ Darlene Hooley, Democrat: Began serving in 1997. ✆202-225-5711; ✐*www.hooley.house.gov*

PITHY POLITICAL POOP
AND SCINTILLATING SCANDAL

Bob Packwood Republican Bob Packwood was first elected to the senate in 1968, and he was reelected four times. But his tenure in office ended with allegations that he had sexually harassed twenty-nine women.

As usual, it was the liberal media that attacked Packwood and made these allegations. But it wasn't the *Oregonian*, Packwood's home state newspaper, that broke the story. It was a free-lance journalist for the *Washington Post*. For whatever reason, the *Oregonian* had buried the story, though the paper had heard allegations of Packwood's sexual misconduct for years. In fact, one of its reporters allegedly was harassed by the senator.

Packwood resigned his senate seat in September 1995, after the senate's Ethics Committee recommended he be expelled. Packwood allegedly made countless advances to congressional aides and interns. The Ethics Committee found evidence to support seventeen of the accusations, which included allegations of groping, forced kissing, and propositioning sex.

In a diary entry, Packwood recounted a time when he supposedly told a woman it was his "Christian duty" to make love to her. And later, when asked by another reporter about the harassment allegations, Packwood claimed he couldn't remember most of his advances because he was drunk at the time.

Remember the Oregon? Though it was built in California, the battleship U.S.S. *Oregon* holds an important place in American history. When the outbreak of the Spanish-American War seemed

imminent, the *Oregon* was sent from the Pacific coast around South America to a base in Florida. The trip took two months, and the *Oregon* played a major role in the destruction of the Spanish fleet. But the length of the trip was one of the major reasons the United States began construction of the Panama Canal.

Oregon Fever Before gold sparked California Fever, many Americans caught Oregon Fever.

Missionary Marcus Whitman led 120 wagons with 200 families to Oregon in 1843. This was called the Great Migration. Stories began to trickle back east about a lush agricultural paradise, and Oregon Fever began to rage.

Some paradise. Whitman and his wife were killed by members of the Cayuse tribe, which blamed them for a measles epidemic.

PEOPLE FROM YOUR NEW STATE
WHO WON'T MAKE YOU FEEL ILL

* Garner Ted Armstrong, evangelist, Eugene
* Mark Hatfield, politician, Dallas
* Linus Pauling, scientist, Portland
* Doc Severinsen, bandleader, Arlington
* Norton Simon, businessman, Portland

PENNSYLVANIA

GOVERNOR, SENATORS, CONGRESS MEMBERS

Governor Edward Rendell, Democrat Rendell became governor in 2003. He served previously as mayor of Philadelphia. Though he's a liberal, it's hard to find much fault with him.

As Philadelphia's mayor, Rendell cut a $250-million deficit. Once elected governor, Rendell announced a plan that sounded eerily like

Johnson's Great Society. But the Plan for a New Pennsylvania actually reduced taxes by $1.5 billion, which led to an average decrease of 30 percent for homeowners. Rendell also passed a prescription drug plan to cover seniors during his first two years in office.

His major failure came in 2004. Rendell wanted to legalize and thus tax slot machine parlors. But the good citizens of Pennsylvania thwarted those plans because the Lord looks askance at gambling. Rendell, who exudes a laid-back, all-around-good-guy image, is among the many Democrats being talked about for a White House run in 2008.

➤ **Contact** ✆717-787-2500; ✑*www.governor.state.pa.us/governor*

Senator Rick Santorum, Republican Santorum served as a congressman from 1991 to 1994. He has been a senator since 1995. You can reelect him in 2006.

Bleeding hearts consider Santorum controversial because he espouses traditional family values and is not afraid to say what he feels about issues such as same-sex marriage.

In a 2003 interview with the Associated Press, he made an even-tempered "slippery-slope" argument about consensual gay sex: "If the Supreme Court says you have the right to consensual (gay) sex within your home, then you have the right to bigamy, you have the right to polygamy, you have the right to incest, you have the right to adultery. You have the right to anything."

Not surprisingly, liberals and the liberal media reacted as though Santorum had advocated burning American flags and using the ashes to line hamster cages. Though he waffled a bit after getting criticized, claiming the AP story was "misleading," Santorum stood by his words.

➤ **Committees** Republican Conference Chairman
➤ **Contact** ✆202-224-6324; ✑*www.santorum.senate.gov*

Senator Arlen Specter, Republican Specter has been a senator since 1981. You can reelect him in 2010. Or maybe you shouldn't.

BLUE STATE
★ ★ ★

Specter is a liberal in conservative clothing. He was as rough as any liberal on John Roberts's nomination to the Supreme Court. You may also remember Specter was the sole Republican to vote against Robert Bork, President Reagan's choice for the Supreme Court. Specter also supports abortion rights and stem-cell research.

➤ **Committees** Chair, Select Committee on Intelligence; Committee on Veterans Affairs; Committee on the Judiciary

➤ **Contact** ✆202-224-4254; ✉ *www.specter.senate.gov*

Congress Members, 109th Congress

★ Robert Brady, Democrat: Began serving in 1997. ✆202-225-4731; ✉ *www.house.gov/robertbrady*
★ Chaka Fattah, Democrat: Began serving in 1995. ✆202-225-4001; ✉ *www.house.gov/fattah*
★ Phil English, Republican: Began serving in 1995. ✆202-225-5406; ✉ *www.house.gov/english*
★ Melissa Hart, Republican: Began serving in 2001. ✆202-225-2565; ✉ *www.hart.house.gov*
★ John Peterson, Republican: Began serving in 1997. ✆202-225-5121; ✉ *www.house.gov/johnpeterson*
★ Jim Gerlach, Republican: Began serving in 2003. ✆202-225-4315; ✉ *www.gerlach.house.gov*
★ Curt Weldon, Republican: Began serving in 1987. ✆202-225-2011; ✉ *www.curtweldon.house.gov*
★ Michael Fitzpatrick, Republican: Began serving in 2005. ✆202-225-4276; ✉ *www.fitzpatrick.house.gov*
★ Bill Shuster, Republican: Began serving in 2001. ✆202-225-2431; ✉ *www.house.gov/shuster*
★ Don Sherwood, Republican: Began serving in 1999. ✆202-225-3731; ✉ *www.house.gov/sherwood*
★ Paul Kanjorski, Democrat: Began serving in 1985. ✆202-225-6511; ✉ *www.kanjorski.house.gov*
★ John Murtha, Democrat: Began serving in 1973. ✆202-225-2065; ✉ *www.house.gov/murtha*

BLUE STATE
★ ★ ★

★ Allyson Schwartz, Democrat: Began serving in 2005. ☎202-225-6111; *www.schwartz.house.gov*
★ Michael Doyle, Democrat: Began serving in 1995. ☎202-225-2135; *www.house.gov/doyle*
★ Charles Dent, Republican: Began serving in 2005. ☎202-225-6411; *www.dent.house.gov*
★ Joseph Pitts, Republican: Began serving in 1997. ☎202-225-2411; *www.house.gov/pitts*
★ Tim Holden, Democrat: Began serving in 1993. ☎202-225-5546; *www.holden.house.gov*
★ Tim Murphy, Republican: Began serving in 2003. ☎202-225-2301; *www.murphy.house.gov*
★ Todd Russell Platts, Republican: Began serving in 2001. ☎202-225-5836; *www.house.gov/platts*

PITHY POLITICAL POOP AND
SCINTILLATING SCANDAL

The Birthplace of Legionnaire's Disease Legionnaire's disease was born in the City of Brotherly Love in 1976. Two hundred veterans, who belonged to the American Legion, were gathered in Philadelphia's Park Hyatt Hotel. They became seriously ill, and doctors couldn't figure out why. Thirty-four of the veterans died from what became known as Legionnaire's disease.

The culprit? Germs breeding in the hotel's air conditioning system. The disease continues to pop up sporadically to this day. It is marked by headache, nausea, aching muscles, and fevers exceeding 104 degrees. Approximately 50 percent of those who contract the disease die from it.

Hail to the Queen Pennsylvania-born President James Buchanan not only was the country's first and only bachelor president, but he may well have been the nation's first homosexual president. Buchanan is known to have had only one relationship with

a woman. In his twenties, Buchanan met and became engaged to Ann Coleman. But she broke the engagement and died soon after. Buchanan stayed away from women after that.

But he shared what he called a "communion" with Alabama-born Senator William Rufus de Vane King. The two shared quarters in Washington, D.C., when both were senators. Behind his back, King was called "Miss Nancy" or "Aunt Fancy" by such red-blooded males as Andrew Jackson.

There are those revisionist historians who also would like to paint Buchanan's successor, Abraham Lincoln, with a homosexual brush. But that's just ridiculous.

The Johnstown Flood Before Hurricane Katrina all but destroyed the city of New Orleans, the Johnstown Flood was second only to the Galveston Flood as the worst natural disaster in American history. To this day, bleeding hearts want to pin the flood on big business.

On the afternoon of May 31, 1889, the 30,000 residents of Johnstown heard a low rumble that grew to a stentorian roar. It had finally happened. For years, folks in the town joked about the lamentable condition of the South Fork Dam, which held Lake Conemaugh in check. That dam will collapse any day, they'd say, with a chuckle. And then it wasn't a joke.

Twenty million tons of water rushed at forty miles an hour toward Johnstown, three miles away. A tsunami-sized sixty-foot wave walloped the town. The death toll was about 2,200. Some bodies weren't found until years after the flood.

Bleeding hearts had two theories. One was that excessive lumbering around the lake clear-cut the surrounding hills, changing the hill's natural drainage and overloading the dam. The other theory pointed a finger at the South Fork Fishing and Hunting Club. Members of the club, which included Andrew Carnegie and Andrew Mellon, had bought Lake Conemaugh, repaired the dam, and raised the water's level. These wealthy industrialists then built cabins along the lake's shore. Folks who survived Johnstown

claimed the wealthy owners hadn't done a good job repairing the South Fork Dam. But that's ridiculous. Besides, no successful lawsuits were ever brought against the captains of industry at the helm of the South Fork Fishing and Hunting Club.

PEOPLE FROM YOUR NEW STATE
WHO WON'T MAKE YOU FEEL ILL

* Edward Goodrich Acheson, inventor, Washington
* Louisa May Alcott, author, Germantown
* Daniel Boone, statesman, Reading
* Bill Cosby, entertainer, Philadelphia
* Robert Fulton, inventor, Lancaster County
* Alexander Haig, politician, Bala-Cynwyd
* Lee Iacocca, businessman, Allentown
* Gene Kelly, entertainer, Pittsburgh
* Tara Lipinski, gymnast, Philadelphia
* George C. Marshall, general, Uniontown
* George McClellan, general, Philadelphia
* Andrew Mellon, businessman, Pittsburgh
* Arnold Palmer, golfer, Youngstown
* Betsy Ross, patriot, Philadelphia
* James Stewart, actor, Indiana

RHODE ISLAND

GOVERNOR, SENATORS, CONGRESS MEMBERS

Governor Donald Carcieri, Republican Carcieri began his first term in 2003. He has aggressively sought to cut taxes in his state by signing an executive order to form the Office of Tax Research and Analysis. The office will seek ways to cut taxes without dipping into essential services. Rhode Island's tax burden is the sixth highest in the

country, despite its being the smallest state. That tax burden has got to be a legacy of former liberal governors of this traditionally Blue State.

➤ **Contact** ☎401-222-2080; ✍*www.governor.state.ri.us*

Senator Lincoln Chafee, Republican Chafee has been a senator since 1999. You can reelect him in 2006. Or maybe you shouldn't. Chafee appeared pretty yellow in 2005 when he voted to make John Bolton the U.S. Ambassador to the United Nations. True, he voted in favor of Bolton. But he repeatedly said things to indicate he did not particularly like Bolton. Though it would hardly be laudable for him to cross party lines and vote against President Bush's wishes, at least it would have shown Chafee to be a man of conviction. Instead, he seemed to want it both ways, waffling as effectively as any liberal.

➤ **Contact** ☎202-224-2921; ✍*www.chafee.senate.gov*

Senator Jack Reed, Democrat Reed served as a congressman from 1991 to 1996. He has been a senator since 1997. You can vote him out of office in 2008.

Reed has proven himself a staunch advocate for public health issues. If he must be a tax-and-spend liberal, at least Reed is trying to spend that money on something other than tree-hugging.

➤ **Contact** ☎202-224-4642; ✍*www.reed.senate.gov*

Congress Members, 109th Congress

★ Patrick Kennedy, Democrat: Began serving in 1995. ☎202-225-4911; ✍*www.patrickkennedy.house.gov*
★ James Langevin, Democrat: Began serving in 2001. ☎202-225-2735; ✍*www.house.gov/langevin*

PITHY POLITICAL POOP AND SCINTILLATING SCANDAL

The Ladies of Newport More than seventy years before Bill Clinton was rightly so lambasted by right-thinking Americans for

favoring gays in the military, another Democrat was alleged to be at the heart of a homosexuality scandal in the military.

The naval base in Newport contained flamboyantly gay seamen known in town as the "Ladies of Newport." These military "men" would sometimes perform in drag during leave. In 1919, Navy officials decided to do something drastic about the situation: they authorized sailors to solicit sex. Naval officials let their moles do anything necessary to get the goods on the Ladies of Newport.

There's debate about the part Assistant Secretary of the Navy Franklin Roosevelt played in the scheme. Either he played a part in making it happen, or he knew nothing about it. Roosevelt, of course, claimed it was the latter.

On the stand during a senate committee, these undercover operatives offered details ad nauseum about their trysts with the Ladies of Newport. Not even the ultraliberal *New York Times* would say much about the testimony, writing about it under a headline that stated "Details Are Unprintable."

The Trials of Buddy Ethnic stereotyping most definitely played a part in the saga of popular Providence mayor, Buddy Cianci.

The Republican first served as mayor from 1974 to 1984. During that time, he was dogged by accusations that he belonged to the Mafia. In 1984, Cianci was forced from office after he pleaded no contest to charges that he assaulted a man with an ashtray, a lit cigarette, and a fireplace log. But can you really blame Cianci? The man he attacked was having an affair with Cianci's wife, or at least that's what the mayor believed.

Cianci stood his ground. He remained in Providence, rather than slinking off to someplace else like your average liberal would do. Cianci became a popular talk radio host, and he was again elected mayor in 1991. After his return to office, an FBI probe led to accusations of racketeering, conspiracy, and extortion. The scandal was dubbed Operation Plunder Dome. And far from

trying to sweep it under the rug, Cianci was very vocal about the situation. He poked fun at it endlessly. Cianci was indicted on twelve counts. He resigned as Providence's mayor in 2002.

During the brouhaha, Cianci's approval ratings never dipped below 60 percent. The city's Italian American community continues to believe that Cianci was a victim of racial profiling.

PEOPLE FROM YOUR NEW STATE
WHO WON'T MAKE YOU FEEL ILL

* George M. Cohan, entertainer, Providence
* Nelson Eddy, entertainer, Providence
* Van Johnson, entertainer, Newport
* Matthew Perry, actor, Newport

VERMONT

GOVERNOR, SENATORS, CONGRESS MEMBERS

Governor Jim Douglas, Republican Douglas followed (chortle, giggle) Howard Dean as Vermont's governor in 2002.

He was appointed governor by the (hooray) Republican-majority state legislature because his race against Democrat Doug Racine was too close to call. Vermont's gubernatorial terms are only two years, and the state has no term limits. Douglas has expressed interest in running for a third term in 2006.

Douglas made national headlines in 2004 when he had a nude statue removed from his desk. The liberal media, as usual, left it at that. The story was, in fact, a bit more complicated.

The statue was part of a lamp on the governor's desk. The nineteenth-century lamp depicted a chained female slave. It was designed to represent the abolitionist movement. But Douglas made the right decision to have it removed. First, he didn't want to have to explain

the naked lamp to visiting schoolchildren. And second, he was afraid the antique would get damaged.

➤ **Contact** ☎ 802-828-3333; 🖉 *www.vermont.gov/governor*

Senator James Jeffords, Independent Jeffords served as a congressman from 1975 to 1988. He has been a senator since 1989. He switched from being a Republican to an Independent in 2001. You can vote him out of office in 2006.

Jeffords's betrayal of the Republican Party handed Democrats the majority in the senate. He claimed that the Republican Party was moving too far to the right for his tastes. Well, gee, Senator Jeffords, we most humbly beg your pardon. On second thought . . . no we don't. Who needs you?

It was most likely sour grapes that led Jeffords to "turn to the dark side." He has a soft spot for spending on special education and apparently didn't feel that enough was being spent on his pet project. Besides, Jeffords is a long-time tree-hugger. He might as well just go all the way and admit he's a liberal.

➤ **Committees** Committee on Labor and Human Resources; Committee on Health, Education, Labor, and Pensions; Committee on Environment and Public Works

➤ **Contact** ☎ 202-224-5141; 🖉 *www.jeffords.senate.gov*

Senator Patrick Leahy, Democrat Leahy has been a senator since 1975. You can vote him out of office in 2010.

Leahy was the senior Democrat on the committee that considered John Roberts's Supreme Court nomination. Leahy made it clear in public statements that he considered Roberts too far to the right.

In addition, Leahy drew the ire of Vice President Dick Cheney. Leahy had the temerity to suggest that Halliburton stands to profit from a stable, post-war Iraq. Apparently, Leahy forgot that Cheney had long since ceased being the CEO of Halliburton. In fact, Cheney dropped out of the oil conglomerate when tapped for the vice presidency by President Bush. But that doesn't stop tongue-wagging liberals like Leahy from suggesting all manner of

wrong-doing . . . without offering a shred of evidence that any wrong is being committed. Why can't these liberals think before they speak?

Fortunately, the vice president can take care of himself. He cursed Leahy on the floor of the senate in 2004, as the body was getting its annual picture made. Leahy whined to the liberal media about the dressing-down, and the media, of course, made this non-story a big story for a short time.

➤ **Committees** Chair, Committee on Agriculture, Nutrition, and Forestry; Committee on the Judiciary

➤ **Contact** ✆ 202-224-4242; ✐ *www.leahy.senate.gov*

Congress Member, 109th Congress

★ Bernie Sanders, Independent: Began serving in 1991. ✆ 202-225-4115; ✐ *www.bernie.house.gov*

PITHY POLITICAL POOP AND SCINTILLATING SCANDAL

The Edmunds Act Vermont-born President Chester A. Arthur was a conservative who understood the importance of traditional family values. The Edmunds Anti-Polygamy Act was passed during his administration. The 1882 act was aimed at the Mormons of Utah, who believed at that time that it was perfectly acceptable to have more than one wife. It isn't, of course, and Arthur knew it. The Edmunds Act made it illegal for a man to have more than one wife. More than 1,300 men were imprisoned for "unlawful cohabitation" following the passage of the act.

Arthur also struck a blow for honest government. Until his time, presidents gave civil service jobs to friends and supporters. The so-called "Spoils System" put a lot of unqualified and unscrupulous men in offices that they used for personal gain. Ironically, Arthur himself had risen in politics in part due to the system. Be that as it may, Arthur oversaw the passage of the Pendleton Civil Service Act. Its main result was the creation of the Civil Service

Commission, a nonpartisan board that creates and administers examinations to applicants for low-level federal jobs. Many states, in turn, formed their own civil service commissions.

Silent Cal Attacks the Police Vermont's other contribution to the White House, Calvin Coolidge, owed his presidency in part to actions in another Blue State.

In September 1919, more than 1,000 members of the Boston Police Department went on strike. The force's wages fared poorly during the period surrounding World War I. Officers began to organize for better pay, shorter hours, and better working conditions. But police commissioner Edwin Curtis refused to sanction a police union and suspended all leaders of the ersatz union from the force. That's when three-fourths of the force went on strike.

Riots and general disorder ensued. Newly elected Governor Calvin Coolidge called in the entire Massachusetts National Guard to break the strike. Coolidge gained a reputation as a strict enforcer of law and order. When the strike ended, Coolidge refused to allow officers who struck to regain their jobs. The jobs instead went to returning servicemen. Ironically, they received better pay and benefits than the officers who had gone on strike.

When union heads complained to Coolidge that he was too harsh on the officers who struck, Coolidge responded, "There is no right to strike against the public safety by anybody, anywhere, any time."

PEOPLE FROM YOUR NEW STATE
WHO WON'T MAKE YOU FEEL ILL

* Chester A. Arthur, president, Fairfield
* Calvin Coolidge, president, Plymouth
* John Deere, inventor, Rutland
* George Dewey, admiral, Montpelier
* Elisha Graves Otis, inventor, Halifax

BLUE STATE
☆ ☆ ☆

WASHINGTON

GOVERNOR, SENATORS, CONGRESS MEMBERS

Governor Christine Gregoire, Democrat Gregoire was not declared governor until early 2005. Her race against Republican challenger Dino Rossi was the closest gubernatorial contest in the nation in 2004.

Gregoire was declared winner by 129 votes. Yes, that's right, just over a hundred votes. Can you say, "The fix is in?" Good. I knew you could. Can you say, "Liberal payback for the 2000 election?" Very good.

➤ **Contact** ✆ 360-902-4111; ✎ *www.governor.wa.gov*

Senator Maria Cantwell, Democrat Cantwell served as a congresswoman from 1993 to 1995. She lost her bid for reelection. She has been a senator since 2000. You can vote her out of office in 2006.

Cantwell is known as Senator "Can't-Smile" because she's your typical deadly serious, tree-hugging, bleeding-heart liberal. Despite claiming that the United States needs to end its reliance on Middle Eastern oil, Cantwell is staunchly against drilling for oil in Alaskan wildlife refuges. She has fought against aspects of the Patriot Act. And she's just too dang intense.

She won her election to the senate by the slightest of margins. Hopefully, she'll lose by a wide margin in 2006.

➤ **Contact** ✆ 202-224-3441; ✎ *www.cantwell.senate.gov*

Senator Patty Murray, Democrat Murray has been a senator since 1993. You can vote her out of office in 2010.

Murray has been outspoken in her support of the so-called morning-after pill, which ought to just be known as the early abortion pill. She and her crony, Senator Hillary Clinton, put out a joint statement in 2005 claiming that the Bush administration ignored scientific research about the pill and made science "take a backseat to politics." It's not politics, ladies. It's a human being. The

Bush administration simply believes in protecting the rights of *all* Americans.

➤ **Committees** Chair, Democratic Senatorial Campaign Committee
➤ **Contact** ✆202-224-2621; ✐*www.murray.senate.gov*

Congress Members, 109th Congress

★ Jay Inslee, Democrat: Began serving in 1993. ✆202-225-6311; ✐*www.house.gov/inslee*
★ Rick Larsen, Democrat: Began serving in 2001. ✆202-225-2605; ✐*www.house.gov/larsen*
★ Brian Baird, Democrat: Began serving in 1999. ✆202-225-3536; ✐*www.house.gov/baird*
★ Doc Hastings, Republican: Began serving in 1995. ✆202-225-5816; ✐*www.hastings.house.gov*
★ Cathy McMorris, Republican: Began serving in 2005. ✆202-225-2006; ✐*www.mcmorris.house.gov*
★ Norman Dicks, Democrat: Began serving in 1977. ✆202-225-5916; ✐*www.house.gov/dicks*
★ Jim McDermott, Democrat: Began serving in 1989. ✆202-225-3106; ✐*www.house.gov/mcdermott*
★ David Reichert, Republican: Began serving in 2005. ✆202-225-7761; ✐*www.house.gov/reichert*
★ Adam Smith, Democrat: Began serving in 1997. ✆202-225-8901; ✐*www.house.gov/adamsmith*

PITHY POLITICAL POOP AND SCINTILLATING SCANDAL

Jim West A gay sex scandal was rocking Spokane as this book went to press.

Mayor Jim West rose up the political ladder as a fiscal conservative opposed to gay rights, abortion, and teen sex. He angered liberals across the country.

That's fine. Heck, that's a *good* thing.

The problem is that it appears West has been a hypocrite for at least a quarter century. A man filed court papers claiming West molested him when the man was a boy and West a Boy Scout leader. More recently, West allegedly hooked up with an eighteen-year-old boy in a gay chat room. Later, a computer expert posed as another eighteen-year-old boy. West allegedly offered this new "young man" all kinds of perks including an internship if he would meet him.

The story was investigated at length by the *Spokesman-Review*. Yes, it was a case of the liberal media attacking a conservative Republican. But this time, it looks like they might actually have had good reason.

PEOPLE FROM YOUR NEW STATE
WHO WON'T MAKE YOU FEEL ILL

* Bob Barker, game show host, Darrington
* Bing Crosby, entertainer, Tacoma
* Bill Gates, businessman, Seattle
* Hank Ketcham, cartoonist, Seattle
* Francis Scobee, astronaut, Cle Elum
* Adam West, actor, Walla Walla

WISCONSIN

GOVERNOR, SENATORS, CONGRESS MEMBERS

Governor Jim Doyle, Democrat Doyle was elected to his first gubernatorial term in 2002. His Web site proclaims that Doyle has worked across party lines to make a positive change in Wisconsin. Hmm.

Well, first let's look at that "positive change" rhetoric. Doyle's 2005 budget cut reimbursement rates by nearly $40 million for

pharmacists filling prescriptions for Medicaid patients. As this book was going to press, pharmacists across the state were threatening to stop serving Medicaid patients altogether in response. Nursing homes also were affected by Doyle's Medicaid cuts.

So in Wisconsin, "positive change" must involve keeping necessary care away from and necessary drugs out of the hands of the elderly.

Republican members of the legislature began to rally in support of the elderly. Several worked to override Doyle vetoes. Those vetoes led to huge cuts in Medicaid reimbursements.

So in Wisconsin, "working across party lines" must refer to acrimonious disputes with Republicans.

➤ **Contact** ✆ 608-266-1212; ✐ *www.wisgov.state.wi.us*

Senator Russell Feingold, Democrat Feingold has been a senator since 1993. You can vote him out of office in 2010.

Feingold has been outspoken in his criticism of the war in Iraq, even making up a bogus withdrawal date of December 31, 2006. He seems to think it's brave to oppose a war that's planting a toehold of democracy in the Middle East and that toppled a ruthless dictator. The date is meaningless . . . it's just something Feingold came up with to get his name championed by the liberal media.

Feingold is perhaps best known for crossing the aisle and joining with Republican Senator John McCain. The two sponsored a bill to reform campaign finance. The McCain-Feingold bill was signed into law in 2002 and took effect in 2003.

➤ **Contact** ✆ 202-224-5323; ✐ *www.feingold.senate.gov*

Senator Herb Kohl, Democrat Kohl has been a senator since 1989. You can vote him out of office in 2006.

Kohl is that rare bird: a businessman *and* a Democrat. His family built the Kohl's department store chain into a hugely profitable business. Kohl owns the Milwaukee Bucs basketball team, and his

wealth is estimated at between $111 and $250 million. Kohl has been particularly supportive of legislation dealing with education.

It's just too bad the guy's with the wrong party.

➤ **Contact** ✆ 202-224-5653; ✐ *www.kohl.senate.gov*

Congress Members, 109th Congress

★ Paul Ryan, Republican: Began serving in 1999. ✆ 202-225-3031; ✐ *www.house.gov/ryan*

★ Tammy Baldwin, Democrat: Began serving in 1999. ✆ 202-225-2906; ✐ *www.tammybaldwin.house.gov*

★ Ron Kind, Democrat: Began serving in 1997. ✆ 202-225-5506; ✐ *www.house.gov/kind*

★ Gwen Moore, Democrat: Began serving in 2005. ✆ 202-225-4572; ✐ *www.house.gov/gwenmoore*

★ James Sensenbrenner Jr., Republican: Began serving in 1979. ✆ 202-225-5101; ✐ *www.house.gov/sensenbrenner*

★ Thomas Petri, Republican: Began serving in 1979. ✆ 202-225-2476; ✐ *www.house.gov/petri*

★ David Obey, Democrat: Began serving in 1969. ✆ 202-225-3365; ✐ *www.obey.house.gov*

★ Mark Green, Republican: Began serving in 1999. ✆ 202-225-5665; ✐ *www.house.gov/markgreen*

PITHY POLITICAL POOP AND SCINTILLATING SCANDAL

Theodore Roosevelt: A Man's Man Former president Theodore Roosevelt proved he was a man's man during a campaign speech in Milwaukee.

Roosevelt had first gained the presidency upon the death of William McKinley. Later, he was elected to a full term. But Roosevelt said he would not run for a second full term under any circumstances. So he left office in 1909. But his successor, William Howard Taft, did such a rotten job that Americans clamored to

have Roosevelt run again. Roosevelt did so, on the short-lived Bull Moose ticket.

Just before he gave a speech in Milwaukee, a saloonkeeper named John Schrank tried to assassinate the former president. Schrank shot Roosevelt, but a glasses case in Roosevelt's pocket deflected the bullet away from his heart. Nonetheless, Roosevelt wound up with a bullet wound in his chest.

Did he start crying and beg to be taken to the hospital? No sir. This Spanish-American War hero *gave the speech with the bullet lodged in his chest.* Could you see John Kerry doing this? No way!

Roosevelt recovered from his wound in about two weeks, and Schrank was committed to a mental hospital.

Roosevelt did not win the 1912 election, by the way. Just as Ross Perot would do some eighty years later, Roosevelt's third-party candidacy split the Republican vote and put Democrat Woodrow Wilson into office.

PEOPLE FROM YOUR NEW STATE
WHO WON'T MAKE YOU FEEL ILL

* Don Ameche, entertainer, Kenosha
* Richard Bong, war pilot, Superior
* Harry Houdini, magician, Appleton
* Tom Wopat, entertainer, Lodi
* Frank Lloyd Wright, architect, Richland Center

Works Cited

Web Sites

Abortion facts, *www.guttmacher.org/pubs/sfaa.html*

Abramoff-Reed, Indian Gambling, *http://64.233.179.104/search?q=cache: XZ6h0m3Rod4J:en.wikipedia.org/wiki/Abramoff-Reed_Indian_Gambling_Scandal+ delaware+political+scandal&hl=en*

Aroostook War, *www.bartleby.com/65/ar/AroostWar.html*

Banned books, *http://digital.library.upenn.edu/books/banned-books.html; http:// home.nvg.org/~aga/bulletin43.html; www.beaconforfreedom.org; and www.floyd.edu/ academics/library/banned/books.htm*

Benson, Craig, *http://72.14.207.104/search?q=cache:V8yOnwFYmCcJ:www.wirenh .com/News/General_News/the_short,_strange_political_life_of_Craig_ Benson_20050105190*

Biden, Joe, alleged plagiarism, *www.washingtonpost.com/wp-srv/politics/ special/clinton/frenzy/biden.htm*

Blagojevich-Mell Feud, *www.dailytexanonline.com/media/paper410/ news/2005/01/26/TopStories/Chicago.Governor.In.Family.Feud.With.InLaw-841470 .shtml*

Blaine, James G., *http://en.wikipedia.org/wiki/James_G._Blaine*

Boston police strike, *www.u-s-history.com/pages/h1348.html*

Bremer, Arthur, *www.pbs.org/wgbh/amex/wallace/sfeature/assasin.html*

Buchanan, James, allegedly gay, *www.planetout.com/news/history/archive/ whitehouse.html*

Cantwell, Maria, *http://usliberals.about.com/od/2006ussenateraces/p/SenCantwell.htm*

Carcieri, Donald, *http://64.233.179.104/search?q=cache:O9UpMlDXZccJ:www.cs geast.org/page.asp%3Fid%3Dweeklynewsbulletin55+donald+carcieri+scandal&hl=en*

Chafee, Lincoln, *http://72.14.207.104/search?q=cache:45u5TQtQMPUJ:slate.msn .com/id/2118601/+lincoln+chafee&hl=en*

Chappaquiddick, *www.gfsnet.org/msweb/sixties/chappaquiddick.html*

Chicago race riots, *www.chipublib.org/004chicago/disasters/riots_race.html*

Cianci, "Buddy," *www.cbsnews.com/elements/2003/11/20/in_depth_politics/ whoswho584748_0_10_person.shtml*

Coleman, Norm, *http://en.wikipedia.org/wiki/Norm_Coleman*

Collins, Susan, on the Air Force Academy, *http://72.14.207.104/search?q=cache:8O cIT6uSNCEJ:hsgac.senate.gov/index.cfm%3FFuseAction%3DPressReleases .Detail%26Affiliation%3DC%26PressRelease_id%3D423%26Month%3D9 %26Year%3D2003+susan+collins+scandal&hl=en*

Corzine, Jon, *www.cnn.com/2005/POLITICS/09/01/corzine.ethics.ap/*

Dayton, Mark, on 9/11, *www.911truth.org/article.php?story=20040805095600503*

Dodd, Christopher, alleged racist comments, *http://washingtontimes.com/upi-breaking/20040407-021034-5250r.htm*

Douglas, Jim, *www.boston.com/news/local/vermont/articles/2004/12/12/nude_statue_to_be_shelved_in_vt_legislative_session/*

Durbin, Richard, on Guantanamo, *http://72.14.207.104/search?q=cache:-izBPosB05MJ:www.aclu.org/news/NewsPrint.cfm%3FID%3D18553%26c%3D280+richard+durbin+scandal&hl=en*

Edmunds Anti-Polygamy Act, *www.u-s-history.com/pages/h734.html*

Euthanasia, *http://en.wikipedia.org/wiki/Euthanasia* and *www.longwood.edu/library/suic.htm*

Family Christian Stores, *www.familychristian.com/locations.asp*

Feingold, Russell, Iraq War withdrawal date, *www.frontpagemag.com/Articles/ReadArticle.asp?ID=19338*

Golden Corral, *www.goldencorral.net/RestaurantFinder.asp*

Gordon, Tom, *www.delawareonline.com/apps/pbcs.dll/article?AID=/20050909/NEWS01/509090346/1006*

Granholm, Jennifer, *www.freep.com/news/statewire/sw121148_20050912.htm* and *http://gaylife.about.com/od/samesexmarriag1/a/granholm.htm*

Gregg, Judd, on "Islamic fundamentalists," *http://64.233.161.104/search?q=cache:QqDPRgBVcyYJ:www.counterpunch.org/jackson03062004.html+senator+judd+gregg&hl=en*

Gun laws, *www.nraila.org/GunLaws/Default.aspx#*

Hawaii, annexation of, *www.state.gov/r/pa/ho/time/gp/17661.htm*

Hawaii, campaign donations scandal, *www.cnn.com/2004/LAW/01/05/hawaii.corruption.ap/*

Hawaiians, native, *www.nativehawaiians.com/fedrecindex.html*

Johnstown Flood, *www.johnstownpa.com/History/hist19.html*

Leahy, Patrick, target of Cheney, *www.cnn.com/2004/ALLPOLITICS/06/24/cheney.leahy/*

Legionnaire's Disease, *www.hcinfo.com/ldfaq.htm*

Levin, Carl, on Abu Ghraib, *www.freep.com/news/nw/levin28_20040528.htm*

Lingle, Linda, *www.forbes.com/business/2005/09/09/economics-hawaii-politics_cz_rk_0909dunce.html* and *www.mercurynews.com/mld/mercurynews/news/politics/12584626.htm*

BLUE STATE
⭐ ⭐ ⭐

Maine, discrimination law, *www.timesargus.com/apps/pbcs.dll/article?AID=/
20050911/NEWS/509110354/1003/NEWS02*

McGreevey, James, "I am a gay American," *www.cnn.com/2004/
ALLPOLITICS/08/12/mcgreevey.transcript/*

Minnesota, government shutdown, *http://cnn.netscape.cnn.com/ns/news/story
.jsp?idq=/ff/story/0001%2F20050701%2F0434354620.htm*

Moscone, George's assassination, *www.heroism.org/class/1970/moscone.html*

Murray, Patty, "Morning After Pill," *www.bloomberg.com/apps/news?pid=10000087
&sid=a08ZfW.AILrs&refer=top_world_news*

Newport Ladies, *http://72.14.207.104/search?q=cache:ukA_OiFd9GMJ:www
.signorile.com/articles/advogc.html+newport+sex+scandal&hl=en*

Oregon, emissions standards, *www.oregonlive.com/news/oregonian/index.ssf?/base/
exclude/112660927457800.xml&coll=7*

Packwood, Robert, *www.cbsnews.com/elements/2003/11/20/in_depth_politics/
whoswho584748_0_7_person.shtml*

Preemption Act, *www.encyclopedia.com/html/P/Preempti.asp*

Pullman Strike, *www.chipublib.org/004chicago/disasters/pullman_strike.html*

Romney, Mitt, *www.boston.com/news/local/massachusetts/articles/2005/09/13/
citing_work_at_home_romney_postpones_trip_to_israel/*

Same-sex marriage, *http://en.wikipedia.org/wiki/Same-sex_marriage_in_the_
United_States* and *http://archives.cnn.com/2000/LAW/05/25/same.sex.marriages/*

Santorum, Rick, on homosexuality, *www.cnn.com/2003/ALLPOLITICS/04/22/
santorum.gays/*

Sarbanes, Paul, *www.washingtonpost.com/wp-dyn/articles/A26762-2005Mar11.html*

Sinclair, Upton, *www.spartacus.schoolnet.co.uk/Jupton.htm*

Smart, Pamela, *www.who2.com/pamelasmart.html*

Smith, Gordon, anti-suicide bill, *www.preventsuicidenow.com/bush-signs-gordon-
smith-suicide-prevention-law.html*

Southern Baptist churches, *www.sbc.net*

Specter, Arlen, *www.pbs.org/newshour/bb/politics/july-dec05/specter_8-24.html*

Spock, Dr. Benjamin's anti-war stance, *www.cnn.com/US/9803/16/obit.dr.spock/*

Stabenow, Debbie, *http://usliberals.about.com/od/2006ussenateraces/p/
SenStabenow.htm*

Watergate, *www.answers.com/main/ntquery;jsessionid=iugllp9us4z1?method=4&dsid
=2222&dekey=Watergate+scandal&gwp=8&curtab=2222_1&sbid=lc05a&linktext=
Watergate%20scandal*

134

West, Jim, *www.spokesmanreview.com/jimwest/*

Wisconsin, Medicaid cuts, *www.channel3000.com/health/4977079/detail.html*

Wyden, Ron, *http://bench.nationalreview.com/archives/072547.asp*

Zangara, Guiseppe, *www.spartacus.schoolnet.co.uk/USAzangara.htm*